AF605937

Critical Dialogues in Southeast Asian Studies

CHARLES KEYES, VICENTE RAFAEL, AND LAURIE SEARS, SERIES EDITORS

Critical Dialogues in Southeast Asian Studies

These new perspectives in Southeast Asian Studies reconsider traditional relationships among scholars, texts, archives, field sites, and subject matter. Volumes in the series feature inquiries into historiography, critical ethnography, colonialism and postcolonialism, nationalism and ethnicity, gender and sexuality, science and technology, politics and society, and literature, drama, and film. This scholarship sheds light on shifting contexts and contests over forms of knowing and modes of action that inform cultural politics and shape histories of modernity.

Imagined Ancestries of Vietnamese Communism: Ton Duc Thang and the Politics of Memory
by Christoph Giebel

Imagined Ancestries of Vietnamese Communism

TON DUC THANG AND THE POLITICS OF HISTORY AND MEMORY

CHRISTOPH GIEBEL

UNIVERSITY OF WASHINGTON PRESS
Seattle & London

in association with

SINGAPORE UNIVERSITY PRESS

Printed in the United States of America
12 11 10 09 08 07 06 05 04 5 4 3 2 1

Published simultaneously in the United States and Singapore.

University of Washington Press, P.O. Box 50096, Seattle, WA 98145
www.washington.edu/uwpress

Singapore University Press, NUS Publishing
3, Arts Link, Ground floor AS3, Faculty of Arts and Social Sciences,
Singapore 117569
Fax: 65-6774 0652 supbooks@nus.edu.sg
www.nus.edu.sg/npu
ISBNs 9971-69-308-9 cloth 9971-69-309-7 paper

Library of Congress Cataloging-in-Publication Data

Giebel, Christoph.
Imagined ancestries of Vietnamese communism : Ton Duc Thang and the politics of history and memory / Christoph Giebel.
p. cm.
Includes bibliographical references and index.
ISBN 0-295-98428-7 (cloth : alk. paper)—ISBN 0-295-98429-5 (pbk. : alk. paper)
1. Tôn, Đú'c Thắng, 1888–1980. 2. Communism—Vietnam—History. 3. Vietnam—History—20th century. 4. Vietnam—Historiography. 5. Presidents—Vietnam (Democratic Republic)—Biography. I. Title: Ton Duc Thang and the politics of history and memory. II. Title.
DS560.72.T66G54 2004 2004041953

The paper used in this publication is acid-free and recycled from 20 percent post-consumer and at least 50 percent pre-consumer waste. It meets the minimum requirements of American National Standard for Information Sciences—Permanence of Paper for Printed Library Materials, ANSI Z39.48–1984.

FOR MY TEACHERS,
WITH DEEP RESPECT AND GRATITUDE

Contents

Abbreviations

BNCLSDTU	Ban Nghien Cuu Lich Su Dang Trung Uong (Central Commission for the Research of Party History)
CCP	Chinese Communist Party
CFRF	Club of Former Resistance Fighters (1986–90)
CPSU	Communist Party of the Soviet Union
DLD	Dang Lao Dong (Vietnamese Labor Party, 1951–76)
DMH	Dong Minh Hoi (Vietnamese Revolutionary League)
DRVN	Democratic Republic of Viet Nam (1945–76)
FCP	French Communist Party
GMD	Guomindang (Chinese Nationalist Party; also KMT)
ICP	Indochinese Communist Party (1930–45/1951)
NXB	Nha Xuat Ban (Publishing House)
OSS	Office of Strategic Services
PRC	People's Republic of China
QDND	Quan Doi Nhan Dan (People's Army of Viet Nam)
SRVN	Socialist Republic of Viet Nam (since 1976)
USSR	Union of Soviet Socialist Republics (Soviet Union)
VFTU	Viet Nam Federation of Trade Unions
VNCP	Vietnamese Communist Party (since 1976)
VNQDD	Viet Nam Quoc Dan Dang (Vietnamese Nationalist Party)
VRYL	Vietnamese Revolutionary Youth League (Viet Nam Thanh Nien Cach Mang Dong Chi Hoi, or Thanh Nien, 1925–29)

A Note on Spelling and Translations

I have chosen to follow Vietnamese usage in separating the syllables of, for example, place names such as Ha Noi, Sai Gon, and Viet Nam. The widespread but never fully uniform Western convention of combining syllables (e.g., Vietnam) appears to be slowly receding. On the other hand, since this book is written in English, I have eschewed providing the Vietnamese diacritics and tone markers (although I might be on the losing end of academic trends in this case). Chinese personal and place names are rendered throughout the study in the pinyin transcription system (e.g., Guomindang instead of Kuomintang in the old Wade-Giles style).

Rather than bringing them into more polished English, I have kept my translations of Vietnamese and French texts in an English form that closely reflects the syntax and tone of the originals.

Acknowledgments

This study owes much to the exceptional guidance and unfailing support of remarkable teachers and mentors, with whom I had the good fortune to work at Cornell University: Keith W. Taylor, David K. Wyatt, Takashi Shiraishi, Sherman Cochran, Kristin Pelzer, and the late Huynh Kim Khanh. I gratefully acknowledge their invaluable advice and generous help.

During the years spent on this project, I have become indebted to a lot of people who helped me in various ways as teachers, sponsors, guides, providers of crucial material, critics, and friends. With sincere thanks I want to mention in particular: Benedict Anderson, John Badgley, Pierre Brocheux, Bui Dinh Thanh, Clare Crowston, the late Do Van Gia, Duong Trung Quoc, the late Stephen Graw, Joseph Hannah and Hoang Thi Dieu Hien, Ho Dinh Thien, Deborah Homsher, Douglas Kammen, Kurihara Hirohide, Hjorleifur Jonsson and Nora Taylor, Micheline Lessard, Bruce Lockhart, Charles Lowery, Hendrik M. J. Maier, Shawn McHale, Michael Montesano, the late Nguyen Anh Que, Nguyen Ngoc Hung, Nguyen Thach Giang, Nguyen Van Kim, Patricia Pelley, Pham Xanh, Phan Huy Le, Hans Stumpfeldt, Hue-Tam Ho Tai, Tran Quoc Vuong, Thaveeporn Vasavakul, Vu Duy Tu, Vu Minh Giang, Tamara J. Wang, the late Oliver W. Wolters, and Peter Zinoman.

For their time, patience, and information, I thank all those who agreed to be interviewed by me. I want to mention in particular Ton Thi Hanh, Ton Duc Thang's daughter; I hope that she will be able to recognize her father in this study.

For their kind and patient assistance, I want to thank the staff of the following institutions: Centre des archives d'Outre-Mer, in Aix-en-Provence (in particular François Bordes, Simone Menager), Services historiques de la Marine in Toulon (Nicole Baronti), Brest (Patrick Petit), and Vincennes, and Sorbonne University, Paris; National Archives Center (Trung Tam Luu Tru Quoc Gia) No. I, Museum of the Revolution, National Library, and Ho Chi Minh Museum, all in Ha Noi; Ton Duc

Thang Museum, Ba Son Shipyard Museum (Pham Tien Xa), National Archives Center No. II, Museum of the Revolution, and Cao Thang Vocational School Museum, all in Ho Chi Minh City; Museum of An Giang Province and Ton Duc Thang Commemorative Area in Long Xuyen and My Hoa Hung; the Echols Collection on Southeast Asia at Cornell University Library, and the University of Washington Library.

I am very grateful for funding and institutional support provided by the Studienstiftung des deutschen Volkes and the Deutscher Akademischer Austauschdienst of Bonn, Germany; the Center for Vietnamese and Intercultural Studies in Ha Noi, Viet Nam; at Cornell University: the Southeast Asia Program (including funds administered for the Luce Foundation), the Department of History (including funds administered for the Mellon Foundation), the Cornell-Hamburg Exchange Program, the Graduate School, and the Center for International Studies; at the University of Washington: the College of Arts and Sciences, the Department of History (including a research grant from the Keller Fund), the Henry M. Jackson School of International Studies, and the Center for Southeast Asian Studies.

In the later stages of this project at the University of Washington, I profited immensely from the ready advice and warm collegiality of, in particular and among others, Laurie Sears, Jere Bacharach, David Biggs, Mary Callahan, George Dutton, John Findlay, Diane Fox, Judith Henchy, Charles "Biff" Keyes, Celia Lowe, Robert Stacey, Sara Van Fleet, and Anand Yang. I am lucky to have found such a supportive and stimulating intellectual environment. Thanks also go to Joseph Hannah, who kindly created this study's maps and ably assisted with the final preparation of the manuscript.

At the University of Washington Press, Michael Duckworth was not only unfailingly encouraging, but also remarkably patient as my teaching, administrative, and renewed parental duties transformed deadlines into moving targets. I am also very grateful for the expert editorial work of Mike Ashby and Marilyn Trueblood. The index was ably prepared by Breffni Whelan. David Chandler, Rita Kipp, and several anonymous readers kindly gave me many insightful comments. Reprint permissions for chapters 6 and 7 by Cornell University SouthEast Asia Program Publications (Deborah Homsher) and the University of California Press (Rose Robinson) are gratefully acknowledged.

Finally, I wish to acknowledge the loving support of my family: Reinhard Giebel, who did not live to see this study's completion; Hanna Giebel of Jugenheim; Hellmut Giebel of Berlin, Germany; and my beloved Tammy Wang and our "auspicious" kids, Sonia Xiarui, Tillman Ruihe, and Beatrice Qirui.

While all of the above have contributed to this study, its errors and shortcomings are entirely mine.

Introduction

In 1926, Nguyen Ai Quoc, a Vietnamese Comintern agent working for the liberation of his people from French colonialism, who would become known in the 1940s as Ho Chi Minh, sent two associates from Canton (Guangzhou) in southern China to Sai Gon. Sai Gon was the capital of the French colony of Cochinchina, an artificial entity the French had created in the 1860s by cutting away the southern third of the Vietnamese kingdom of Dai Nam. To the Vietnamese, "Cochinchina" remained simply Nam Ky, the South.[1]

During the previous year, in 1925, Nguyen Ai Quoc had begun organizing anticolonial Vietnamese youths living in southern China in the Viet Nam Thanh Nien Cach Mang Dong Chi Hoi, the Vietnamese Revolutionary Youth League (hereafter Thanh Nien or VRYL). This radical party is usually seen as the "proto-communist" forerunner to Vietnamese communism, which would not formally organize itself as such until 1929/1930. In 1926, Nguyen Ai Quoc's two emissaries were to establish a southern Thanh Nien branch in Cochinchina and actively recruit new members.

In Sai Gon, they soon came into contact with a trained mechanic, Ton Duc Thang, who was reputed to be leading lively efforts in organizing the city's growing numbers of workers. In early 1927, at age thirty-eight, Ton Duc Thang was admitted into Thanh Nien. A little over two years later, in the summer of 1929, Ton was arrested by the French, along with scores of his fellow Thanh Nien members and other southern anticolonial radicals. Tried and then incarcerated at the infamous Con Lon Island penitentiary off the Vietnamese coast, he would remain jailed for more than sixteen years. The Vietnamese Revolution of August 1945 finally freed him.

A committed communist, Ton subsequently became one of the best-known leaders of the Communist Party-led, independent Vietnamese state. Despite his prominence, what triggered his arrest and imprisonment in 1929 is a well-kept secret of the party. The episode has thus far remained murky and requires a lot more diligent research, but from several, partially conflicting versions, the following sketch is drawn:[2]

Once admitted into the party in 1927, Ton Duc Thang became a member of the Sai Gon party cell. Much to his own surprise, he was promoted after three months to become the representative of the VRYL's Cantonese Central Committee with the party's Regional Committee of Cochinchina. The chairman of the latter committee, Le Van Phat, who supposedly was a professional practitioner of traditional medicine, soon became Ton's rival. Ton believed that he had a more justified claim on the leading VRYL post in the south because of his seniority and experience. Le Van Phat in turn arrogantly urged him to abandon his wife and children for more effective party work, a demand that almost made Ton Duc Thang quit the VRYL. For a time Le Van Phat even had Ton put under surveillance.

In 1928, a young woman, Tran Thu Thuy, joined the VRYL, and either Ton himself, as the French claimed then, or, as Vietnamese historians insist now, another party member, Do Dinh Tho, fell in love with her. However, she was soon forced by Le Van Phat to live with him and become his mistress. After several unsuccessful attempts to bring the matter before the Regional Committee, Ton and a few close comrades accused Le Van Phat of abuse of a "sister" and of violations of party rules. With like minds from both the Regional and the Sai Gon Committees, a party court was convened. Although Ton himself might have opted for sending Le Van Phat to Canton to be disciplined by the Central Committee of the VRYL, a majority decided that Le Van Phat had to be eliminated.

On 8 December 1928, Le Van Phat was first drugged by Nguyen Trung Nguyet [3] and then killed by Tran Truong, Tran Van Cong, and Ngo Thiem in a house in Sai Gon's rue Barbier. Ton afterward gave the assassins instructions to make the murder look like a crime of passion. Highly disturbed by the incident, the VRYL's Central Committee dissolved the Regional Committee in the same month. It also sent Pham Van Dong, a trusted lieutenant of Nguyen Ai Quoc who much later would become prime minister of independent Viet Nam, to Sai Gon to build a new regional party organization in Cochinchina. It is possible, but hitherto unsubstantiated, that Ton Duc Thang actually left the VRYL in the wake of the killing and founded a rival organization, the Nam Ky Kong Hoi (Cochinchinese Labor Union).

The French, who had been looking for some time for a pretext to crack down on an increasingly restless, radical anticolonial scene in Cochinchina, never fell for the ruse of a crime of passion. The murder was a golden chance to net political activists on charges of a common crime. In the course of about ten months, almost the entire networks of the VRYL and other anti-French groups and parties were smashed in Cochinchina. Ton Duc Thang was arrested on 23 July 1929. In mid-July 1930, forty-four defendants stood trial for forming "secret societies," seven among them also for the *crime de la rue Barbier.* The three assassins were all condemned to death and executed on 21 May 1931. Ton barely escaped the death sentence; as the alleged instigator of the murder of Le Van Phat, he was condemned to twenty years of forced labor and sent to Con Lon.

TON DUC THANG was born on 20 August 1888, the first child of well-to-do peasants on Ong Ho Island in the lower Mekong River. Just a few kilometers away was the town of Long Xuyen, the center of a western province in the French colony of Cochinchina. He died on 30 March 1980 as his country's president in Ha Noi, the capital of the independent and united Socialist Republic of Viet Nam. Viet Nam has multiple histories, many of them touched and influenced Ton's life. Yet, framed by these dates and data, terms and places, his life belongs most of all to the histories of Viet Nam's twentieth-century movements for national independence and social revolution. Clearly, Ton Duc Thang himself conceptualized his life in, and fully devoted it to, this paradigm.

Among Viet Nam's communist leaders, Ton Duc Thang stands out in several ways: He was the oldest and, with Ho Chi Minh, who was two years his junior, one of the only two who were born long before 1900. He was one of the very few who had deep roots in the working class. Furthermore, he endured the longest incarceration under the French. Among the small number of southerners in the post-independence leadership, he held the most positions of prominence: chairman of the National Assembly, chairman of the Fatherland Front, the country's vice president under Ho Chi Minh, and then its president, to name a few. Finally and notably, among those who held prominent posts, Ton Duc Thang exerted the least amount of influence in policy-making circles of the party—and never exhibited any discernible ambition to gain such influence.

As one of its central intentions, the following inquiry will pursue the question why one of the most visible exponents of the communist regime so conspicuously lacked actual power, or, vice versa, why someone with positions of only a rather reactive, passive nature was among the communist party's most celebrated and accomplished representatives. Ton Duc Thang gave the party an identity that no one else apparently was able to provide. His life addressed some of the core assumptions of the party's self-image. In this regard, a study about Ton Duc Thang is not a biography in the narrow sense, even though it regularly needs to introduce and discuss biographical information. Rather, it is also an investigation into the history of Vietnamese communism: how did the party think of itself and shape its self-identity, how did it portray itself—in concrete and symbolic ways—to the outside, and how did it explain that it had a legitimate claim to power?

In this study, the term "Vietnamese Revolution" denotes the long *process* in which Vietnamese national liberation was achieved and an independent, communist-led country established. The term therefore describes a historical development as much as a historical vision, both of which date back to the early twentieth century, certainly culminated in the decade between 1945 and 1955, and, in a way, are still ongoing and being pursued.[4] Post-independence historical writing in Viet Nam has long been under the tight control of the Communist Party and dictated by the strict determinism of the Marxian historical materialist model it advocated. Consequently, the multiple histories of Viet Nam's recent past have been oriented toward, and subordinated to, the privileged story of the party-led Vietnamese Revolution. National and party histories often are portrayed as, and collapsed into, one. Therefore, a study of the communist celebrity Ton Duc Thang in large measure concerns the historiography of postcolonial Viet Nam as well.

Ton Duc Thang's life came to be defined by three famous episodes and achievements, which were intimately connected to his later rise to prominence:

(1) his alleged participation, perhaps even decisive role, in the French navy mutiny in the Black Sea in 1919, which helped end the Allied anti-Bolshevik intervention in the Russian civil war following the October Revolution of 1917;

(2) his organization of a so-called "secret labor union" in Sai Gon in the early 1920s, identified by some as the country's first labor union; and

(3) his union's supposed leadership of a strike at the Sai Gon navy shipyard in 1925, usually portrayed as the first political strike in Viet Nam.

This study argues that each of these episodes established imagined ancestries, or origins, for Vietnamese communism. They spoke directly to the party's ideal image and had a powerful grip on the imagination not only of communist revolutionaries but of the Vietnamese public in general. Some of the defining stories of Ton Duc Thang's life were embraced by the entire party, while others were contested and became instrumentalized in intraparty factionalism.

I have divided this study into three parts. Part 1, with three chapters on "constructions," examines the ways in which Ton Duc Thang's most well known biographical episode—his participation in the Black Sea Mutiny—came about originally and how it was utilized by various interests over time. Chapter 1 discusses the Black Sea Mutiny in the late colonial moment, before and during Ton Duc Thang's early party career prior to the August Revolution of 1945. The story's genesis will be traced, when Ton's professed involvement in the French navy revolt became an essential part of his (self-)image as a revolutionary.

Chapters 2 and 3 follow the story of Ton's role in the Black Sea Mutiny through the revolutionary and post-recognition moments, when the communist-led Democratic Republic of Viet Nam (DRVN) appropriated Ton's story. The Black Sea episode now came to symbolize some of the revolutionary characteristics of the state, and it was mainly directed at the potential and, after recognition, acknowledged political and ideological allies of the Vietnamese Revolution.

Part 2, with two chapters on "contestations," describes the process in which certain tales from Ton's life no longer remained within the exegetic domain of the central party. Instead they were claimed by regional factions within the Revolution, and opposing interests began to challenge them.

The strike at the Sai Gon navy shipyard in 1925 was first propagated in the late 1950s, and chapter 4 analyzes this episode in the context of the post-partition moment, that is after the division of Viet Nam following the Geneva Conference of 1954 and the establishment of a rival southern regime in Sai Gon, which forced many southern revolutionaries into a northern exile of yet unknown duration.

Historiographical debates on the so-called "secret labor union" of Sai Gon did not take place until the late 1970s and early 1980s and heated up toward the mid-1980s. Chapter 5 describes the debate in the framework of the post-unification moment, when, after 1975, the Vietnamese Revolution had extended its authority over the southern half of the country as well, and a southern revolutionary identity was able to express itself more assertively.

Part 3, comprised of two chapters on "commemorations," juxtaposes two distinctly different approaches to the commemoration of the deceased Ton Duc Thang. As detailed in chapter 6, in the immediate posthumous moment of the early 1980s, a biography commissioned by the central party apparatus in Ha Noi sought to establish an official, national image of Ton Duc Thang's revolutionary heroism. By contrast, chapter 7 looks at the mid- to late 1980s, the post-socialist moment, when southern commemorative efforts became vehicles for a nostalgic critique of the country's political course. In the changing environments of Vietnamese society, economics, and politics, the symbolic meanings of Ton's life are increasingly lost—just like Ton Duc Thang himself is largely forgotten in contemporary Viet Nam.

THIS BOOK COMBINES ITS DISCUSSION of the historical contexts in which the central episodes of Ton's life appeared with historical research into the stories and a close analysis of the narrative and textual conventions in which these imagined ancestries came to be expressed and recalled. By way of a biographical case study, it thus seeks to gain a deeper understanding of the historiographical construction of the self-images of Vietnamese communism. All too often, our understanding of the Vietnamese Revolution is based on assumptions and assertions that have never been seriously tested. With the possible (and only partial) exception of some biographical inquiries into Ho Chi Minh's life or analyses of the Vietnamese communist genre of prison memoirs,[5] no systematic attempt has been undertaken thus far to shed light on the inner "workings" of Vietnamese historiography in constructing those images that seek to explain the nature, the origins, and the ultimate trajectory of Vietnamese communism.

Historical revisionism is, of course, not lacking, nor is it something entirely new. In recent decades, structuralist and post-structuralist theories, subaltern and postcolonial studies, feminist and postmodern modes of analysis—to name a few approaches of historical inquiry—have opened up fresh ways in which to (re-)interpret the past. This study certainly seeks to participate in processes of resituating, interrogating, and deconstructing fields of knowledge and discourses of power. In the following pages, dearly held "truths" of Vietnamese communism will be debunked. But more than that, I am interested in the very processes in which myths have been created, a concern that all too often remains unaddressed in the literature.

A study that seeks to combine, among other things, history, historiography, and biography is faced with various chronologies that, far from running parallel, often rub against each other: Ton Duc Thang's personal chronology, the Revolution's chronology, as well as the chronologies of the various tales. I decided to concentrate primarily on the trajectories of the episodes, even if that meant that biographical and revolutionary chronologies were at times disrupted and had to loop around the main argumentative thread. In that sense, this book is neither a conventional biography nor a complete account of the Vietnamese Revolution. Rather, by way of analyzing a particular set of historical-biographical writings and at the same time examining pertinent and new information from the archives, it is a thorough reevaluation of the history of Vietnamese communism that seeks to crack the thick walls of the party's historiographical rhetoric.

The best way to analyze the various imagined ancestries associated with the tales of Ton Duc Thang's revolutionary exploits is to position them within their respective historical (and historiographical) *moments*. The concept of "moments" that I employ throughout the book constitutes my particular engagement with Keith Taylor's idea of "surface orientations."[6] Like Taylor's surface orientations, "moments" highlight the temporal and local specificities that determined the ways in which ideas were received and discussed and people made their choices. A sensitivity to a particular terrain—geographically, intellectually, and historically—can best free us from explanatory mega-narratives of "nation" and "revolution" and cut through the fog that such larger paradigms throw up to enforce self-legitimizing standard interpretations of the past, a past to which, we are made to believe, we are intimately and meaningfully linked.

Another historical work that particularly inspired my study in this regard is Glenn May's *Inventing a Hero*.[7] Similar to my work, May is concerned with the discursive strategies, nationalist teleologies, and at times outright manipulations employed by commemorators of a Filipino national-revolutionary hero. May and I share an acute interest in the processes of historical engineering, in the ways in which myths of power and authority are created and circulated. More so than May's, however, my study on the politics of history and memory production focuses on two hitherto under-recognized issues: first, how regionalism is an influential factor in modern Vietnamese historiography (which nationalist narratives emanating from the center of power habitually seek to obscure), and second, how unstable even seemingly hegemonic narratives can become. Regionalism and other, related communal interests have a way of latching on to and embellishing, redirecting, or undermining discourses of authority and legitimacy. As this book shows, soon enough such powerful stories can develop dynamics of their own and slip outside the control of those in whose interests they were propagated. The following detailed examination of a certain body of historical texts shows that, even in the case of a biography of a model revolutionary, the history of the Vietnamese Revolution continues to be contested and reshaped, and its ancestries imagined in multiple ways.

Finally, an inquiry of the kind this book is attempting is not without pitfalls. It lies in the nature of seeking to reach a better understanding of the inner workings of historical and propagandistic production that at times "smoking gun" evidence is lacking. But this should not deter us. Conjecture, context, supposition, and circumstantial evidence have a place in such an undertaking, as long as the evidentiary bases and the process of their interpretation remain transparent. In that sense, I am offering here a set of hypotheses on Ton Duc Thang's experiences and the developments of the various tales that do not exclude variant readings.

PART I

Constructions

CHAPTER 1

The Black Sea Mutiny in the Late Colonial Moment

LIKE SO MANY OTHERS, my story has, perhaps inevitably, no real beginning. Among various possible pathways, I have chosen one that will set out from a secret guerrilla base amid the rugged mountains of northern Viet Nam in 1947.

In early November of that year, thirty or so men came together for a meeting in or near the small town of Vo Nhai, about thirty kilometers northeast of Thai Nguyen, the administrative center of Bac Thai province,[1] and roughly eighty kilometers north of Ha Noi, the country's capital then occupied by the French, their mortal enemies. Most of the men gathering in Vo Nhai held highest or high ranks in the government and other political organs of the Democratic Republic of Viet Nam, which had declared its independence from French colonial rule in September 1945 following a brief, successful revolutionary upheaval. But the French had returned to reestablish their control, and after much maneuvering, war had broken out between the two sides in December 1946. Soon, the DRVN had been forced to retreat to resistance strongholds in the countryside, mostly in the mountainous terrain of northern and north-central Viet Nam, from where it conducted a guerrilla campaign.

On that November day in Vo Nhai, however, the men convened not in their capacity as DRVN representatives, but as leading cadres of the Indochinese Communist Party (ICP), which had continued to function clandestinely since its voluntary, yet only nominal, dissolution in November 1945. We can assume that among those likely to have participated in the gathering were Ho Chi Minh, Le Duan, Truong Chinh, Pham Van Dong, Vo Nguyen Giap, Le Duc Tho, Ton Duc Thang, Pham Hung, Le Van Luong, and Hoang Van Hoan. The reason for their meeting was a commemoration, and the occasion was provided by the thirtieth anniversary of the Russian October Revolution of 1917.

Before describing what transpired at the commemorative gathering in Vo Nhai in November 1947, I should stress that the only information about the event was provided, during an interview with me, by Duong Van Phuc, who claimed to have been present as Ton Duc Thang's adjutant, then in his early twenties. A few months later, he would also become Ton's son-in-law when he married his boss's oldest daughter, Ton Thi Hanh.[2] No independent sources could be found to corroborate Duong Van Phuc's story.[3]

According to Duong Van Phuc, then, it was during this meeting in commemoration of the thirtieth anniversary of the Russian October Revolution that Le Van Luong addressed the gathered ICP leadership roughly along the following lines: There actually was in their midst one person who had personally been involved in an important event connected with the October Revolution. In 1919, comrade Ton Duc Thang had been a seaman on a warship in the Black Sea where French naval forces operated in support of counterrevolutionary White armies. At Sevastopol, Ton had taken part with French sailors in the famous and successful mutiny aimed at ending the intervention and thereby defending Soviet Russia. He even had been in contact with André Marty, the well-known navy officer who instigated the mutiny and later, after his release from prison, became a communist.

Upon hearing Le Van Luong relate the story of the mutiny, everybody at the meeting—again according to Duong Van Phuc—was very proud of their comrade Ton Duc Thang. Supposedly, it was only at the Vo Nhai commemorative event that many of the ICP leaders learned about Ton's exploits for the first time; Duong Van Phuc explained the novelty of the tale with reference to Ton's modesty and lifelong habit of rarely talking about his past.

Over time, the story of Ton Duc Thang in the Black Sea would become famous both domestically and abroad as representing one of the most heroic deeds by a Vietnamese radical activist and one of the clearest and earliest manifestations of the Vietnamese spirit of revolutionary internationalism. Indeed, in this episode we can find the first and perhaps most important instance in which Vietnamese communism imagined its ancestry through the life of Ton Duc Thang. If Duong Van Phuc is correct about the gathering in 1947, those communist leaders at Vo Nhai heard a tale that would establish the earliest and most direct link between the very core of their own political enterprise and their ultimate historical and ideological model, the deeply revered Russian

October Revolution of 1917–20 they were commemorating at that very moment.

The meeting in Vo Nhai marked a turning point for the story of Ton Duc Thang's participation in the Black Sea Mutiny. Yet, in order to explain the qualitative change in 1947, we need to take a big step back in time and first trace the tale's genesis. This chapter will therefore lay the evidentiary basis for my discussion (in chapter 2) of how revolutionary internationalism during the October Revolution became one imagined ancestry of Vietnamese communism. Here we will pursue the following questions: What was the Black Sea Mutiny? What was Ton Duc Thang's connection to the mutiny? How did the tale become known? And how did Ton put the story to use?

THE BLACK SEA MUTINY, 1919

The Russian October Revolution is insufficiently understood if we focus solely on the events of 6/7 November 1917,[4] when the Bolsheviks under Vladimir Ilich Lenin and Leon Trotsky seized power in the Congress of Soviets convening in Petrograd[5] and did away with the more moderate provisional government, then led by Aleksandr Kerensky, which had ended the rule of the czar in March 1917. The initial success of the Revolution *as act* must be seen in the light of the uniquely favorable conditions produced by the total disintegration of the czarist army on the eastern front of World War I and the rapidly rising social disorder among a starving and war-weary population. But beyond that, the Russian Revolution *as process* is also remarkable because it managed to hold on to power beyond the coup of 1917, consolidate, against greatest odds, its regime during 1918 and 1919, and by 1920/21, firmly control the huge territory that would be called the Soviet Union. The gravest adversities should briefly be mentioned: Lenin had to extricate Russia from World War I at all costs lest total defeat also sweep his regime away; he signed the humiliating Treaty of Brest-Litovsk with Germany in March 1918. For the next two years, the Bolshevik Red Army fought counterrevolutionary White armies in a bloody Russian civil war that would not turn decisively in the Red Army's favor until late in 1919. At the same time, the World War I Allies—an especially eager France, Japan, Britain, and the United States—intervened with joint military expeditions on four fronts and by supporting the White armies.

Further consideration must be given to the ideology of class struggle and socialist development propagated by the Bolsheviks (soon called communists). The Revolution had for the first time successfully institutionalized a powerful counter-paradigm to the two prevalent capitalist models, the closed spheres of influence of colonialism and the Wilsonian free-market liberalism that paid little more than lip service to notions of self-determination. The appeal of the Soviet paradigm was immense among the poor working classes of Europe as well as radicals in and from the colonies—among them Nguyen Ai Quoc, who later called himself Ho Chi Minh—who found in it answers to the problems of both national liberation and social revolution. In sum, the Russian October Revolution should be appreciated in the context of three main factors: it was aided by the chaos of World War I, it successfully defended itself against powerful counterrevolutionary forces, and it constituted a new and appealing counter-model in world politics.

The events in the Black Sea in the spring of 1919 were closely related to the same three factors.[6] The Allied intervention in the Ukraine, the Crimea, and southern Russia from late 1918 to mid-1919 was partly a result of the end of World War I; armistice provisions called for the disarmament of German troops and their evacuation from those regions. But strong anti-Bolshevik designs were equally fueling Allied military operations. Allied forces supported the White armies and were not infrequently engaged in direct hostilities with an advancing Red Army. On the other hand, the mutinous sailors were largely motivated by an overwhelming desire to return home to France after World War I and deeply resented being kept on duty in an undeclared war. But pro-Soviet sympathies also were an important driving force for their protests.

Because of the great notoriety the story of Ton Duc Thang's exploits in the Black Sea has achieved, a detailed look at the Black Sea Mutiny will be necessary. The French navy and other Allied units, mostly British and, to a lesser degree, Greek and Romanian, had been operating in the Black Sea since the end of 1918. There were no hostile naval forces; the flotilla mainly transported troop detachments from bases outside the Black Sea to the occupied coastal areas of the Ukraine, the Crimean peninsula, and southern Russia and provided subsequent logistical support. In March 1919, however, Red Army units advanced toward the region, and Allied and White forces had to retreat beyond the

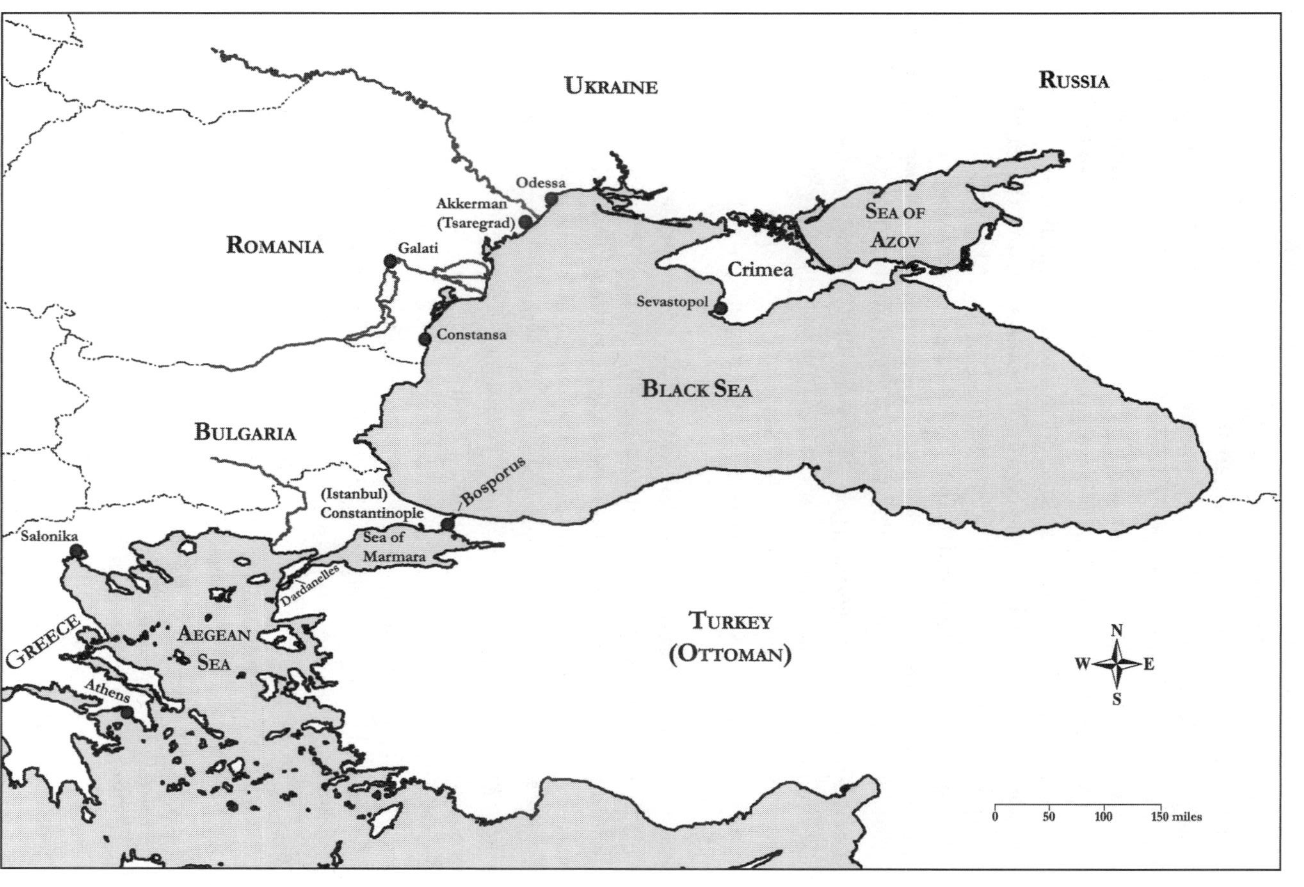

The Black Sea and the Aegean Sea, 1919

Dniester River southwest of Odessa. French vessels were instrumental in the hasty evacuation of Odessa in early April and, thereafter, imposed a blockade on the Ukrainian coast. In mid-April, at the Crimean port of Sevastopol, Allied warships were shelling Red Army troops further inland that were pushing toward the city.

Considerable morale problems among French units had been apparent for a while. Contributing factors were uncertainty over the extent and aims of the ongoing operations so long after the armistice, compounded by deteriorating living conditions on board, and the exposure of the crews and troop detachments to the charged environment of the Russian Revolution and to French anti-interventionist agitation. In April, things came to a head. First, hoping to trigger widespread revolts and bring about the collapse of the Allied intervention, André Marty, an officer (first engineer) on the torpedo boat *Protet,* plotted to take command of the ship and hand it over to the Bolsheviks. But the plan was foiled, and Marty and a few associates were arrested on 16 April. Only a few days later—although quite independent of the Marty incident—mutinies broke out on about eight to ten French navy vessels at Sevastopol. Crews demanded, most of all, the immediate return to France, defiantly sang the "Internationale," and protested against the Allies' "dirty" counterrevolutionary war. On three armored cruisers, the *France,* the *Jean-Bart,* and the *Justice,* red flags were even hoisted. In late April, in another serious incident, sailors on the heavy cruiser *Waldeck-Rousseau,* on patrol only about half a nautical mile off the piers of enemy-held Odessa, voiced similar demands and threatened to turn the ship over to the Red Army. To a lesser degree, the crews of two torpedo boats and a cruiser in the proximity of the *Waldeck-Rousseau* also rebelled and briefly refused to follow orders. In a series of aftershocks, isolated and shorter outbreaks of insubordination happened on the torpedo boat *Dehorter* in May east of the Crimea, on the armored cruiser *Condorcet* in June off Odessa, and finally in August, at the very end of Allied operations in the Black Sea, on the torpedo boat *Touareg.*

These were the instances of mutinies in the Black Sea in connection with the French anti-Bolshevik intervention that came to be known as the Black Sea Mutiny. More protests and mass insubordinations would occur from May to August on warships at French and other Mediterranean navy bases.[7] But they will not concern me further at this early point because Ton Duc Thang's story specifically mentions the Black Sea. One should, however, keep in mind that the southern French port of Toulon was among those places where this second wave of mutinies and organized mass actions occurred.

Except for the unrest on the *France,* which lasted for more than ten days, all other mutinies in the Black Sea were over after one, two, or three days. Some crews lost their courage and resumed their duties; in other cases, commanders managed to defuse the crisis by combining intimidating pressure tactics with paternalistic appeals to "reason." Yet, several ships had to be withdrawn, if only to navy bases further south in the Black Sea. By leaving the vicinity of enemy forces, for which volatile crews had voiced sympathies, the specter of ships being commandeered and turned over to the Red Army was banished. And, accompanied by vague promises to consider a return to France, departures as such already restored a measure of calm.

Philippe Masson has convincingly pointed out that the whole affair exhibited characteristics more akin to labor strikes than to mutinies (in the narrow sense of sailors rebelling and taking command of a ship).[8] The crews—at least those at Sevastopol and those involved in incidents after April—staged protest rallies and refused to work as long as their demands were not met. Although threats were used on both sides, acts of violence or sabotage on board the ships were rare and small in scale. Indeed, essential services were maintained.

By early May, just after the most serious revolts, most French warships had left the Black Sea. With the Red Army now controlling the regions east of the Dniester, only a naval blockade was enforced. But the mutinies alone hardly caused the end of Allied operations. More accurately, they hastened the process of the thinly veiled retreat already under way. From its start, the intervention had lacked clear goals, adequate supplies, and domestic support (so soon after the long World War). Thus too limited to aid the counterrevolution effectively, the involvement of foreign troops in the civil war instead strengthened the Red Army's nationalist appeal. In fact, the habitual ruthlessness with which Allied forces moved against suspected revolutionary "elements" in occupied zones not only alienated large portions of the population but also led to the first serious instances of insubordination among French landed troops—even before unrest spread to the flotilla. The counterproductivity of the limited intervention is further revealed by the ironic fact that White Russian armies, once they were left with much *less* Allied support, temporarily reoccupied Odessa and the Crimea in the summer of 1919.

But even if the revolts alone were not so decisive in ending Allied Black Sea operations—ineffective as the campaign was anyway—they still had an important impact. By revealing widespread morale and discipline problems, they put troop reliability very much in question, and any potential French re-intervention in the Russian Revolution was rendered infeasible.[9]

Contesting interpretations of the events in the Black Sea were emblematic of the growing ideological and organizational split among the Left, which was to become disastrously paralyzing in the face of rising European fascist movements. For the radical Left, which was soon to found communist parties and organize in the Third Internationale, the Black Sea Mutiny of 1919 became an icon of revolutionary, proletarian internationalism. I suggest that the mutiny was all the more propagated as proof of the validity of this concept so central to Marxian ideology, precisely because proletarian internationalism had utterly failed at the outbreak of World War I in the summer of 1914. Then, most European workers, labor unions, and socialist parties (of the Second Internationale) quite enthusiastically supported their national war efforts, which, after all, would see millions of working-class soldiers shooting at their "brothers" across blood-soaked trenches.

The Black Sea Mutiny was used to heal the trauma brought on by the utter failure of proletarian internationalism in 1914. Now the theme of transnational revolutionary class solidarity, pro-Soviet support, and anti-imperialist sentiments of the mutinous crews became greatly amplified and recast and celebrated as a heroic, epic struggle that defeated the intervention.[10] Consequently, what became downplayed was the sailors' widespread desire to finally return home so long after the armistice (likely their predominant motivation somewhat irrespective of the specific circumstances of the Allied operations) and the undermining of the campaign by inherent problems the mutiny only compounded.

Not unexpectedly, the more moderate Left of democratic socialists of the Second Internationale accentuated the events of the Black Sea differently. The fiasco of internationalism in 1914 had happened on its watch, and it was unprepared to admit that only the new Soviet model might be successful in bringing about that loftiest of working-class sentiments. Instead, true to their social reformist agenda, socialists defended—not celebrated—the sailors' actions by emphasizing deplorable conditions on board. And reflective of their strategy of working within the system, they further explained the revolt with reference to the long-delayed demobilization and the unconstitutionality of the intervention.

French military and state authorities were clearly rattled by the mutiny, the potential for disaster, and the authorities' near impotence when faced with mass unrest. After the event, they struck back with unfettered vengeance. In the ensuing court-martials of the "instigators" of the mutiny, André Marty received the longest jail sentence, twenty years. (A handful of soldiers, who had disobeyed orders during combat situations on land, actually received death penalties, later commuted to long prison terms.) Other navy mutineers initially received sentences of up to fifteen years. Still, the majority of followers got away with lighter disciplinary measures. Perhaps because he was of a higher military rank, or for reasons of his excellent public relations skills, André Marty became a cause célèbre in the polarized postwar social and political climates. An amnesty campaign finally freed Marty in 1923. He joined the French Communist Party soon after, was elevated to its politburo in 1931, and, in 1935, worked in the Comintern secretariat.[11]

TON DUC THANG AND THE BLACK SEA MUTINY

We will recall, following Duong Van Phuc, what Le Van Luong told ICP leaders during the 1947 meeting in Vo Nhai in commemoration of the thirtieth anniversary of the Russian October Revolution: in 1919, Ton Duc Thang had been on a French warship in the Black Sea and, at Sevastopol, participated in the successful, internationalist mutiny in defense of Soviet Russia. And he had been in contact with André Marty, the famous alleged instigator. What evidence can be found to substantiate the story of Ton's exploits in the Black Sea?

The revolts in the Black Sea, which were deemed so serious that court-martials were held afterward, took place on the following French warships:[12]

- — the *Protet,* foiled at Galaţi, Romania, 16 April (A. Marty);
- — the *France,* at Sevastopol, 19–23 April, and on sea, 23–30 April;
- — the *Jean-Bart,* at Sevastopol, 19–21 April;

— the *Justice,* at Sevastopol, 20–22 April;
— the *Algol,* at Sevastopol, 21 and 22 April;
— the *Waldeck-Rousseau,* off Odessa, 27 and 28 April; and
— the *Touareg,* off Odessa, 7 and 8 August.

In addition, Masson's and Marty's detailed accounts of the events conform with one another in describing far less serious incidents on the following vessels:

— the *Du Chayla,* at Sevastopol, 19–21 April;
— the damaged *Mirabeau,* at Sevastopol, around 21 April;
— the *Vergniaud,* at Sevastopol, 21 and 22 April;
— the *Scarpe,* at Sevastopol, 22 and 23 April;
— the *Bruix,* at Tendra, an island off Odessa, 28 April;
— the *Dehorter,* off the Crimea, early May; and
— the *Condorcet,* at Tendra, 13 and 14 June.

Marty and Masson differ, however, on the question of a few other navy units marginally involved in the unrest. In these cases, crews had made no plans of their own; rather, nearby mutinies triggered the crews' spontaneous and short-lived insubordinations. For these least important instances, Marty, but not Masson, names the following warships:

— the *Escaut,* at Sevastopol, 20 and 21 April;
— the *Fauconneau,* off Odessa, 27 April; and
— the *Mameluck,* off Odessa, 27 April.

On the other hand, Masson describes brief unrest on two ships, about which Marty remains silent. These are:

— the *Hussard,* at Sevastopol, 24 April; and
— the *Chamois,* unspecified (April/May?).

The French navy kept detailed crew registers *(rôles d'équipages)* of their vessels on board. They were large, heavy books filled with blank, preprinted lists. Among other data, the full names, ages, identification numbers, and dates and ports of service of the officers and all the lower ranks were entered in ink into the register. The *rôles d'équipages* for the year 1919 of most of the navy vessels in question were available to me, and French archivists examined a few more crew lists at my request.

The only unavailable register was that of the *Condorcet* (of category 2). Since Ton might have used the alias Dinh Cong Thang at some point before 1929,[13] the *rôles d'équipages* were searched under the names TON Duc Thang, DINH Cong Thang, and THANG, Ton Duc/Dinh Cong. But none of the possible entries appear in those lists.[14]

On this evidentiary basis, four initial conclusions can be drawn: First, Ton Duc Thang was not on board those ships on which the most decisive revolts broke out. Second, neither before, during, or after the Black Sea Mutiny could Ton therefore have been in contact with André Marty, who had been serving on the *Protet* (category 1) since September 1917.[15] Third, Ton Duc Thang did not take part in any of the mutinies at Sevastopol. And fourth, with regard to far less serious incidents on other warships, we can rule out Ton's participation except for the *Condorcet*—a minor and geographically isolated case, however, that occurred two months after the main wave of unrest.

Not only was Ton Duc Thang on none of the ships for which crew registers were available, but none of these vessels had any Vietnamese crewmen at all on board during their Black Sea operations. Sailors from other French colonies (Senegalese and northern African), however, are included in several *rôles*. The crew lists on which Vietnamese sailors do appear (as *marins indigènes*) need to be read carefully: they show that Vietnamese "third rank" seamen, most of them unskilled *(matelots de troisième classe sans specialité)*, and navy cadets *(apprentis marins)* were transferred during the intervention to French navy bases in Salonika (Greece) and Constantinople just outside the Black Sea. In January 1919, for example, the *Bruix* brought fifteen "Tongkinese" (i.e., from northern Viet Nam) cadets to Constantinople and to the *Patrie* (which was based there and did not see crew unrest until June, outside the Black Sea). Only after the Black Sea operations would Vietnamese seamen be assigned to vessels on which insubordinations had occurred earlier in the spring.

Thus, in September and October 1919, about fifty Tongkinese navy cadets, all of whom had been recruited for three years of duty in the summer of 1918, came on board the *Waldeck-Rousseau* from Constantinople and Salonika. A few months later, many of them were transferred to other warships like the *France* and the *Jean-Bart,* which had already received more than one hundred new Vietnamese crew members from Salonika earlier in the fall of 1919. These men included two quartermasters and about equal numbers of cadets and unskilled sailors who had been recruited in Sai Gon (or more generally in Indochina) in the fall of 1918. Finally, in October and November 1919, the *Du Chayla* received nine Tongkinese unskilled seamen from Constantinople. Even among these Vietnamese sailors who served on navy vessels *after* the end of the Allied anti-Bolshevik intervention, Ton Duc Thang is not listed.

We can therefore conclude that Ton Duc Thang did not participate in any of the core revolts in the Black Sea in 1919. His presence on only one warship with a belated, minor incident of unrest at an isolated navy base cannot be fully ruled out. Yet, in the light of Vietnamese seamen being assigned to warships only after the large-scale demobilization of French reservists, in September and October of 1919, it is highly unlikely that Ton Duc Thang was on this one ship for which no crew register could be checked. We will revisit the events of 1919 and test my conclusions in chapter 3, in which I will discuss Ton's "recollections" of his involvement in the Black Sea Mutiny.

Even though the story of Ton's revolutionary deeds in the Black Sea is false, the tale has always carried a certain amount of credibility. Ton Duc Thang could potentially have been in the Black Sea, because he was a colonial worker at the French navy base in Toulon from 1916 to about 1919/20, right before or even during the times of the mutinies. In the next sections, we will look at the following questions: How did Ton end up serving in France? What do we know about his sojourn there? And is there a connection between his sojourn in France and the Black Sea Mutiny?

TON'S ENLISTMENT FOR WARTIME SERVICE

All biographers agree that Ton moved from his parents' place near Long Xuyen to Sai Gon in 1906, at the age of eighteen. As the oldest son of well-to-do peasants, he had been privately tutored in Long Xuyen in classical studies (Chinese script, Chinese history and philosophy) and had learned some French in a public school. As is the case with many other aspects of his life, little of a concrete nature can be said at all about the next nine years of his life. From 1906 on, Ton allegedly became a worker in Sai Gon, doing "a bit of everything for a living," including a job as a servant.[16] Later in his life he claimed to remember little of those years. One of his memories, however, was his enrollment in the only vocational school in Indochina, the École des mécaniciens asiatiques de Saïgon (Sai Gon School for Asian Mechanics).

Ton's name indeed surfaces in a document from the École des mécaniciens asiatiques. According to the school's register, which lists all the diplomas for specialized training *(brevets d'études techniques)* for 1906–66, Ton enrolled in 1915 for a training course scheduled to be completed after two years *(promotion de 1915–1917)*. His birthplace is listed as "Anhoa Longxuyen," and his age as twenty years, even though he was already twenty-seven years old at that time.[17] A possible explanation for the discrepancy is that the École des mécaniciens asiatiques imposed an age limit for admissions, which Ton might have circumvented by passing himself off as younger. The only other entry in the list is a grade, "16.44," for his performance with "machines." Otherwise, neither grades for additional courses of instruction nor a diploma are recorded.

A second document from the École des mécaniciens asiatiques accounts for the absence of a final course degree for Ton Duc Thang. The school's matriculation rolls for 1907–18 mention that Ton took courses in "electricity" and "automobiles." But in the middle of his training program, in September 1916, he left the vocational school "to serve in France," from where he returned only in August 1920.[18] Before we look at Ton's sojourn in France, we need to discuss his departure from the École des mécaniciens asiatiques and its relation to the Black Sea story.

The matriculation record in 1916 does not suggest any coercive mobilization for wartime service. The entry states "Engagé pr [pour] Servir en France." "Engagé" means, quite neutrally, "recruited," and would rather imply voluntariness than pressure.[19] On the other hand, after the rediscovery in 1980 of the old school register, Ton Duc Thang's biographers have usually argued that he was mobilized *(bi dong vien)* for war service in 1916, and they imply by the use of the negative passive form *(bi)* that he was drafted against his will, or at least without a choice. Others even say that Ton was "forced to go" *(bi bat sang)* to France.[20] Clearly, the question whether Ton's and, for that matter, other Vietnamese workers' recruitment to aid France during World War I happened by coercion or on their own volition cannot be answered at this point and warrants further inquiry. But the disconcerting image of a future revolutionary serving his colonial masters most likely necessitated the biographical move toward coercion.

This discomfort about Ton Duc Thang's association with a colonial institution was also likely the reason for the following biographical oddity. Prior to the discovery of the school register in 1980, biographical sketches maintained that Ton was involved *in 1912* in several early protest strikes at the Sai Gon navy shipyard *(xuong Ba Son)* and at the École des mécaniciens asiatiques. In danger of being arrested by the French because of his involvement in the walkouts, Ton then left the country under a false name. During the next seven years abroad, he at first worked on a French merchant ship, then became a ship mechanic in the French navy, and thus finally, in 1919, played his part in the Black Sea Mutiny.[21] In 1957, Ton recalled these "experiences" in the following way:

> At that time none of the rich kids wished to enter those schools for dirty, oily vocations. Therefore the French . . . had to select *us* poor youths. And while we were taught little, we had to work a lot as ship repairmen. This means that they used the good name of studying to exploit our labor. . . . *We* urged *each other* to stage a school strike, which also was a work strike. Without ship repairmen, [they] forced the workmen of Ba Son to come and work. We mobilized the fellow workers to leave as well and not to work. When the French colonialists in turn fired some of those fellow workers, we again mobilized all of the Ba Son workmen to strike immediately. . . . The struggle was victorious, yet we did not know what to do next. . . . We lacked an ideal, the Party.[22]

The same image of someone who then had the will but not the means is presented in another statement made by Ton in 1957:

> I remember the day I left the country. . . . At that time the strikes of the students of the Sai Gon Industrial School and of the Ba Son workers were victorious. It was also the time when I boarded a French ship *in disguise* to evade the enemy's pursuit. A *life on the sea* began then. With patriotic fervour, I *hoped I might learn* truly a lot in order to return later and fight more effectively.[23]

Three points need to be made here: First, in Ton's recollection, he himself clearly is a student of the vocational school during the strike ("we," "us"). Second, he did not date his activism at the École des mécaniciens asiatiques, but we know, of course, that Ton Duc Thang enrolled in 1915. And third, his departure was supposedly caused by his anticolonial struggles at the vocational school and French attempts to arrest him. Yet, the school register shows that Ton, under his own name, was simply recruited by the French.

What happened here is an act of biographical obfuscation. Ton and/or his biographers sought a version of this period in his life that would directly connect the two desirable elements—(a) his proletarian background at the vocational school and (c) his participation in the Black Sea Mutiny—and erase the undesirable event in between, that is (b) recruitment and service for the French. Thus, Ton's affiliation with the colonial school had to be marked by cynical French exploitation and heroic Vietnamese struggle. Biographers moved his departure from the École des mécaniciens asiatiques to 1912, two years before the massive military recruitments caused by World War I. And it is imminent danger that compels Ton Duc Thang to leave the school and begin "a life on the sea"—a necessary discursive springboard to get Ton into the navy without having to introduce the recruitment scene at the school. The subsequent service in the French navy is unpleasant from the narrator's point of view, but unavoidable in order to arrive at the mutiny. It is thus rationalized, on the one hand, by Ton's patriotic desire to hone his anticolonial skills, and, on the other, cushioned by his disguise; in a sense, the disguise implies that an incognito Ton Duc Thang does not really serve the French.

For an episode of a shipyard/school strike in 1912, however, no archival evidence could be found.[24] I propose that the incidents of 1912 were invented and figured simply as a narrative device to move on to Sevastopol in the least conspicuous manner, and that Ton actually "remembered" events that were transposed from 1916, the year of his recruitment for service in France.

Once the evidence from the school register appeared in 1980, Ton's official party biography (discussed in chapter 6) tried frantically to make the unfitting fit. The year 1912, the transposed event of 1916, had to be maintained, but with the new information in circulation, the real departure for France in 1916 needed acknowledgment as well. To do so and still be able to narratively drop Ton off at his desired destination in the Black Sea, the party authors inserted a biographical loop, a chronological duplication, so to say, by having Ton *return* to Sai Gon before being mobilized into the navy. They thereby made 1912/1916 into two separate yet curiously parallel-identical events, as shown in the juxtaposition below:

First cycle (1912–15)	*Second cycle (1915–19)*
school strike in 1912	school enrollment in 1915
forced departure in 1912	forced mobilization in 1916
life on sea	life in the navy
learns from proletariat abroad	learns from French class struggles
brief return to Sai Gon	arrival in the Black Sea

To explain the 1915 enrollment at the École des mécaniciens asiatiques, however, Ton Duc Thang needed to become previously unknown at this place, since a reinstatement of a known troublemaker from 1912 would be unconvincing. Consequently, the biography had to overlook Ton's claim that he himself was a student of the vocational school during the strike of 1912. Instead, he was made to organize the 1912 protests from outside, and, thus unknown to the French, had no more need to disguise his identity; the very passage to that effect in the original "recollection" therefore was ignored.[25] Faced with such an utter mess, biographers later in the 1980s simply disregarded the alleged events of 1912 altogether and resigned themselves to the disconcerting images of 1916, since an enlistment in the navy was necessary for the Black Sea story. But, as discussed earlier, they made sure to portray Ton Duc Thang's wartime service in the French navy as coerced.

THE SOJOURN IN FRANCE, 1916–20

The little information we have about Ton Duc Thang's time in France was largely provided by Vo Van The, a former coworker at Toulon, during an interview in 1979 with Luu Phuong Thanh of the Ho Chi Minh City branch of the Commission for Research of Party History.[26] According to Vo Van The, a total of eighteen students of the École des mécaniciens asiatiques were selected for wartime metropolitan service from the graduates of 1916 and the trainees of Ton's class of 1917. In September 1916, they left by ship for France. After their arrival and a few days of rest in Marseilles, they were brought to the Mediterranean port city of Toulon and assigned as ship mechanics to various work

Ton Duc Thang and friends in Toulon, 1917.
Back, left to right: Doan Cong Su, Vo Van The, Nguyen Van Khanh. *Front, left to right:* To Cong No, Nguyen Van Giao, Ton Duc Thang.
Source: Tran Van Giau, Tran Bach Dang et al. (eds.), Dia chi van hoa thanh pho Ho Chi Minh, vol.I: lich su, Ho Chi Minh City: NXB Thanh pho Ho Chi Minh, 1987, 282. Identifications by Luu Phuong Thanh, May 11, 1992, Ho Chi Minh City.

units within its huge navy shipyard, also called the arsenal. Among his expatriates in Toulon, Ton was particularly close to five younger Vietnamese coworkers, to whom he became a kind of surrogate older brother. Of them, Doan Cong Su, who had been a classmate at the École des mécaniciens asiatiques,[27] was Ton's best friend. Vo Van The stressed Ton's sincerity, selflessness, and sense of duty in Toulon, and how he was a model of propriety to his friends.

A photo of the six men taken in the summer of 1917 in Toulon conveys the curious simultaneousness of closeness and distance that came with Ton's dual role as friend and older guardian. Most striking is the difference in attire: while Ton Duc Thang chose to wear a formal, white uniform with a stiff, high collar and long military boots for the photo, his friends were dressed much more casually in dark civilian clothes and shoes. And unlike the five younger men, whose body language shows them to be open and relaxed—they are leaning toward one another, with hands visible and touching shoulders—Ton hides his hands behind his back and appears more withdrawn, watchful, and tense.

The time in Toulon produced two significant changes in Ton's life. First, Ton's dear friend and colleague Doan Cong Su fell gravely sick and eventually succumbed to his disease. Ton made sure that his friend received a proper burial and thereafter sent letters and a photo, presumably of the grave, back to Doan's family. According to Ton Duc Thang's daughter, Doan Cong Su became in death a matchmaker: in his last letter to his family, Doan asked that his older sister be given in marriage to his friend Ton Duc Thang. It is not clear if Ton knew of this last wish. In any case, after his return from France, Ton visited Doan Cong Su's grateful family in the village of Vinh Kim near the provincial town of My Tho, south of Sai Gon. In 1921, Ton Duc Thang and Doan Kim Oanh were married.[28]

Second, his work at the arsenal and life among the French laboring class of Toulon, the capital of the "red" *département* of Var, supposedly radicalized Ton's thinking. His biographers usually point out that he learned of the importance of organizing by witnessing strikes and other labor union activities. And after his arrest, Ton admitted to having been introduced to politics by French workers and by reading leftist journals like *l'Humanité*.[29] Ha Huy Giap even claims (without proof) that Ton was already in contact in Toulon with the radical socialist André

Marty, who later became one of the instigators of the 1919 Black Sea Mutiny; supposedly Ton's work unit was under Marty's command.[30] The politicization of colonial workers and soldiers in France was indeed a widely recognized phenomenon. In 1935, André Dumarest wrote about the matter:

> They had been influenced by new ideas and political and social aspirations; . . . upon their return, they possessed to a certain degree the worker's *esprit,* the constitutive element of the working class.[31]

French authorities closely monitored the new political currents. Typical of French attitudes at the time, the May 1919 *Rapport du contrôle postal indochinois,* in a paragraph on strike information found in intercepted letters Vietnamese workers tried to send home, reads as follows:

> The theories of blind socialism have certainly sunk in with our natives, and *especially with those who have associated with the French worker. . . . They dream of perfecting themselves in France, so that, upon their return, they will be able to demand profit-sharing, a portion of the revenues which their "labor capital" will have given their employers.* If the [industrialist] does not accept these conditions and demands, one will do as [workers do] in France![32]

The quotation lends credibility to Ton Duc Thang's notion, quoted earlier, that abroad he "hoped [he] might learn truly a lot in order to return later and fight more effectively." Indeed, the idea seems to have been widespread and was very likely influenced by earlier and ongoing efforts like Phan Boi Chau's Dong Du (Travel East) movement that sent students to Japan, or the growing orientation of other intellectuals toward France in particular and the West, including the Soviet Union, in general.[33]

If it was true, against all evidence, that Ton Duc Thang took part in the events of the Black Sea in 1919, at some point before he must have been transferred from his work assignment at the Toulon arsenal to ship mechanic's duties on board a navy vessel. Not surprisingly, there is absolutely no evidence for such a transfer, not even a workable recollection of Ton's, and his biographers therefore must gloss over the total lack of explanation and documentation.[34] What they do report, however, is Ton Duc Thang's claim, later in the 1950s, that he was expelled from the navy after the mutiny and worked "for the car company Renault" until his repatriation to Sai Gon.[35] Here again, nothing further is known: In which city was the job? Was the job at a local car repair shop, or at a larger assembly site? And for how long did Ton hold the job? He never provided specific details.[36]

One item remains to be discussed briefly in this section: Ton Duc Thang's return date to Sai Gon. During his interrogation in July 1929, Ton stated that he had worked at the Toulon arsenal until January 1919, when he was repatriated to Cochinchina, "at the rank of quartermaster" *(maréchal des logis)* on board the *Général Galliéni.* At the arsenal he had taken mathematical and mechanical courses, but without getting a diploma. Back in Sai Gon he obtained a *permission libérable,* visited his parents, learned to drive at the École des mécaniciens asiatiques, and took a job at Ateliers Kropff & Cie, where he became the "chef d'atelier pour la partie mécanique."

On the other hand, the matriculation roll of the École des mécaniciens asiatiques, as shown earlier, dates Ton's return at August 1920. The same entry continues to describe that Ton actively sought his continued education at the school, which the wartime service in France had interrupted in 1916. Under the label "untrustworthy person" *(sujet de peu de confiance),* it notes that Ton appeared at the school after returning from France and demanded his training toward the diploma. He promised to work as the school's driver in exchange for free tuition, room, and board. But then he abruptly left the school. The entry does not clarify whether he suddenly left when he was about to be admitted, or when he was about to become eligible for the degree.[37]

Just as biographers and archival documents do not accord on Ton's recruitment in 1916, similar interpretative differences appear with regard to his return to the École des mécaniciens asiatiques. For example, contrary to school records, his official party biography assigns to him a passive role, because it is likely more becoming a radical anticolonialist. It claims that the French actually wanted Ton to work again at the vocational school "in order to bribe and monitor" him, but that he had refused.[38]

If we disregard January 1919 as a possible month of his repatriation from France, as claimed under interrogation, Ton's police statement and the school records can be put together in remarkable correspondence. First, both documents mention that he drove a car at the vocational school, suggesting that he did spend some time at the school. And second, if Ton indeed traveled on board the *Général Galliéni,* a return date of August 1920 becomes even more likely. According to the daily port bulletin of the Sai Gon Chamber of Commerce, which listed ship movements as well as expected arrival dates, the *Général Galliéni* did not sail to Sai Gon during the first months of 1919. But in early July 1920, the bulletin reported the *Général Galliéni*'s departure from Marseille in the last days of June. With passages from Marseilles to Sai Gon taking about five weeks, the *Galliéni* was expected to arrive around 1 August 1920.[39]

IN SUMMARY, what can be learned from the often insubstantial and even contradictory information about Ton Duc Thang during the 1910s? And is there a connection to the Black Sea Mutiny? In the early 1910s, Ton, then about twenty-five years of age, lived in the small but growing working-class milieu of Sai Gon-Cho Lon and showed an active interest in improving his education and skills. His enlistment to serve in France during World War I interrupted his training as a mechanic at the École des mécaniciens asiatiques. At the navy arsenal in Toulon beginning in the fall of 1916, he was exposed to French leftist politics and unionized labor activities, and his political views became more radical and much more sophisticated in consequence.

But there also emerged in Toulon a personal trait in Ton that was to become a pattern of behavior in the future: his preferred association with younger, like-minded Vietnamese, for whom he played multiple roles as older brother, confidant, role model, guardian, tutor, and authority figure. This orientation in Ton's social life toward the younger and more impressionable will reemerge in Sai Gon in the early 1920s—in the so-called "secret labor union" (the subject of chapter 5)—as well as in the late 1920s in the Cochinchina branch of Thanh Nien, the Vietnamese Revolutionary Youth League.[40] A similar role is ascribed to Ton Duc Thang during the long years in the penitentiary of Con Lon,[41] and, in certain ways, even during his post-1945 political career in representational functions and as the old revolutionary "uncle" second only to Ho Chi Minh.

Most likely, Ton Duc Thang returned to Sai Gon in August 1920. Only for a brief moment did he then seek to realign his life with a colonial institution, but soon realized, perhaps, that his newfound convictions demanded otherwise. When he abruptly left the École des mécaniciens asiatiques, it seems that he also finally turned his back on any thought of accommodation with colonialism. In this move may lie the beginning of a political and personal hardening that led to stark contrasts in perceptions observers have gained of the man. To Ton's opponents, he seemed ruthless vis-à-vis outsiders, an unbending, orthodox true believer. But to those who belonged to Ton's in-group, he was a model of warmth, loyalty, and support.

GLIMPSES OF THE GENESIS OF THE BLACK SEA STORY

What does all this mean with regard to the Black Sea Mutiny? We have already seen that, with one unlikely exception, Ton Duc Thang was on none of the warships involved in the unrest. And in the absence of any evidence to support an eventual transfer of Ton's from the Toulon arsenal to a French warship—an absolutely crucial move to establish the credibility of the Black Sea tale—the chances that Ton Duc Thang actually witnessed any of the revolts in the Black Sea are remote. After all, not even his coworker and friend in France, Vo Van The, mentioned such a change in assignments and location.

On the other hand, Ton Duc Thang lived and worked for several years in the center of the "red" Var, a stronghold of radical socialism, labor union activism, and proletarian self-assertion. His political views were profoundly affected by his experiences there. If it is true that he was not repatriated until mid-1920, and that he instead stayed in Toulon throughout 1919, we can—indeed must—assume that he witnessed the serious public unrest and navy mutinies in Toulon in May and June of 1919.

In early May, news of the large-scale insubordinations in the Black Sea began to trickle back to France, where opposition to the armed intervention among a war-weary public was widespread—and pronounced among the Left. Throughout the month, warships involved in the revolts returned to French bases, and firsthand accounts of the events thus multiplied. At the same time, military authorities started to hold the first court-martials in an apparent mood of vengeance, and solidarity with the mutinous crews grew stronger. These feelings added to the growing impatience of naval troops with their delayed demobilization and created an explosive mix. In early June in Toulon, amid the agitation and anger gripping troops and workers of the navy base and its arsenal, some ships were ordered to sail to the Black Sea to replace units that had been withdrawn earlier. Thereupon, especially from 8 to 12 June, the city, its port, and the arsenal became the sites of mass demonstrations, strikes, and clashes between mounted riot police and protesting workers and sailors in the narrow streets of the old quarters. Several units of naval troops stationed in Toulon refused to obey orders. And in the most serious incident to take place on the warships at anchorage, the crew of the admiral's flagship *Provence* remained in a state of open, partly armed mutiny for two days. More demonstrations and labor stoppages in Toulon occurred into late June. Thereafter, an amnesty campaign for the convicted mutineers, foremost among them André Marty, continued to stir emotions and hold the public's attention.[42]

I propose, therefore, that the event in which Ton Duc Thang took part in 1919 did not belong to the Black Sea Mutiny but to the second wave of mass protests in Toulon in the aftermath of the Black Sea incidents. Detailed and perhaps embellished stories of the mutinous ships at Sevastopol would have circulated around the arsenal for him to remember, and André Marty became the most recognizable of the tales' heroes. He could have read newspapers of various political orientations that ran articles on the disturbances in the Black Sea and at home and engaged in polemics over the events' significance and proper interpretation. But most important, the things he had learned about in the process of his politicization—workers' rights and interests, strikes and protests, organization and tactics, class solidarity and labor unions, et cetera—were all at once staged for him to witness, immerse himself in, and experience. By participating in sustained mass confrontations with French state power—so seemingly invincible in Indochina—Ton might have played out fantasies of Vietnamese anticolonialist struggles. And his determined, courageous coworkers provided him with powerful role models for his political aspirations and future actions.

These must have been heady days in the "red" Var for Ton Duc Thang. The excitement and liberation felt in mass action likely became for him one of those exceptional experiences from which human beings draw inspiration and energy for a long time to come. The strikes and mutinies in Toulon lacked only one important ingredient: the originality of the mutinies in the Black Sea with their connection to the Russian October Revolution and, thus, their immediacy as a symbol for anti-imperialist struggle and proletarian internationalism.

WHAT HAPPENED TO THE STORY of Ton Duc Thang in the Black Sea between 1919 and 1947, when it resurfaced in Vo Nhai? There is little to work with, and conclusions can be drawn only tentatively. First, there is Vo Van The, Ton's coworker and friend in Toulon. In his conversation with Luu Phuong Thanh of the Commission for Research of Party History in 1979, Vo Van The mentioned that he returned to Sai Gon from France in 1919, independently of Ton. About a year later, the two men met again in Sai Gon and renewed their friendship. Ton Duc Thang had begun working at the colonial enterprise Kropff & Cie by then. It was only at that time, late in 1920 at the earliest, that Ton supposedly told Vo Van The about his involvement in the Black Sea Mutiny.[43]

The secondhand character of this episode needs to be emphasized here: Luu Phuong Thanh, the party historian, told me in 1992 that Vo Van The told him in 1979 that Ton Duc Thang told him in 1920 or 1921 . . . And Luu Phuong Thanh's information only came at a point in our meeting when I voiced doubts about Ton's participation in the Black Sea Mutiny. But if Vo Van The really mentioned the episode to Luu Phuong Thanh, why did the latter not include it in his 1987 publication that incorporated Vo Van The's other recollections? After all, Vo Van The was the only known historical witness of those times in Toulon; and Ton Duc Thang told this former coworker about the Black Sea when they met again in Sai Gon. Did that fact not suggest a very real possibility that the two men had already lost contact in France, that Ton had left their joint assignment at the Toulon arsenal at some earlier point? Was this not, finally, evidence of Ton's transfer onto a French warship—the crucial but thus far missing link between Ton's job at the arsenal and his alleged presence in the Black Sea? But even at the symposium on Ton Duc Thang in Long Xuyen in 1988, where that very question received much attention, Luu Phuong Thanh did not reveal the information he would give me during our meeting four years later.[44]

I suppose that Luu Phuong Thanh remained silent about that part of Vo Van The's recollections because his informant had failed to provide the missing link. In 1979, Vo Van The either did not mention or did not remember any transfer of Ton's away from the arsenal or, worse yet, denied that such a transfer occurred before Vo Van The's departure. In this scenario, the two friends must have been together in Toulon until Vo Van The's repatriation in 1919. Ton Duc Thang stayed behind in France, probably until the following summer, as discussed earlier. Back in Sai Gon, Ton then explained to his friend what supposedly had "happened" to him after Vo Van The's departure. But this scenario had two problematic effects. Without Vo Van The as a witness, there still was no concrete evidence for Ton's reassignment. Instead, the window of opportunity for the transfer had shrunk from perhaps one and a half years—Ton's picture was taken in Toulon in the summer of 1917—to a few weeks: even if Vo Van The left France as early as January 1919, Ton Duc Thang would have had to board a navy ship very soon after to be able to witness the mutinies at Sevastopol in April.

There are some further indications that Ton Duc Thang talked about his participation in the Black Sea Mutiny once he came back to Cochinchina, but they are, again, not fully reliable and somewhat contradictory. In 1992 in Ho Chi Minh City, Duong Quang Dong, a senile eighty-seven-year-old retired worker, insisted that Ton Duc Thang had told him the story of the Black Sea exactly on 15 February 1920. On that day in 1920, Ton had met with a few young men, Duong Quang Dong among them, at Binh Dong temple on the outskirts of Sai Gon to practice martial arts with rattan swords and to organize the first Vietnamese "red" labor union *(cong hoi do),* which was maybe also called the "red workers and peasant union" *(cong nong hoi do).*[45]

Duong Quang Dong had achieved some fame during the 1980s in local party circles because of his assertion that he had belonged to Ton's entourage of young men during the early 1920s. He was interviewed by historians several times and regularly became a featured speaker at commemorative events for Ton Duc Thang.[46] The party rank and file and cadres adored and celebrated him as an old revolutionary fighter, as somebody, perhaps, who had been touched by history. Party historians, however, in private were infuriated by Duong Quang Dong's sycophantic act. His initial basic claim of having associated with Ton Duc Thang was credible. Yet it became clear to these historians that he also read through all kinds of historical accounts, including long-outdated and refuted ones, to "refresh" his memory and better prepare for his performances, in which he clearly reveled. The result was a hodgepodge of incredible combinations of people and associations, illogical dates and "events," and other inaccuracies and contradictions. With rising fame and privilege as well as advancing age and ossification, Duong Quang Dong became a historian's nightmare. Self-important and long-winded, he was obstinate in insisting on every detail of his saga.[47] It was practically impossible to recognize and distinguish genuine recollections from imagined actions, but, as Luu Phuong Thanh confided, even though Duong Quang Dong was "totally wrong," historians had to put up with him politely "because he was an old, accomplished party member."[48]

It would be easy to dismiss Duong Quang Dong's notion that Ton Duc Thang told him of the Black Sea Mutiny had not a few other, more credible historical witnesses said similar things. Ha Huy Giap, who became a member of Thanh Nien in December 1926 and, later on, an organizer and leader of the ICP in the south, remembered that, in 1926, he heard people in Sai Gon talk about Ton Duc Thang, who had become "very popular." People both of communist and anticommunist leanings supposedly "paid attention" to him "because of the things Uncle Ton did in the Black Sea."[49] Ha Huy Giap met Ton soon after, in March 1927. In the 1930s, both were held on Con Lon, but in different prison blocks. Ha Huy Giap later became a party historian.

Phan Trong Binh and Nguyen Van Loi, the two Thanh Nien recruiters whom Nguyen Ai Quoc sent from Canton to Sai Gon at the end of 1926, met Ton Duc Thang in 1927. They heard of him as the leader of a circle *(nhom)* of workers who were clandestinely organizing labor union cells around Sai Gon. A few initial meetings took place with Ton, to check him out, so to say, before they would admit him and his closest friends into Thanh Nien. It was then, according to Phan Trong Binh's recollections in 1984, that Ton mentioned the Black Sea story to Nguyen Ai Quoc's emissaries.[50]

In 1929 or 1930, Ton Duc Thang told a prison mate about his participation in the Black Sea Mutiny. Both men were being held in the central prison in Sai Gon in the aftermath of the Thanh Nien-internal killing at the rue Barbier. Ton's fellow prisoner was Pham Van Dong, who later became an ICP leader, close lieutenant of Ho Chi Minh, and longtime prime minister of the DRVN. After the murder in December 1928, an angered central Thanh Nien in Canton had dissolved the Cochinchinese branch of the organization and sent Pham Van Dong to Sai Gon to build a new branch. But he was soon caught in the ensuing French crackdown. Before their arrests, Ton and Pham knew of one another, but had never met due to the secrecy of their assignments and Ton's going into hiding for a few months after the incident.[51]

During the long years on Con Lon prison island, from 1930 to 1945, Ton Duc Thang apparently talked to more of his comrades about the Black Sea tale. For example, Tran Tu Binh indicated in his memoirs that Ton's role in the mutinies of 1919 was known among his fellow prisoners.[52] Curiously though, Le Van Luong, who was in the same ICP cell at the penitentiary with Ton for many years, and whom Tran Tu Binh mentions as well in this context, claimed to have heard about the Black Sea event only after 1945;[53] he would, of course, introduce the tale to the ICP leadership in 1947 in Vo Nhai. Nonetheless, as mentioned by the historian Nguyen Thanh, a number of former prison mates confirmed later that they had heard Ton tell the story of the Black Sea on Con Lon.[54]

Finally, Ton Duc Thang's daughter, Ton Thi Hanh, made two points in that respect. First, her father supposedly met a Frenchman on Con Lon, who had also been involved in the navy revolt in the Black Sea; only thereafter did her father tell his comrades about his own participation in the mutinies. However, Ton Thi Hanh could neither recall whether the Frenchman had been an inmate or a staff member of the penitentiary, nor whether the Frenchman and her father had known one another in 1919, nor how exactly she heard about the meeting on Con Lon. Second, it was only at some point after 1945, when the family had relocated to the north of Viet Nam, that Ton Thi Hanh learned of her father's role in the Black Sea Mutiny. But since her father rarely talked about his past with the family, she was not surprised and, indeed, found such a deed "normal" in times when a lot of Vietnamese had to act heroically.[55]

IN CONCLUSION, despite the unreliable evidence, it appears that Ton Duc Thang began telling the story of his part in the revolt of the Black Sea soon after his return from France. In the early 1920s, he slowly gathered around himself a circle of young working-class men, which might have served social as much as political purposes. Physical exercise was combined with extolling the virtues of solidarity and mutual aid. During meals together one could talk of revolution and dream, perhaps, about a strong workers' movement, and outings in the environs of Sai Gon were used to read newspaper articles and other materials and explain new concepts and ideas found therein. As had happened with his Vietnamese friends and colleagues in Toulon, Ton became the young men's surrogate older brother, counselor, coach, and tutor—a social role and association Ton seems to have felt most comfortable with.

I suggest that the story of the Black Sea became Ton Duc Thang's credentials among these youths. He had become a radical anticolonialist and labor union observer in Toulon and, back home, apparently planned gradually to organize idealistic, enthusiastic, and impressionable working youth into a viable force for socioeconomic as well as national liberation. In the early 1920s the task must have been daunting, given the very small size of the working class in Sai Gon, its utter lack of organization and politicization, the power of the French colonial regime, and the prevalence of collaborationist and elitist, self-proclaimed Vietnamese spokespersons. But also in personal terms, Ton Duc Thang's task was difficult. During those years, Sai Gon students slowly began to become more active politically. But Ton never was a man of many words or drawn to abstract intellectual debates; consciously, or perhaps instinctively, he steered away from those circles and turned to the working youths. By now he was in his early thirties and thus a dozen or so years older than those he wanted to organize and lead. With little to show for what made him interesting, how could he attract an entourage that would take him seriously and be trusting and loyal?

The tale of the Black Sea Mutiny could achieve just that and establish Ton Duc Thang's authority with (and over) these youths. Unlike the strikes and protests in Toulon in June 1919 with their mainly French focus, the earlier revolt in the Black Sea related both to French labor struggles and to the Russian October Revolution. Thus the story of Ton's presence in the Black Sea portrayed him standing up both against French power and for the protection of the Soviet Union, the new revolutionary force that promised liberation and salvation. Furthermore, the unrest in Toulon produced no outcome that could be transmitted or comprehended in a simple, condensed form. In contrast, the withdrawal of the flotilla from the Black Sea provided a potent image for Ton Duc Thang's success. The tale gave Ton a certain curious mysteriousness and depicted him as possessing experiences and personal traits of unusual power, charisma, and courage that held the promise of future achievements as a leader. To such a person others would be drawn, with such a man others could throw in their lots in hopes of improving their situations.

Ton Duc Thang's use of the Black Sea story should not be misconstrued as boasting. After all, it was genuine modesty that observers time and again found so remarkable about this man. Yet, with Ton's preferred role as the older, guiding "brother" came the need to set himself apart. Vis-à-vis his younger peers, he cultivated a realm of difference in his personality and thereby fostered characteristically unequal friendships, at once authoritative and close. Perhaps the white uniform in the photo from Toulon in 1917 was such a device of difference. The story of the Black Sea must have been another. Far from boasting of individual heroism and bragging about personal fame, the tale rather simply asserted how Ton took part in a great instance of mass political action. It thereby aimed at instilling quiet awe, commanding deep respect and establishing unquestioned authority. Furnished with such credentials, Ton's leadership did no longer have to prove itself; he could be the usually unassuming and modest adviser and concentrate on his central objective of propagating and organizing among the working people of Sai Gon.

When Ton Duc Thang came into contact with the Thanh Nien recruiters in 1926/27, the story of his participation in the mutinies served similar purposes. In Phan Trong Binh's recollections, the sense of awe and relief over having found somebody with Ton's excellent revolutionary credentials is apparent. To these trained revolutionaries, the aspect of proletarian internationalism in the mutinous act must have been particularly impressive. However, after the murderous blunder of the southern Thanh Nien in 1928 and the destruction of its party apparatus in its wake, the Black Sea story took on a certain defensiveness. Ton bore some responsibility for the demise of the southern party branch. When he met Pham Van Dong, the emissary of the central party, in prison, he might have likely thrown the Black Sea story into the balance to counter the negative impressions of him the killing at the rue Barbier must surely have produced.

During his long incarceration on Con Lon, Ton Duc Thang became an orthodox communist. Unlike political prisoners, most of whom were at least temporarily freed in the amnesties of the mid-1930s, Ton was always held in the prison complex for inmates who, like himself, had been tried and convicted as common criminals. In 1933, he was admitted into the ICP and, soon after, became one of the leaders of its prison organization. In fact, he remained one of the most reliable pillars of the party cell. Biographers usually credit him for his untiring work of lifting morale among the incarcerated communists and for keeping in touch with developments in the outside world through clandestine contacts with sympathetic intermediaries, like sailors who worked on ships that brought supplies to the island. Tran Tu Binh's memoirs of his prison times capture Ton in his familiar role as a compassionate older brother, selfless friend, and encouraging teacher of the young ICP inmates. In no small part, Ton's authority and stature among the incarcerated revolutionaries must have been built on the tale of the Black Sea, as suggested by the deep impression his professed past credentials made on Tran Tu Binh.[56]

By September 1945, when the Vietnamese August Revolution finally freed him and many of his comrades, at least a small number of ICP inmates knew about Ton Duc Thang's alleged part in the Black Sea Mutiny—and most likely had no doubts about its accuracy. At that point, it was still Ton's own, personal story. But as my discussion in the following chapter will show, he was soon to lose control over it.

CHAPTER 2

The Black Sea Mutiny in the Revolutionary Moment

IN THE PREVIOUS CHAPTER, I set out from the ICP leadership meeting in Vo Nhai in 1947 and traced the tale's development from the original event in 1919 and Ton Duc Thang's sojourn in France, through his life in Sai Gon in the 1920s, his incarceration on Con Lon during the 1930s and 1940s, and up to 1945. We will now first accompany Ton Duc Thang and his account of the Black Sea Mutiny from Con Lon Island via Ha Noi to Paris, and then back to Vo Nhai, where the story was set on a significantly different course and underwent a substantial qualitative change. What was the environment for the tale's reception in 1947? What was its utility to the party? And what happened to the story after 1947?

TON'S CAREER FROM 1945 TO 1947

About four weeks after the 1945 August Revolution of the communist-led "League for the Independence of Viet Nam," the so-called Viet Minh, and about two and a half weeks after Ho Chi Minh's 2 September 1945 declaration of independence of the Democratic Republic of Viet Nam, Ton Duc Thang regained his freedom. Now at age fifty-seven, he had spent more than sixteen years under harsh conditions in French captivity. As we will see, his liberation from the island penitentiary of Con Lon (Poulo Condore) off Viet Nam's southeastern coast came in the nick of time. Harold Isaacs captured the drama of the DRVN's rescue mission for several thousand of its jailed comrades:

> A fleet of seagoing junks was hastily mobilized [by the Viet Minh] and sent off to the island penal colony. . . . But the Viet Minh ruled in Saïgon for only one month. By the time the prisoners of Poulo-Condor approached the coast in their fleet of junks with their brown-patched sails, they landed, not to join a freely functioning republic but to enter a harshly renewed struggle to be free.[1]

After Japan's surrender that ended World War II, nominally neutral British-Indian troops had moved into the southern half of Indochina in order to disarm Japanese occupational forces there. But itself part of a colonial power, the British command was hostile to the Viet Minh and their claim to national independence of a reunified Viet Nam and openly supported French attempts to regain control of the "lost" colony.[2] Only hours after Ton set foot as a free man on the mainland near Soc Trang, rearmed French soldiers staged a coup against DRVN authorities in Sai Gon on 23 September 1945 and soon went on the offensive in all of Cochinchina. They were actively aided by the British, who made brazen use of Japanese troops that should long have been disarmed, and received generous logistical aid from the United States. DRVN/Viet Minh forces, which had a much more tenuous hold on power in the south than in the north, were defeated by early 1946, tried to regroup in the central highlands around Ban Me Thuot (Buon Ma Thuot), or withdrew further north.

The months from September 1945 to March 1946 were tumultuous and dangerous for Ton Duc Thang. He became secretary of the ICP regional committee for Cochinchina (Xu Uy Nam Ky) in October and, in December, was appointed to the newly formed Executive Committee for the Southern Resistance (Uy Ban Khang Chien Mien Nam).[3] He clearly earned these leadership positions because of his untiring work for the party during his imprisonment, when he had become an absolutely trusted and orthodox communist. From November in particular, Ton's responsibilities likely kept him constantly on the move throughout the south, where more and more territory formerly held by the Viet Minh came under French attack or even outright French control.

Possibly as early as October, in DRVN-held My Tho, Ton underwent surgery on a tumor (or lump) that had developed over the years as a result of beatings he endured in 1929 in the prison of Sai Gon. When French forces targeted My Tho soon after, he was brought to his wife's home village of Vinh Kim nearby to recuperate.[4] In November, despite the great dangers posed by the French on the way and by the violently anticommunist Hoa Hao sect that controlled the Long Xuyen area, Ton managed to slip into his native village of My Hoa Hung near Long Xuyen for one night. This brief visit after so many years on Con Lon was the last time he saw his mother (she died in 1947; his father had died in 1938 during Ton's incarceration).

By November, Ton Duc Thang fully assumed his functions in the anti-French resistance.[5] But by year's end, the struggle for control of Cochinchina was decisively turning against the DRVN loyalists, and in early March 1946, Ton Duc Thang arrived in Ha Noi. The official reason for his move north was his selection in the DRVN's only all-Vietnamese elections in early January 1946 to represent Sai Gon (and its Chinese-Vietnamese twin city Cho Lon) at the first National Assembly.[6] On 2 March 1946, when the National Assembly met in Ha Noi, Ton even assumed the post of vice-chairman of its Standing Committee under the former high-ranking mandarin of the Nguyen court, Bui Bang Doan. Bernard Fall, however, disputes Ton's initial election to the National Assembly:

> The Presidium of the National Assembly . . . was ruled by Ton Duc Thang, an ICP stalwart of long standing. His position is the more interesting as—while occupying the high posts of President of the Presidium and Vice-Chairman of the Permanent Committee—his name does not appear on the list of *elected* members of the Assembly published in the *Official Journal* of the D.R. on April 13, 1946. It is therefore most likely that he was directly appointed to either his membership in the Assembly, or to his high political post.[7]

Not surprisingly, as Friedrich Sembdner has shown, all the major groups participating in the elections were maneuvering since the Viet Minh and anticommunist nationalist parties and factions were in a grim competition then, and each group took care to get adequate representation in the various organs of the new state.[8] On the other hand, orderly elections for an organ of the DRVN could hardly have been possible in French-held Sai Gon. Nonetheless, Viet Minh activists apparently attempted improvised elections in the city at great risk to their lives.[9] The uncertainty about Ton's electoral status might thus be rooted in the atmosphere of anti-DRVN violence that prevailed in the south during the elections.

Why and how did Ton Duc Thang relocate north, when, after all, he had only recently assumed a leading role in the troubled southern resistance? I suggest that at some point after the National Assembly elections, perhaps in late January or early February 1946, the men around Ho Chi Minh decided not to employ Ton in the military-political capacity he had been assigned to only weeks before. Instead, perhaps on the recommendation of those who knew him well from shared prison experiences, they planned to use the best talent that Ton had so clearly exhibited over the last three decades—namely, to be the selfless counselor, unassuming guide and role model. Rather than the older brother, however, he would, at age fifty-seven, now take on the functions of a national father figure.

Before discussing the reasons the DRVN/Viet Minh/ex-ICP leadership changed how Ton Duc Thang would serve the Revolution, a brief look at the chronology of events is needed to establish that such a decision must have been made.[10]

Late in 1945, by order of the central party, the Southern Resistance Committee was established and the region under its command was divided into four military zones; Ton was put in charge of supplies and logistics. At the same time, with the struggle in the south on the verge of defeat, Ban Me Thuot, a town in the central highlands, was chosen as the southern resistance's "long-term base," just as the northern Vietnamese mountains had been before the August Revolution. Around the same time, attempts to hold the elections for the National Assembly were made in the south, and Ton received the mandate to represent Sai Gon-Cho Lon.

In January of 1946, the remaining scattered southern Viet Minh forces formed three groups or columns to make their way to Ban Me Thuot. Huynh Van Tieng and Hoang Quoc Viet (also known as Ha Ba Cang) led two smaller advance groups that set out north, probably from the provinces of Long An, west of Sai Gon, and Dong Nai, east of the city. Ton Duc Thang was to lead the main column from the western delta province of Dong Thap Muoi. Had these units moved north on land toward Ban Me Thuot, however, they would have had to fight their way through enemy lines, as the narrow stretch between Sai Gon, the Cambodian border, and the Mekong delta lay within the French perimeter. Ton therefore first gathered his Viet Minh forces south of the Mekong, either in the port of Rach Gia or the town of Ca Mau.[11] Around 1 February, after Tet 1946, the lunar New Year holidays, the troops boarded several barges, made their way on canals to the sea, and sailed north to the port of Phan Thiet. From there they were to march to the highland base. Phan Thiet was the landing point likely because it was about as far north as shallow, calmer coastal waters permitted the barges to go.

As an elected representative of Sai Gon-Cho Lon, Ton was to assume

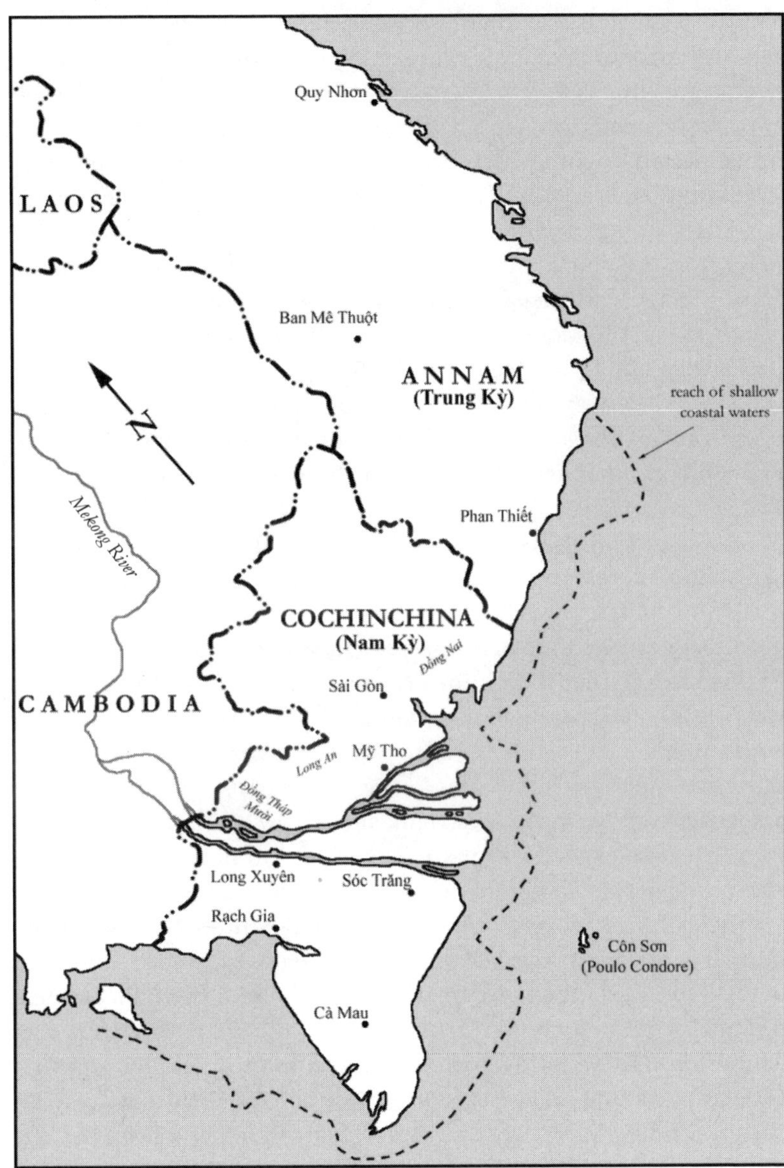

Southern Viet Nam, 1945/46

a leading role in the southern resistance base of Ban Me Thuot, but in early February in Phan Thiet he received orders to hurry instead to Ha Noi and to the National Assembly. Thereupon, Ton Duc Thang, his two grown daughters, who had come along with their father,[12] and other elected assembly members from Cochinchina made their way through jungles and over mountains to Quy Nhon, a trip of several hundred kilometers, which, partly on foot, must have consumed most of February. Having finally reached Quy Nhon, they took a train to Ha Noi. Afflicted with malaria, Ton arrived there only days before the National Assembly convened on 2 March 1946. The revolutionary journalist Thep Moi ("New Steel," the nom de guerre of Ha Van Loc), who was present, conveys a sense of the suddenness of Ton's appearance in Ha Noi and of Ton's unexpected rise to the leadership of the National Assembly: just before the convention, "nobody yet paid attention to Ton Duc Thang."[13]

The reasons for the decision to have Ton rush north lie in two critical political developments of late 1945 and early 1946:[14] (1) the intense rivalry in which the Viet Minh found itself with anticommunist nationalist parties like the Viet Nam Quoc Dan Dang (VNQDD) and the Dong Minh Hoi (DMH); and (2) growing French ambitions to make Cochinchina a separate entity again and thus deny DRVN claims of authority over the south. With regard to the first question, the Viet Minh required Ton Duc Thang for his seniority and ability to attract an "entourage" (as he had accomplished in 1920s Sai Gon); in other words, he was expected to unite people behind him. With regard to the second problem, the DRVN intended to utilize Ton as a southerner.

When Chinese troops loyal to the Chinese Nationalist Party (Guomindang, or GMD) occupied the northern half of Viet Nam in the fall of 1945 to disarm the Japanese, they brought with them Vietnamese nationalist parties whose orientation was threefold: they were pro-Chinese, intensely anti-French and anticommunist. Though enjoying little popular support, the VNQDD and the DMH had the powerful backing of the GMD troops and so were viable competitors for the Viet Minh during the first nine or so months of the DRVN's existence.[15] In January 1946, Ho Chi Minh formed a provisional coalition government with the VNQDD and the DMH. And although the Viet Minh had overwhelmingly won the elections of 6 January, the VNQDD and the DMH were assured a certain number of seats in the National

Assembly. During these dramatic months in Ha Noi, amid mutual suspicions and sporadic violence, an atmosphere of forced compromise and cooperation prevailed. Thus, to assure that communists exerted a controlling influence over the legislative assembly, the (now officially dissolved) ICP sought to place a trusted comrade in the parliament's future leadership who could win wide acceptance and who had a certain status and authority.

Because of his seniority, Ton Duc Thang was uniquely qualified to play such a role. Except for Ho Chi Minh, who was head of the DRVN executive branch, all other ICP leaders were in their late thirties or early to mid-forties and did not yet possess the kind of authority that older age bestows. When Ton Duc Thang was elected to the powerful Standing Committee of the National Assembly, he joined noncommunist committee members who were also of advanced age. With these men, such as the former imperial court mandarin Bui Bang Doan or the Catholic priest Pham Ba Truc, Ton became part of an assembly leadership easily and widely recognizable as the nation's guiding elders, who lent legitimacy to the DRVN and yet supposedly stood above the petty political divisions of the day. Furthermore, Ton's talents as a bridge builder and selfless moderator earned him additional respect, to the advantage of the ICP-controlled Viet Minh.

Equally, as one of the elected chairmen of the National Assembly, Ton Duc Thang was in a highly visible and prominent position to counter French designs to undermine the newly established unity of Viet Nam. Cochinchina had fallen under French control again, and there was now a very real danger that the south, regarded by the French as their colony, would once again be separated from the rest of the country. The courageous and costly attempts in Sai Gon to hold the elections for the National Assembly, as well as the hasty journey of southern members of that parliament to Ha Noi, are indications that the DRVN government was desperate to show to the Vietnamese people, the French, and the world in general that it legitimately represented the aspirations of the entire nation. There existed, of course, a very distinct underrepresentation of southerners in the ICP, the Viet Minh, and many DRVN institutions. As one of the chairmen of the DRVN parliament, Ton Duc Thang thus came to symbolize most powerfully the south's essential oneness with the rest of Viet Nam.

The first session of the National Assembly convened for only one day, on 2 March 1946; its most important task was to give a new government under Ho Chi Minh a popular and democratic mandate. This central scene, as witnessed by Thep Moi in the following quote, captures the double function of Ton as authoritative figure for the Viet Minh and as representative of the south:

> Bui Bang Doan and Ton Duc Thang were presiding over the meeting. Uncle Ho announced the resignation of the Provisional Government. Bui Bang Doan accepted [*or* confirmed] it. The person to proclaim the [vote of] confidence in Ho Chi Minh to form a revolutionary government of resistance and national reconstruction was Ton Duc Thang. The southern compatriots and the compatriots of the whole country thus entrusted Uncle Ton to give this historic speech. In the current political circumstances, the voice of the south was of utmost importance.[16]

After a brief stint in military and political decision-making positions, Ton Duc Thang had been assigned a role that best suited his abilities and personality. And so, in this crucial moment in March 1946, the tone was set for what would subsequently become an amazing career. Ton would serve the Vietnamese Revolution in *representational* functions, both internally and externally, and both as a southerner and as an older, respectable authority figure who symbolized a nation united behind Viet Minh (and later openly communist) leadership. In these symbolic roles—and, I should emphasize, only in these—Ton would be second only to Ho Chi Minh in prominence and public visibility.

Ho Chi Minh and Ton Duc Thang were the only party leaders of the generation born long before 1900. In the early years of the DRVN, they were therefore the only two communists who had the seniority required to pose convincingly as the nation's protective fathers and guiding elders. In their division of symbolic labor, the two men complemented each other almost perfectly: on the one hand was Ho, the man from north-central Viet Nam, on the other Ton, the man from the south; Ho the revolutionary with the longest record of international activism, Ton the revolutionary with the longest record of incarceration under the French; Ho the intellectual, Ton the laborer; Ho the voice of government, planning, decision making, and implementation, and, in Ton, the voice of the masses, of giving input, approving, and supporting; the leader of leaders on the one hand, and the leader of followers on the other.

Ton Duc Thang's people-centered, representational, and essentially reactive functions ensured that (a) the DRVN government received the maximum amount of support, domestically and abroad, and (b) the various groups of society were kept in line with the Revolution and its vanguard party. A list of his most important appointed and elected posts attests to this:

- 1946–60: vice-chairman, then acting chairman, finally chairman of the Standing Committee of the first National Assembly, that is president of the DRVN's parliament (until he became vice president of the country).
- 1946–77: vice-chairman, then chairman of the national committees of successive United Front organizations: the Lien Viet Front (1946–51), the expanded Lien Viet Front (1951–55),[17] and the Fatherland Front (established 1955), for which Ton was of even greater symbolic value as a southerner after the de facto partition of the country.
- 1948–55: head, Central Department for Patriotic Emulation.
- 1949: lifelong honorary chairman, Vietnamese General Confederation of Labor.
- 1950–51: chairman, Vietnamese section of the Stockholm Appeal, a Soviet-led international peace campaign.[18]
- from 1950: chairman, Vietnamese-Soviet Friendship Association.
- 1955–61: member of the World Peace Council.
- 1955: lifelong honorary president, Vietnamese Committee for the Defense of World Peace.
- lifelong honorary chairman, Vietnamese Committee for Adolescents and Children.
- 1960–69: vice president of the DRVN under Ho Chi Minh.
- from 1969: president of the DRVN (after 1976: SRVN).

By contrast, Ton Duc Thang held only one post connected to the executive branch; from 1947 to 1949, and for some time in 1951, he was inspector general of the Government Inspectorate.[19] And briefly, from April to October 1947, after the death of the minister of the interior, Huynh Thuc Khang, Ton became acting minister until Phan Ke Toai, a former imperial court mandarin, could assume these duties, which were "reserved for a personality from [Nam Bo, i.e., Cochinchina]."[20]

After his election as the country's Vice President, Ton Duc Thang (right) receives President Ho Chi Minh's congratulations (1960).
Source: So Van Hoa va Thong Tin An Giang (An Giang culture and information department), ed. *Chu tich Ton Duc Thang (1888–1980)* (President Ton Duc Thang). An Giang, 1988, 9.

Equally, despite his high visibility, Ton's actual political influence was limited. After the reconstitution of the Communist Party as the Vietnamese Labor Party (Dang Lao Dong, or DLD) in February 1951,[21] he always remained only a member of the party's Central Committee and never made it into its politburo.

In sum, already by 1946, Ton Duc Thang's path in the service of the Revolution was prescribed. Occupying prominent functions of the DRVN's National Assembly and United Front organizations, yet with only limited political weight in the party, he was a symbol of the south and of the DRVN's claim to authority over a united Vietnamese nation. His role as symbol was especially important in 1946/47, when the French were attempting to turn Cochinchina once again into an artificially separate entity, and after 1955, when the U.S.-backed government in Sai Gon sabotaged the Geneva Accords and hopes for a peaceful unification of the country were dashed. After 1960, Ton's vice presidency must be seen in the same context.

In addition, with his seniority and the cultivation of his image as a widely respected father figure, Ton could use his posts in the assembly and especially the United Front to ensure that often competing interests within Vietnamese society were streamlined toward the party-led DRVN government. In particular, Thep Moi credits Ton's untiring efforts in moderating, reaching out, and uniting the people as chairman of the Fatherland Front for the party's success in riding out the difficult years 1955–57, when the excesses of the land reform program and widespread internal DRVN political and cultural dissent seriously challenged the party's monopoly on power.[22]

TON DUC THANG AND ANDRÉ MARTY, 1946

Ton Duc Thang's interrelated functions as a symbol for the Vietnamese south and as one of the elders of a united Vietnamese nation were put to use again soon after the first session of parliament, when he became part of a delegation of the National Assembly that traveled to France in April and May 1946. It was during his visit to France that the story of his involvement in the Black Sea Mutiny resurfaced.

On 24 March 1946, Ho Chi Minh and the French high commissioner for Indochina, Thierry d'Argenlieu, signed a statement that specified preparatory steps for the ill-fated Franco-DRVN negotiations at Da Lat and at Fontainebleau during the spring and summer of 1946. One of the provisions of the communiqué stipulated that a "friendship mission" of ten delegates of the DRVN's National Assembly would pay a goodwill visit to the French Constitutional Assembly in Paris. After much internal maneuvering, the ten men were chosen, and Ton Duc Thang and Huynh Van Tieng, another leader of the Southern Resistance Committee who, like Ton, led a Viet Minh column out of Cochinchina, were among them. The friendship delegation, led by Pham Van Dong, stayed in France from 26 April to 16 May 1946. After almost twenty-six years—more than sixteen of which were spent in jail—Ton was in France again.

The goodwill mission was of great importance for Ho Chi Minh's government. French propaganda continued to falsely portray the Viet Minh as initially installed, armed, and directed by the Japanese, or simply as bandits. Furthermore, the French government tried to keep the Franco-DRVN negotiations as far from public scrutiny as possible. And the French colonial lobby was actively advocating to declare Cochinchina a separate political entity again. The National Assembly delegation, on the other hand, was supposed to drive home to the metropole the reality of the DRVN's existence. As parliamentarians, the group could show that Ho Chi Minh's government had a democratic legitimacy and a popular mandate. A gesture of goodwill from assembly to assembly could further demonstrate that the DRVN considered itself France's equal, as a fully constituted state in general and as a future negotiation partner in particular. Finally, the delegation comprised Vietnamese from all of the country's regions, including so-called Cochinchinese like Ton and Huynh Van Tieng, and thus symbolized the nation's unity and desire to remain united.

The French were fully aware of the symbolism of the delegation's visit and its public relations value to the DRVN. In consequence, the Vietnamese visitors were shuttled from one dazzling reception to the next but kept at arm's length from the general public. During the delegation's sojourn, *Le Monde,* for example, published only three very brief and neutrally worded articles on the topic; in fact, the third article only reported Ho Chi Minh's telegraphic thanks for the friendly treatment of the delegates.[23] The account of Jean Sainteny, an idealistic yet ardent colonialist and the chief French intermediary with Ho Chi Minh, reflects the predominant French attitudes well. He downplayed the trip to nothing but a "getting in touch" visit and framed the Franco-Vietnamese contacts in the usual paternalistic relationship the colonial mind seemed unable to transcend: noteworthy for Sainteny was that the delegation, before flying home and after having been wined and dined at length, "spontaneously struck up a racy *Marseillaise*."[24] Furthermore, the French colonial lobby attempted to sabotage the assembly delegation's visit by sending a "mission of autonomous Cochinchina" to Paris at exactly the same time.

As can be expected, Huynh Van Tieng paints a different picture of the delegates' experiences. They met a few French communist politicians, scientists, and journalists as well as some Vietnamese colonial soldiers, who were distressed over having helped liberate a country that had now turned to attacking their own nation. The parliamentarians witnessed a May Day parade where overseas Vietnamese and French workers displayed a few DRVN flags; Pham Van Dong burst into tears, but Ton Duc Thang simply said: "There, that's the working class for you." And when the goodwill delegation realized that the upcoming conference at Fontainebleau could not succeed because of France's ill will, it supposedly decided, on Ton's initiative, to return home.[25]

One of the meetings the delegation had with French communists is noteworthy because it brings us back to the Black Sea Mutiny. At some point, the delegates came together with none other than the most famous mutineer of 1919, André Marty, who was a high-ranking French Communist Party (FCP) cadre in 1946. Huynh Van Tieng remembered the meeting as follows:

> Uncle Ton met André Mart[y] *again*, his old fighting friend *in the Black Sea*. The two friends embraced and kissed each other warmly. André Mart[y] told Uncle Ton and us [other delegates] straight away: "It's okay that you came here [to France], but you should have no illusions; they [the French government] will strike over there [in Viet Nam]. Return to prepare for the resistance!"[26]

We will recall that André Marty made a political career out of revolutionary internationalism. His own account of the Black Sea Mutiny framed the event as a primarily internationalist, pro-Soviet, and anti-imperialist revolt. He joined the FCP after his amnesty and rose to the party's politburo. In the mid-1930s, Marty became a member of the Comintern secretariat in Moscow and a volunteer of the international brigades in the Spanish civil war. In 1946, despite the FCP's aloofness from the Vietnamese Revolution (because the party was part of the French ruling coalition), André Marty, who was the FCP's "specialist on Indochinese affairs,"[27] probably saw it as his internationalist duty to lend his support to the Vietnamese delegation.

As discussed in the previous chapter, André Marty and Ton Duc Thang could not have met in the context of the mutinies, since Marty worked on the *Protet* from September 1917 until his arrest, and Ton can be ruled out as a crew member of this ship. And in his detailed accounts of the navy revolt, Marty never mentioned any possible role of Ton's in the historic event. On the other hand, at least one among Ton's co-delegates, Pham Van Dong, had heard about the Black Sea story before. Furthermore, the story's Vo Nhai version of November 1947, at the latest, included the claim that some contact between André Marty and Ton Duc Thang had occurred in the Black Sea.

But were André Marty and Ton indeed old acquaintances? The two "old friends" could have met "again" only if they worked together at the Toulon arsenal for some time between about November 1916 (Ton's arrival) and September 1917 (Marty's boarding of the *Protet*).[28] Yet, regardless of whether Marty and Ton knew one another in Toulon, they certainly were not "fighting friends in the Black Sea," and before their meeting in 1946, Marty would not have known about Ton's claim to a role in the navy revolt.

Was Marty, then, made aware of Ton's alleged participation in the revolts of 1919? If he was, Ton would have told Marty at their meeting in 1946, much as he had been telling his Vietnamese comrades since 1920. And, for the first time, the story would have gained impressive credentials not only for Ton in particular but for the DRVN in general. But what would Marty's reaction to Ton Duc Thang's fine internationalism in the Black Sea likely have been? Would he not have done more than just exhort the delegates to prepare for war? Huynh Van Tieng, in fact, did not recall that André Marty made any reference to the mutiny during their meeting. And would the exemplary, committed internationalist Marty not have mentioned such a telling episode in his book's next edition, in 1949?

It is therefore much more likely that André Marty was unaware of Ton's story during their meeting. The two older men—one was sixty, the other almost fifty-eight at the time—simply embraced and kissed in the usual manner of communist-internationalist greetings, and the mutinies of 1919 were never an issue at their meeting. At what point, then, did the false detail of Ton's Black Sea contacts with Marty enter the story? Either it was added sometime between the Paris encounter with Marty in the spring of 1946 and the conference in Vo Nhai in November 1947, at the latest, or the revolutionary contacts with the famous André Marty had long been a false ingredient of the Black Sea story Pham Van Dong, among others, had heard from Ton. In the latter case, surprised by the appearance of the real Marty, Ton Duc Thang had to forestall Pham Van Dong's possibly embarrassing questions by enacting the tight embrace of two "old fighting friends" with an unsuspecting if perhaps puzzled Marty.

Whatever the case might have been, it is clear that Ton Duc Thang was losing control over his story. His rising prominence as cochairman of the DRVN's National Assembly and, by late May 1946, of the Lien Viet Front propelled him into a public—indeed an international—arena where a story of such powerful imagery and symbolism could no longer remain simply his own. Ton had evolved from the pre-1945 anticolonial activist and communist prisoner to the post-1945 highly visible, southern, elder father figure representative of a united, independent Vietnamese nation. What had formerly been personal credentials for his authority over a younger entourage now became, in a parallel development, revolutionary credentials for the newly independent and communist-led DRVN.

VO NHAI AND BEYOND: THE DRVN IN 1947–49

If Ton Duc Thang began losing control over his story in the spring of 1946, he had lost it entirely by November 1947. At the commemorative gathering of the ICP leadership in Vo Nhai on the thirtieth anniversary of the Russian October Revolution, Le Van Luong introduced the top DRVN/ICP leaders to Ton's account. He spoke of Ton's participation in 1919 in the anti-interventionist French navy mutiny at the Black Sea port of Sevastopol, which successfully defended young Soviet Russia, and of Ton's contacts then with the famous French communist André Marty. If Duong Van Phuc, Ton's adjutant who witnessed the meeting, is correct, many of the leaders may have heard the story for the first time.

It must have caused quite a stir. Here was a comrade who, on account of his seniority and his southern background, had been made an important exponent of their independent, united, and communist-led country the Vietnamese August Revolution of 1945 had established. And now it was said that he had been involved in a heroic, revolutionary act linked to the Russian October Revolution—the very object of commemoration at this moment in Vo Nhai. The men undoubtedly were aware of the highly celebrated status that the Black Sea Mutiny enjoyed in the Third Internationale as one of the purest manifestations of proletarian internationalism. Through his physical presence at Sevastopol and his individual contribution, Ton Duc Thang had directly connected the Vietnamese Revolution with the October Revolution, the venerated Mother of communist revolutions, their historical-political model and source of inspiration and ideological guidance.

To be sure, a number of the men present at the meeting in Vo Nhai had lived in the Soviet Union and had been trained there. But none of them, not even Ho Chi Minh, the longtime anticolonial activist and Comintern agent, could provide a connection with the October Revolution that reached as far back and was as personal and immediate as Ton's. Then again, Ho Chi Minh (as Nguyen Ai Quoc) had participated in highly significant events, like his attempt to be heard at the Versailles Peace Conference in the summer of 1919, or his role in the founding of the French Communist Party in 1920. But Ton's activism in the Black Sea invoked for Vietnamese communism a symbolic imagery of internationalism and revolutionary solidarity that far surpassed these other deeds.

It remains unclear what else took place at the meeting in Vo Nhai in November 1947, or what, if any, decisions were made regarding Ton Duc Thang's story, or when the story was propagated for the first time. But I propose it was at this point, in this fluid, perilous *revolutionary moment* that his heroic internationalism in the Black Sea Mutiny became an imagined ancestry of Vietnamese communism. It was here that the Vietnamese Revolution appropriated Ton's tale, took control of it away from him, and used it to establish the DRVN/ICP's credentials in the international arena. For a better understanding of the motivations behind that move and for its expected benefits, the historical environment of the Vietnamese Revolution around the end of 1947 needs to be considered.

Just like the Bolsheviks in Soviet Russia, the Vietnamese revolutionaries and the independent country they established found themselves under attack and in complete international isolation almost from the very beginning. As Harold Isaacs observed in November 1945 in Ha Noi: "The Annamite [Vietnamese] Communists I met were men bitten deeply with the bitterness of having been abandoned by their ideological comrades overseas. . . . They were oppressed, in common with all the non-Communist . . . nationalist leaders, by a fearful sense of loneliness."[29]

Clearly, the nations of Indochina were only on the periphery of fast-moving post-World War II developments. International politics focused most of all on the power struggles in Europe and the beginning Cold War, which would freeze most of the world in two hostile camps and, in tragic consequence, take the question of decolonization hostage. The French neocolonial war of aggression in Viet Nam, begun in 1945 in the south and continued in late 1946 in the north, was an outgrowth of, and made possible by, these overriding political developments.

In France there existed the very real possibility that the Left would be able to form a Popular Front government, in which the communists could wield considerable influence. Already included in a broad postwar governing coalition since November 1945, the FCP remained preoccupied with metropolitan politics. It was therefore distant to the DRVN's independence claim lest the FCP appear unpatriotic in the eyes of the French electorate and hurt its chances of metropolitan influence. Even after its ouster from the government in May 1947, the FCP hoped for some more time to return to the cabinet. Only by about 1949 would the FCP finally take a clear antiwar and pro-DRVN stance.[30]

Further, except for the small extreme Left, none of the political parties, including the FCP, were willing to relinquish French overlordship altogether and abandon the colonial project right away. In late 1945 Harold Isaacs asked ICP leaders, in this connection, about their assessment of the FCP. One of them

> snorted with disgust. "The French Communists . . . are Frenchmen and colonialists first and Communists after." [. . . Another one] spoke contemptuously of Thorez [the FCP General Secretary], who . . . had said he was in favor of the Annamites "finally arriving at their independence." He laughed sourly. "A fine rubber phrase, is it not? . . . No, I am afraid we cannot depend on these fine gentlemen. They

> are the dominant party in France now. And look what Frenchmen are doing now in Indochina."[31]

So bruised was the French national psyche by military defeat and shameful surrender, Vichyite collaboration with German and Japanese fascist occupiers, and liberation mostly at the hands of others, that restoring France's honor and *grandeur* and continuing its "civilizing mission" held a strong appeal far into the political Left. Under these conditions, the French military, the political Right, and the colonial lobby found it quite easy to start the piecemeal process of reconquering "their" colony, sabotage any attempt to come to a peaceful arrangement between France and the DRVN, and provoke the all-out war at the end of 1946.

Vietnamese independence was also sacrificed to early Cold War politics in Europe, where France became one of the primary contested grounds. The Soviet Union, which had sustained the heaviest losses and devastation in World War II, focused on internal reconstruction and on a European order that would guarantee the security of the Soviet Union's most vulnerable western flank. With the FCP so close to coming to power through the electoral process, Stalin was hardly inclined to weaken the FCP's position by supporting Vietnamese independence. Vietnamese revolutionaries were keenly aware of Soviet coolness to their cause and, again in Harold Isaacs's personal observations of late 1945,

> unusually frank and cynical about the Russians. Even the most orthodox among them, like [. . . Tran Van Giau], the partisan organizer, granted that the Russians went in for "an excess of ideological compromise," and said he expected no help from that quarter. . . . "The Russians are nationalists for Russia first and above all," another . . . Communist said with some bitterness. "They would be interested in us only if we served some purpose of theirs."[32]

Isaacs further reported that French communists in Sai Gon "stood aside" during the August Revolution and hid behind the perceived demands of Soviet foreign policy. In September 1945, they advised the ICP to be patient and refrain from "premature adventures." Vietnamese independence was subordinated to Soviet policy requirements, which "might well include France as a firm ally of the U.S.S.R. in Europe, in which case the . . . independence movement would be an embarrassment."[33] In addition, the Soviet Union eyed the ICP-led August

Revolution itself with a good deal of suspicion; Ho Chi Minh's political line had long been criticized, and continued to be seen, as emphasizing national liberation over social revolution. Stalin and Ho Chi Minh apparently did not settle their differences until February 1950, shortly after the Soviet Union's recognition of the DRVN, when Ho secretly appeared at the Stalin-Mao summit in Moscow.[34]

From the United States' perspective, the beginning Cold War made its wartime anticolonial rhetoric quickly obsolete. The United States would eventually force the Netherlands to grant independence to Indonesia with its noncommunist leadership. But France was too important a cornerstone in the U.S. design for a postwar European order to oppose its colonial reconquest. The United States instead gave logistical and financial support to the French in Indochina beginning soon after the Japanese surrender. In addition, despite the short period of good relations and cooperation between the Viet Minh and the U.S. Office of Strategic Services (OSS, the forerunner of the CIA) in the summer of 1945, the DRVN and its Ho Chi Minh-led government fell victim to the growing U.S. anticommunist obsession during 1946 and 1947. Not surprisingly, DRVN feelers toward the Truman administration in the spring and summer of 1947, which were accompanied by policy changes intended to portray the DRVN as flexible and hardly radical, solicited no response;[35] they came at a time when the Truman Doctrine and the Marshall Plan were announced and "containment" of communism became the guiding principle of U.S. foreign policy.

The Chinese Communist Party (CCP) under Mao Zedong, another of the DRVN's potential allies, was engaged in a civil war with the GMD under Jiang Jieshi (Chiang Kai-shek) in northern China. Thus, only limited, local contacts existed in the borderlands between the DRVN and smaller CCP units until late in 1949.[36] The CCP's victory over the GMD and the founding of the People's Republic of China (PRC) in 1949 would, of course, radically alter the course of the French war in Indochina in favor of the DRVN, but in 1947, when the GMD was at the peak of its military might and had even succeeded in driving the CCP from its Shaanxi Soviet around Yan'an, the CCP instead appeared near defeat. The DRVN could expect no assistance from the CCP at that point.

Therefore, at several instances during 1947, Ho Chi Minh pragmatically tried to appeal to the GMD for anti-French support. His hopes might have been based on a shared anti-imperialism of the two Asian nations and on the many contacts between the Viet Minh and the GMD during the anti-Japanese resistance of the early to mid-1940s and in the first ten months of the DRVN's existence, when Chinese Nationalist armies occupied the northern half of Viet Nam. But many of the GMD officials, who had been sympathetic to the Viet Minh then, had been transferred from the border region, and the GMD in general was, once again, more decidedly anticommunist. Throughout 1947, several DRVN attempts at contacting the GMD either failed, produced no tangible results, or ended in the temporary arrest of its emissaries in southern China.[37]

With the DRVN thus isolated from, or ignored by, the major powers in 1947, the newly emerging independent nations of Asia could, for the most part, only offer moral support; at the Asian Relations Conference in New Delhi in the spring of 1947, the DRVN delegation, led by Tran Van Giau, received no more than friendly attention and sympathy. As the only other assistance of limited scope, some arms smuggling was arranged for a while via Thailand. In Bangkok in September 1947, a forum of potential utility to the DRVN, the Southeast Asia League, was founded by Pridi Phanomyong and Tran Van Giau to assist in regional anticolonial and nationalist cooperation. But the organization was short-lived. By November 1947, a military coup—probably fueled by early Cold War anticommunism—replaced the Left-leaning, pro-DRVN Free Thai government with a prominent rightist leader, Phibun Songkhram, who was openly hostile to the Viet Minh. Subsequently, DRVN arms procurements shifted to deals made across the Chinese border and to maquis-based production in simple workshops.[38]

Turning to the domestic situation around 1947, military and political developments of that year had put the DRVN on the defensive. After the outbreak of large-scale Franco-Vietnamese hostilities in December 1946, the DRVN was forced to abandon Ha Noi and to try to salvage and reestablish the remnants of its state structure and government apparatus in the rugged terrain of the northern guerrilla base. Thep Moi specifically credits Ton Duc Thang for the National Assembly's Standing Committee—vested with far-reaching powers to act on behalf of the entire parliament (which would not reconvene until 1953)—safely reaching the maquis.[39] But in general, the transition from an urban to a guerrilla government proved extremely difficult for the

DRVN during the first year of the resistance war, when it was subjected to intense military pressures by its enemy.

The French launched several offensives in the spring, summer, and fall. The last one, begun in October 1947 and ongoing at the time of the Vo Nhai commemorative gathering, was the largest and most sustained French effort to decide the war in its favor. It only narrowly failed in its objectives, but scattered the Viet Minh forces and even forced some units into Chinese border sanctuaries, where the Viet Minh had to seek accommodation with ragtag gangs of bandits, smugglers, and armed political sectarians who controlled these areas. DRVN forces, however, were able to regroup soon after. By early 1948, the defensive war largely gave way to equilibrium. The stalemate would last until 1950, when the PRC began assisting the DRVN's war efforts.[40]

Politically, developments throughout 1947 and into 1948 did not look promising. First, in May 1947, Emile Bollaert, the new French high commissioner for Indochina, sent one of his advisers, the Orientalist scholar Paul Mus, to the maquis to deliver to Ho Chi Minh France's conditions for a cessation of hostilities. In Nguyen Khac Vien's words, however, the terms "were tantamount to a [Viet Minh] capitulation." Consequently, Ho Chi Minh rejected them outright: "There's no place in the French Union for cowards. If I accepted these conditions, I'd be one." Paul Mus conceded that he himself would not have acted differently.[41]

Second, what came to be called the "Bao Dai solution" slowly took shape in the summer of 1947: a renewed attempt by Vietnamese anticommunist nationalists, among them the VNQDD, to form a broad-based alternative Vietnamese government under the ex-emperor Bao Dai that might be more acceptable to the French than the DRVN and so achieve limited independence for a reunited Viet Nam within the framework of the French Union. It proved to be acceptable to such a degree that France co-opted the movement and its model during the autumn of 1947 and more or less directed it thereafter. The more ardent among the nationalists thereupon abandoned the project, and popular support, which had looked promising at first, waned. During 1948 and 1949, the "Bao Dai solution" would get bogged down in political maneuvering. Never able to fully shake off their image as French puppets, its Vietnamese exponents did not achieve a measure of national independence (as the "State of Viet Nam") and governmental autonomy until 1950, when the war had shifted irreversibly in the DRVN's favor.

Nevertheless, for a while in 1947 and into 1948, the "Bao Dai solution" made, in Neil Jamieson's words, "spectacular progress in the south" by drawing various religious beliefs and sects into the anti-DRVN nationalist camp; it also began making headway in the north. To the DRVN, the possibility of "another formally established Vietnamese government, which had a plausible claim to legitimacy," seemed quite real at that time. On 23 December 1947, France publicly ruled out any further contacts with Ho Chi Minh's DRVN and was fully committed to the "Bao Dai solution."[42]

Thus, in late 1947, at about the time of the meeting in Vo Nhai where Ton's story of the Black Sea was told, the fortunes of the DRVN had reached their lowest point. A year after the outbreak of war, the regime was still weak, and its organizational structure was in shambles. Successive French offensives had pushed the Viet Minh far into the mountains and cut the resistance government almost entirely off from vital outside communications. Any compromise solution through Franco-DRVN negotiations was now illusory, and a nationalist alternative to Ho had to be reckoned with.

Perhaps even more important, the DRVN remained in complete international isolation. Some potential allies like the CCP or the new independent Asian nations had no means of effectively assisting the Viet Minh. Others like the FCP wavered on the colonial question and were more annoyed than pleased by the communist-led Vietnamese Revolution. The Soviets, whose October Revolution the men in Vo Nhai were commemorating in reverence, viewed Ho Chi Minh's revolutionary line with suspicion; in addition, Moscow had thus far subordinated its support for the DRVN to the power struggles in France. Similarly, the beginning Cold War hostilities all but killed hopes—remote as they had been anyway—of receiving anticolonial support from the United States or Nationalist China.

The setbacks of 1947 clarified the diplomatic-political options for the Viet Minh. The door to accommodation with France, the GMD, and the United States was now completely shut. On the other hand, the FCP had recently been expelled from the French government. Even more important, the Communist Information Bureau (Cominform), an organization for international communist cooperation, was founded in Wilcza Góra (Poland) in September 1947. There, the increasing Cold War polarization of the world found its most pronounced expression yet in the famous speech by Andrei Zhdanov, the CPSU's second in rank after Stalin, on the need for armed opposition to imperialism and on the world's division into two hostile camps—the Soviet-led East versus the U.S.-led West, socialism versus capitalism, democracy versus imperialism, and love of peace versus belligerence.[43]

I suggest that the leaders of the DRVN/Viet Minh/ICP realized in the critical situation of late 1947 that they had no other option than to redouble their efforts to align themselves with the communist bloc, despite their present de facto isolation from it. Indeed, this was not just a last option but a promising new chance to break out of their isolation. The Cominform constituted the first institutionalized manifestation of revolutionary internationalism since the Comintern's demise during World War II. Did not Andrei Zhdanov's passing mention of the Vietnamese anticolonial resistance war signal that the communist movement with the Soviet Union at the helm was now, after all, prepared to listen in earnest to appeals for help from the Vietnamese Revolution? In J. H. Brimmell's opinion, the creation of Cominform marked a "policy switch" of major proportions: "The Soviet Union was now ready to throw its strength into the struggle whose lines had been thus [by the "two camps"] demarcated. In drawing up the battle order the Soviet leaders remembered the nationalist movements of Asia, and once more, after twenty years, began to pay serious attention to them."[44]

Furthermore, true to the new Cominform line, Zhdanov criticized the FCP "for wanting to return to the [coalition] government." Instead, he urged the European communist parties, including the FCP, "to identify more closely with overseas movements."[45]

The "two camps" concept found worldwide resonance and had a greatly encouraging effect on the Vietnamese Revolution. When news of Zhdanov's programmatic speech finally reached the maquis at the low point described above, it must have appeared to rectify what grievances the Viet Minh had with the FCP and the Soviet Union: the DRVN's subordination to the FCP's political needs would end, and Soviet disinterest would turn into genuine attention. Already in January 1948, at the ICP's enlarged Central Committee meeting, the party formally endorsed the Cominform's "two camps" concept.[46] All that the party had to do now was to announce and prove itself as part of the Soviet-led camp.

It did so in several ways. First, at the February 1948 Conference of Southeast Asian Youth in Calcutta, the Viet Minh delegation emphasized armed revolution in what was regarded as the conference's "keynote message."[47] Second, at another conference of ICP cadres in August 1948, an "Asian Cominform" was proposed; furthermore, in Motoo Furuta's words, "the basic character of the Indochinese revolution was redefined as a 'new democratic revolution'." This Maoist concept of 1940 now "meant a 'people's democratic revolution' possessing the potential to evolve into socialism under communist-party direction." Despite the alignment of the (still officially dissolved) ICP with the Cominform, however, the much more open character of the DRVN and even of the ICP-controlled Viet Minh continued through 1949. Furuta notes that the "application of the concept of a people's democratic revolution to the Vietnamese revolution was a gradual process that did not affect the reality of the situation in Vietnam until 1950."[48]

Nevertheless, Vietnamese communism from early 1948 on defined and announced itself consciously as part of the new communist order. But what about the internationalist support that the ICP-led resistance so urgently needed at this critical stage in late 1947 and early 1948? What about lingering Soviet doubts about the ICP's previous revolutionary record with its emphasis on national liberation? Enter Ton Duc Thang's story. Ton's alleged internationalism in the Black Sea Mutiny became known at the most opportune moment, in late 1947, when the Vietnamese Revolution desperately needed to present credentials in order to be found worthy of communist, internationalist help.

At this lowest point in the revolutionary moment, Ton Duc Thang's story of his internationalist gesture toward revolutionary Russia became an imagined ancestry of Vietnamese communism. Ton's part in the glorified Black Sea Mutiny firmly rooted the Vietnamese Revolution in the original Bolshevik victory and in the purest sentiment of communist militants, revolutionary internationalism. But not only could internationalism, as exhibited by Ton in the Black Sea, be imagined as a fundamental and long-standing ingredient of Vietnamese communism, in the critical months of 1947, Ton's tale also encouraged the imagining of the DRVN/ICP in the role of the "infant" Soviet Union.

The parallelism of Soviet Russia in 1919, two years after the October

Revolution, and the DRVN in 1947, two years after the August Revolution, cannot have gone unnoticed in Vo Nhai. Both of the new regimes were attacked by foreign and domestic counterrevolutionary forces bent on their destruction. Both experienced total isolation at first. For the Bolsheviks, however, help had come in the form of vigorous internationalist struggles waged by radicals of many nations, including the Vietnamese Ton Duc Thang. But revolutionary solidarity and internationalist support had so far not materialized for the DRVN.

Therefore, at some time between the gathering in Vo Nhai in November 1947 and, at the latest, 1949, the story of the Black Sea Mutiny was broadcast abroad as part of attempts by the ICP to seek aid and recognition as a legitimate, long-standing, and accomplished member of the international communist movement. There is no indication that the story was propagated domestically before 1957. Clearly, its chief addressees were the Soviet Union, which quite suddenly had rediscovered its interest in the Asian revolutionary movements for national liberation, and the FCP, which recently had been admonished by the Cominform for its politics of compromise and of neglecting the colonial question. Now, with no hopes of returning to the government, the FCP could make amends.

Vis-à-vis both the DRVN's potential allies, Ton Duc Thang's revolutionary actions in 1919 served as a legend of origins for the ICP. As in all legends of origins, the essence of its subject—here of Vietnamese communism—was transmitted via a highly symbolic image in which its various meanings were condensed. The story of the Black Sea had all the right ingredients: the mutiny signified revolutionary internationalism focused on the Bolshevik Revolution, the warships stood for the defeated Western power and imperialism, and André Marty was a trope for the true revolutionary radicalism of the sailors (as opposed to the self-interest of those who simply demanded their return to France and their demobilization). The essence of Vietnamese communism, therefore, lay in its ancestry with the Russian October Revolution, in its anti-imperialism, its revolutionary militancy, and its internationalism. In addition, it was personified by Ton Duc Thang, cast as one of the elders of the Vietnamese people, who represented not only the ICP but also—through his chairmanships of the United Front and the National Assembly—the promising revolutionary potential of a united and heroic nation. The Vietnamese Revolution thus showed impeccable credentials.

Vis-à-vis Moscow, the Soviet Union centeredness of Ton's internationalism was likely emphasized as well. The symbolic significance of the mutinous act directly engaged Stalin's long-held suspicion about the nationalist orientation of the ICP. In addition, the portrayal of the DRVN as the mirror image of the embattled young Soviet Union underscored the ICP's appeals for internationalist support. The implicit message was that Vietnamese revolutionary activism had already paid its dues with the October Revolution back in 1919. Now it was time for the Soviet Union to reciprocate and help protect the August Revolution, with whose present critical situation the Soviet Union could easily empathize out of its own experiences from 1917 to 1921.

Vis-à-vis the FCP, Ton's story emphasized an imagined brotherhood of the two communist parties. After all, the FCP, too, sought to trace its ancestry in part to the glorified Black Sea Mutiny. The subtle affirmation of the two parties' equal status as brothers (in contrast to colonial paternalism) was reinforced by the image of Ton Duc Thang fighting side by side with his French comrades, among whom had been the FCP's famous André Marty. Further, potential FCP doubts over the revolutionary reliability of the south of Viet Nam, where a nationalist alternative to the DRVN undeniably had a certain measure of support, were countered in the person of Ton, the "Cochinchinese" revolutionary mutineer. In the struggle for Vietnamese independence, there should be no ambiguity over whom the FCP had to support. It could only be the communist-led DRVN, and the FCP was urged to defend it with just as much determination as French sailors had fought for Soviet Russia in the Black Sea.[49]

After Vo Nhai in 1947, Ton Duc Thang's story had become a legend of origins for the ICP and its revolutionary state, the DRVN. Ton himself likely had no more control over it. Although no evidence could be found to clarify when and how exactly the story was utilized in the manner described, we know of its propagandistic transmission abroad through the feedback the story elicited from overseas communist allies. These reactions will be discussed in the following chapter. As will be seen there as well, after about 1955 Vietnamese communism in turn began losing its control over the tale.

CHAPTER 3

The Black Sea Mutiny in the Post-Recognition Moment

AT SOME POINT between late 1947 and 1949, Vietnamese propagandists began transmitting the story of Ton Duc Thang's participation in the Black Sea Mutiny of 1919 abroad. Their primary targets as audiences were the Soviet Union and France. This chapter will first discuss foreign reactions to Ton's story. These responses were for the most part connected to trips Ton Duc Thang took to China, in 1951, and to Eastern Europe and the Soviet Union, in 1955/56 and 1956. Based on the feedback from abroad, it is apparent that a significant development took place in the 1950s with regard to the contents of the propagated story. This chapter will chart the changes that were made to the tale and discuss the dramatic effects they had on Ton Duc Thang. After an analysis of the only known published "recollections" of Ton's involvement in the navy revolt, which were published in 1957, a synthesis of the evidence from chapters 1, 2, and 3 will be presented.

THE BLACK SEA STORY ABROAD, 1950–56

In May 1951, when Ton Duc Thang undertook an official trip to China, tremendous changes had occurred in comparison to the perilous days of 1947–49. The CCP won the civil war against the GMD and established the People's Republic of China in October 1949. Once its People's Liberation Army reached the Vietnamese border in December, the DRVN was no longer encircled by hostile powers. And after the end of its geographic insularity, the diplomatic isolation of the Vietnamese Revolution was finally broken when, in January 1950, first the PRC and then the Soviet Union and the other East European countries recognized the DRVN. The DRVN was firmly in the communist camp now and began its long balancing act between Moscow and Beijing. In May 1950, Ton became the chairman of the newly formed Vietnamese-Soviet Friendship Association.

Also during 1950, the two-year-long military stalemate with France turned into a resistance war in which the DRVN—thanks to extensive assistance from its new northern neighbor, the PRC—went on the offensive. In one of France's biggest colonial defeats ever, a Viet Minh offensive during the autumn secured the entire border regions and the northern highlands. Then, in February 1951, the Communist Party reconstituted itself openly as the Vietnamese Labor Party (Dang Lao Dong, or DLD). Ton played a prominent role at the founding congress.[1] And when the party had resurfaced and no longer needed to work through the Viet Minh, the Lien Viet Front absorbed the Viet Minh at a unification congress soon after.

Thus, at the time of his trip to China, Ton Duc Thang was one of nineteen full members of the Central Executive Committee of the "new" Communist Party, the reelected chairman of the enlarged Lien Viet United Front, and acting chairman of the National Assembly. It is not clear in which exact capacity or for what reason Ton paid that visit to Beijing. Important for our purposes here, however, is that the Soviet ambassador to the PRC organized a formal reception for the visiting Vietnamese communist as well. A stunning scene occurred during the event, and an apparent eyewitness, Thep Moi, the revolutionary journalist who by then had risen to the top echelon of the DLD's main organ, *Nhan Dan* (The People), described it as follows:

> Zhou Enlai and Liu Shaoqi were not present at the reception, but Vice-Premier Chen Yun and other persons of high caliber attended. When everybody had arrived and taken their places just before dinnertime, a phone call by Stalin came in from the Kremlin. Stalin requested that the first toast should be from the Central Committee of the CPSU and the Soviet state in honor of Ton Duc Thang, the Black Sea fighter of old times! This had great significance. Stalin's praise of Ton Duc Thang taught those Maoists a lesson; it elevated the position of Viet Nam so that China had to hold it surely in high esteem![2]

The Black Sea story, as utilized by the Vietnamese Revolution, had fulfilled its purpose. It had received the attention of the Soviet Union and, indeed, of Stalin himself. Vietnamese communism had announced itself as a truly revolutionary movement in which internationalist consciousness had been an essential ingredient from the beginning. In addition, through the scene in the Black Sea, where internationalism was focused on the October Revolution, it had paid its respects to the leadership role of the Soviet Union, which in turn now acknowledged the legitimate place of the DRVN in the communist world.

Stalin's phone call must have been carefully planned and timed. And Thep Moi's last comment reveals why the call was made: Viet Nam became contested territory between Moscow and Beijing. The CCP under Mao Zedong had long insisted on its own revolutionary line and came to power entirely on its own. It owed the Soviet Union no political debts, so to say, and saw itself as the CPSU's equal. After the founding of the PRC, the CCP propagated its revolutionary line as the only one applicable to the various Asian anticolonial revolutionary movements. Moscow had gone along with that for a while, but in 1951, the rivalry between the two communist powers was heating up.

This was Stalin's apparent lesson to the Chinese communists at the reception: his demonstrative praise of Ton Duc Thang's pro-Soviet internationalism reiterated Moscow's claim to be the primary center of world communism (which the CCP openly challenged). And Stalin's "elevating the position of Viet Nam," presumably to the PRC's level denied that the Maoist line had anything to teach the Vietnamese Revolution. Instead perhaps, the People's Republic of China might have something to learn from the (in Moscow's view, well-behaved) Vietnamese and their past accomplishments. Ton Duc Thang's tale of the Black Sea Mutiny became the example in this lesson.

In 1988, when anti-CCP feelings were still pronounced in Viet Nam, and Thep Moi remembered the event at the Beijing reception, the scene of the teacher Stalin, the irreverent student CCP, and the class nerd Ton (i.e., the Vietnamese Revolution) might have been exaggerated. It is not clear how the DRVN, which always tried to steer clear of the Moscow-Beijing rivalry, reacted back in 1951. After all, Maoism exerted a strong influence during the first half of the 1950s on Vietnamese communist policies. Yet, even in its instrumentalization in the CPSU-CCP contest, the story of the Black Sea continued to be transmitted and rebroadcast and established impressive credentials for the Vietnamese Revolution.

The next known instance in which Ton Duc Thang's story of the Black Sea became acknowledged abroad was Philippe Devillers's 1952 publication in France of the *Histoire du Viêt-Nam de 1940 à 1952.* All that Devillers wrote was that Ton, the chairman of the Lien Viet Front, was an "old sailor of the Black Sea and an ex-prisoner, during 19 years (1926–1945), of Poulo Condore." Since Devillers wrote the preface to his book in March 1952, he had most likely received his information about Ton already by 1951 at the latest.[3]

In 1953, the FCP weekly *Regards sur le monde du travail* portrayed Ton Duc Thang in wording almost exactly like Devillers's. *Regards* either copied its information from Devillers or based it on the same unknown source that Devillers had used.[4] Two other French authors, the anti-communist Bernard Fall and the pro-communist Jean Chesneaux, in 1954 and 1955, connecting Ton's imprisonment directly to his participation in the Black Sea Mutiny, cited *Regards* as their source, although *Regards* had not made that claim.[5]

In late 1955 and early 1956, Ton Duc Thang visited East Germany and the Soviet Union. The trip culminated on 21 January 1956, in Moscow in the conferral of the Stalin Prize on Ton Duc Thang.[6] It was the highest Soviet decoration a Vietnamese had thus far received. Ton's participation in the Black Sea Mutiny figured prominently in the eulogy.[7] Only a month later, at the twentieth congress of the CPSU, Nikita Khrushchev famously denounced Stalin and his personality cult. He characterized previous Stalin Prize winners as Stalin's "sycophants in Russia and abroad," and the award was soon renamed International Lenin Peace Prize.[8]

During the two years prior to Ton's trip to Eastern Europe, major developments had taken place in Viet Nam. In the spring of 1954, DRVN forces besieged and finally stormed the French bastion at Dien Bien Phu. This historic victory over a deeply humiliated France ended the First Indochina War; almost a century of French colonialism came to a close. The subsequent conference at Geneva resulted in the division of Viet Nam along the 17th parallel—a division explicitly meant to be provisional until all-Vietnamese elections in 1956 would produce a unified nation, state, and government. Vietnamese troops of Bao Dai's regime and the French left the north, along with several hundred thousand anti-DRVN civilians, many of them Catholics. In turn, about one hundred thousand southern DRVN loyalists—troops, cadres, and civilians—regrouped north of the 17th parallel. However, what was expected to be a two-year-long sojourn in the north, until reunification, became an exile of over twenty years for many of these southern revolutionaries.

In the south, Bao Dai's prime minister Ngo Dinh Diem, with active U.S. encouragement, quickly moved to sabotage the Geneva Accords and the all-Vietnamese elections. During 1955, he replaced the French with U.S. overlords and Bao Dai with himself as head of the southern state, soon to be proclaimed as the Republic of Viet Nam. Domestic rivals, like the Binh Xuyen gang, were eliminated. One year after Geneva and one year before the deadline for elections, which Ho Chi Minh's government was expected to win easily, it became clear that the southern regime would permit no elections. By 1955, the temporary division of Viet Nam for armistice purposes had turned into a permanent and complete separation.

In the north, the DRVN resistance returned to Ha Noi after almost seven years in the maquis. Its highest priority was to reestablish and consolidate the state structure in the northern half of the country. For several years after Ngo Dinh Diem's cancellation of the elections, the DRVN thus still sought peaceful means to achieve reunification. Even more so than before, Ton Duc Thang became a representative of these DRVN policies focused on peace and unity. In the summer of 1955, Ton cofounded the Vietnamese Committee for the Defense of World Peace, which named him lifelong honorary president. And in July, the Helsinki congress of the communist-dominated World Peace Council elected him a member.

Further, in direct response to Ngo Dinh Diem's reneging on all-Vietnamese elections, congresses of both the Lien Viet United Front and the DRVN National Assembly were convened in Ha Noi in September 1955. The Lien Viet now became the "Vietnamese Fatherland Front" with an even broader patriotic appeal.[9] Three months before his trip to Eastern Europe, Ton Duc Thang, the most prominent southern revolutionary and a national father figure, was reelected chairman of the National Assembly and the Fatherland Front. After the Cold War division of the country, Ton's role as a symbol of the south carried an even greater significance than before; Ton personified national unity and the DRVN's claim to legitimate authority over all of Viet Nam.[10]

For my discussion of the public life of the Black Sea story, Ton Duc Thang's trip to Eastern Europe and to Moscow in 1955 and 1956 is of interest because it provides the first instance where the tale's most dramatic detail appeared: not only did Ton's European hosts in their welcoming communiqués recall his part in the internationalist revolt of 1919, but now he was even credited for personally raising a red flag on his mutinous warship![11]

What can be made of this? Neither Stalin in 1951, nor Devillers and the FCP weekly *Regards,* whose source for Ton's Black Sea involvement likely dated from 1951 or even earlier, made reference to a red flag when they talked about the story. But would they not have done so, had they known about the red flag then? An image of such powerful political and emotional symbolism would surely have been noticed and mentioned had it been part of the story before 1951.[12] I therefore suggest that the detail of the red flag raised by Ton during the Black Sea Mutiny was first propagated abroad by the DRVN at some point in or after 1951.

Before considering the reasons the red flag was added to the story, we should briefly recall the main aspects of the Black Sea Mutiny. During the unrest, around 20 April 1919, red flags were hoisted on three armored cruisers, the *France,* the *Jean-Bart,* and the *Justice,* which were all at anchorage in Sevastopol at that time. None of the men who raised the flags are known, but Ton Duc Thang can be ruled out as a crew member on all three ships. In the only other incident involving a red flag, at Toulon in June 1919, the flag flew only briefly on the *Provence* during one night five days *before* the mutiny broke out on this ship. And during the revolt on the *Provence,* an attempt to raise a red flag was unsuccessful. In this case, however, the name of the man is known, a certain Yacomo.[13] Thus, even if Ton had been involved in any of the unrests, he certainly did not hoist a red flag. This new detail of the story was definitely wrong.

A likely explanation for the dramatic embellishment of Ton's Black Sea story can be found in the reconstitution of the Communist Party in 1951 as the Vietnamese Labor Party (DLD). King C. Chen has pointed out how Maoist influences were predominant in the DRVN by 1950, after the founding of the PRC and its establishment of relations with the Vietnamese resistance government. According to Chen, the Maoist revolutionary line included a formula that "was prepared for exporting to colonial and semi-colonial countries." The formula, as espoused in Mao's tract on the "People's Democratic Dictatorship," was "composed of three elements, namely, a well-disciplined party armed with the theory of Marxism-Leninism, an army under the command of such a party, and a united front of all revolutionary classes and groups under the leadership of such a party."[14]

The DRVN, of course, possessed both a communist-led army and a communist-led united front. But the party itself, the ICP, officially dissolved late in 1945; unofficially, however, it continued to operate through Marxist study groups, occasional cadre conferences, and, most important, through the Viet Minh Front. It was the Vietnamese Revolution's acceptance of the Maoist revolutionary formula that led to the disposal of the Viet Minh in the merger with the Lien Viet Front and the founding of the DLD as an openly reconstituted Communist Party in February 1951. Not only did the PRC applaud the DLD's founding as proof of Vietnamese adherence to the concept of the three essential factors, but Vietnamese communism itself also repeatedly acknowledged its indebtedness to Maoist thought in general, and to Mao's formula for successful revolutions in particular. For example, presiding over "Viet Nam Soviet Chinese Friendship Month" in January 1954, Ton Duc Thang invoked those "three lessons" learned from Maoist thought.[15]

As discussed before, the ICP *as a party* already in early 1948 accepted the Cominform's "two camps" model. But the DRVN *as a resistance government* in its weak and embattled state continued to be broad-based, open, and politically flexible and only gradually drew practical consequences from such a firm alignment. Only during 1950, when the geographical and diplomatic isolation of the Vietnamese Revolution was broken, did the DRVN unequivocally align with the communist camp. With Maoist influence came a turn to much tighter political control and ideological orthodoxy; as Chen reports, Ho Chi Minh in 1950 "dropped his pre-1949 notion of a 'coalition' and 'independent' Viet-Minh government."[16]

The embellishment of the Black Sea story likely occurred in a parallel development. Before the founding of the DLD, the red flag was not yet included. In 1948 and 1949—those critical years of the resistance—the story emphasized the pro-Soviet internationalist sentiment in Ton Duc Thang's involvement in 1919 and thereby appealed for reciprocal internationalist assistance. After the founding of the DLD, the addition of the red flag shifted the story's emphasis. The desperate need for internationalist support had been satisfied, and the DRVN had taken the initiative in the war. Now, the red flag introduced the DRVN to its allies as an orthodox member of the communist world. A similar demonstration of orthodoxy was the naming of the reconstituted party as the Vietnamese *Labor* Party. Equally, the red flag in Ton Duc Thang's story of the Black Sea now stood for *proletarian* internationalism. It clarified the class base and revolutionary depth of Ton's act.

The red flag (or, Red Flag) is a signifier for the working-class revolution in a manner comparable to the ways in which the Coca Cola bottle represents American-centered corporate capitalism. The Red Flag is universally recognizable as a marker in which a multitude of related associations and images collapse into one quintessential symbol of the proletarian revolution. In the Black Sea story's earlier version, Ton had simply participated in the internationalist navy revolt. His commitment was still somewhat open to interpretation—just as the Viet Minh government was in relation to the communist world before 1951. But hoisting the Red Flag entailed a deliberate, conscious, and personal act that would dispel doubts, if there ever had been any, over Ton's exact motivations to take part in the mutiny. His class alignment was clarified by the Red Flag, just as the DRVN, in 1951, committed itself fully to the communist camp. In other words, it was necessary that Ton Duc Thang raised the Red Flag in 1919 in the story's new version because the DRVN raised the Red Flag of a "new" Labor Party in 1951.

After 1947, in the bleak and dangerous revolutionary moment of the DRVN's isolation, Ton Duc Thang's radical act of internationalist solidarity dating all the way back to the Bolshevik October Revolution became an imagined ancestry of Vietnamese communism. After 1951, in the more confident post-recognition moment of the DRVN, the Red Flag in the Black Sea stressed Ton's proletarian background as another imagined ancestry of the reconstituted party.

TON DUC THANG'S "RECOLLECTIONS"

What about Ton Duc Thang's role in the progressing career of what had once been his story of the Black Sea Mutiny? Out of the few available glimpses emerges a general picture of unease and dissociation on Ton's part. Not only had he lost control of the tale already, but now it even became adorned with a highly symbolic detail his own experiences could not at all sustain. The Red Flag took on a propagandistic life of its own that was increasingly in danger of getting out of hand. After the party had appropriated his story, only a few instances are reported in which Ton himself still was willing to talk about the Black Sea: once to younger cadres during the resistance war, and then around the time of his "recollections" of the incident in 1957. Otherwise, Ton was widely known as someone who preferred to remain silent about the past, either gruffly evading questions about the mutinies or claiming that he had forgotten everything.

Ton's excuse of poor memory was clearly a subterfuge. After all, he would at other times remember details even from his life prior to the sojourn in France. If the navy revolt really was the one defining moment of Ton's youth, it is inconceivable that his memory of this crucial event would fail him when other, less memorable ones could in fact be recalled. Finally, his daughter and sons-in-law also insisted that, despite beatings in prison, illnesses, and several operations, Ton retained excellent powers of recollection until very old age. Instead, Ton Duc Thang's family attributed his unwillingness to talk about the past to his humility, genuine modesty, and the conviction that so many others had contributed equally or even more to the revolutionary cause.[17]

But much more was involved than mere modesty. For example, Tuong Bich Truc, one of Ton's sons-in-law, recalled how he had sometimes teased his father-in-law to tell him about the Black Sea or the years in prison. But Ton

> never talked [or wrote] about himself. . . . He just told me, "I have already forgotten, I don't remember. I might misrepresent something, and others could refute it. That would be very embarrassing. Enough *[thoi]*, if people want to write something, they have to write that I can't recall."[18]

Ton's resentment over being made a propaganda tool speaks from these sentences. A Red Flag had been saddled on his story, and—to stay in the metaphor—he was bucking. Ton was supposed to invent awkward "memories" of that new part of the story, and the possibility of being proven wrong was great. Now he had "enough." He refused to cooperate with those people who authored the Red Flag. He could not prevent them from "writing something," but he for his part would remain silent or feign poor recollection.

Thus, for example, the Museum of the Revolution in Ha Noi proposed in early 1966 that then DRVN vice president Ton Duc Thang write a short autobiography. The museum's unsuspecting vice-director Tran Van Trinh attached to this initial inquiry a list with eight suggested topics of greatest historical interest, including the Black Sea Mutiny. Nothing came of this initiative.[19] And the author Le Minh reports that she was forced to rely exclusively on other historical witnesses when she conducted research for her semi-fictional biography of Ton Duc Thang. Although she was personally close to Ton, he and his family (who might, after all, have known a few things, as Le Minh implies) did not help her out:

> He would not talk to anybody about his life, not even to his children at home. Whenever someone asked him about those old tales that so many people knew, Uncle [Ton] always only had a single answer: "Already forgotten." Uncle often told his children, "there's nothing to tell," and therefore the children at home went along with that.[20]

What can we learn from the instances where Ton actually did "recall" the mutiny? One example is, again, provided by Thep Moi, the leading journalist of the party's mouthpiece, *Nhan Dan*. After the victorious military offensive in the autumn of 1950, large parts of the north of Viet Nam were secured for the DRVN, and a safe guerrilla base for the party leadership was established in 1951 near Dinh Hoa, about fifty kilometers northwest of Thai Nguyen. Ton Duc Thang lived in this base and, just as he had done throughout his adult life, liked to spend time with, and give good guidance to, a younger entourage; in this case, these were junior cadres who had assignments in the base. Thep Moi remembered the following scene to have taken place in 1951 or perhaps a bit later—that is, just when the Red Flag was added to the party-propagated story: "Uncle [Ton] talked about the Black Sea. But he did not speak about hoisting any flag. The important point was to tell how the sailors on the ship landed on shore and fraternized with the people of that port."[21]

This little episode confirms that Ton Duc Thang himself would not mention a Red Flag when recounting the events of 1919. Other unknown propagandists added the detail of the Red Flag to the story around 1951. Significantly, most notable to Ton was not his own contribution to the navy revolt but the association and interaction with the revolutionary masses. He told the young cadres a didactic tale of staying close to, and learning from, the people. Yet, during the mutinies of 1919, where, in fact, were sailors able to land and mingle with the people in a manner that impressed Ton Duc Thang so profoundly? Considering that a number of mutinies occurred on the high seas,[22] there are merely two possibilities: First, during the April revolts, in Sevastopol, where, as shown before, Ton was not present, and second, during the unrest in May and June 1919 in French ports—including Toulon!

What makes Thep Moi's recollection so credible is Ton's narrative preference for the people and against the pompous, self-congratulatory Red Flag, conforming with Ton's personality and modest social style mentioned frequently by others. As previously argued, Ton never seemed to employ the Black Sea story for the purpose of bragging about individual heroism or fame. Instead, it was a rather subdued tale of marvelous personal experiences gained at a time and in a place beyond his audience's reach. Ton Duc Thang thus created a realm of difference from which to assert his authority. The contrast between his mysterious past and the genuine modesty and simplicity he exhibited in daily life attracted a loyal following much more effectively than boastful self-congratulations could have done. Ton's memories at Dinh Hoa of heady moments in 1919 where he felt one with the masses are consistent with his personality. They point even more strongly to Toulon as the actual location of Ton's participation in the navy unrest.

If Ton never mentioned the Red Flag on his own initiative, he clearly exhibited unease when asked to "recall" that detail. In 1992, Ha Huy Giap, the Thanh Nien member, southern ICP organizer and leader, and fellow prisoner, described a meeting with Ton Duc Thang around 1956. At that time, Ha Huy Giap was a party historian and asked Ton detailed questions about the Black Sea. Ton first answered teasingly: "So are you people at the Research Commission for Party History really asking all these details for your historical writing? I've long forgotten." But Ha Huy Giap pressed his friend for specifics: surely he must have fought ardently to earn the great distinction of being chosen to hoist the Red Flag. Ton reacted evasively: "Those guys were competing over who'd raise the red flag. Then they resolved that this little Annamite chap would climb up there. All the sailors agreed." Ha Huy Giap did not believe Ton and thought he was only being modest.[23]

The Red Flag version of the story was picking up speed. Although it was still transmitted only abroad, a few people in higher DRVN circles took note. Of course, Ton Duc Thang would never have considered exposing the party's propaganda lie; but neither did his aversion to self-applause allow him to just go along and brag about a nonexisting revolutionary achievement. With some resentment, he tried instead to avoid the story, fake forgetfulness, or, in a few instances, continue to tell his own version without the flag. When cornered, however, as in the example with Ha Huy Giap, Ton became evasive and tried to make the least possible out of the episode. But the Red Flag had such a powerful grip on people's imagination that nobody believed his attempts to play down what had "happened." The Red Flag was True, and Uncle Ton was just being his usual modest self.

IN OCTOBER/NOVEMBER 1956, nine months after receiving the Stalin Prize, Ton Duc Thang was back in the USSR leading a delegation of the National Assembly. The visit culminated in the thirty-ninth anniversary celebrations of the October Revolution on Moscow's Red Square. Huynh Van Tieng, who had already accompanied Ton to France in 1946 and witnessed the curious meeting with André Marty, traveled along. He later recalled: "In the Soviet Union, the Soviet reporters wanted to interview Uncle [Ton] about his hoisting the flag in the Black Sea in 1919. But he declined. He thought it was improper to talk about his individual achievement while he was in the Soviet Union."[24]

Here we find the familiar reaction again: Ton avoided making any statement about the Red Flag lest it embarrass him later. And he excused himself by referring to his sense of propriety as a guest of the Soviet Union, thanks to whose October Revolution the Vietnamese Revolution had been made possible. But the Red Flag story could no longer be stifled, and Ton could not help but play along. His hosts brought him to Odessa to "revisit" the scene of some of the glorious moments of the mutinies. And in Leningrad Ton met a veteran of the Russian civil war, who had participated in the battles on the shores of the Black Sea.

One year later, on the fortieth anniversary of the October Revolution, Ton Duc Thang's official "recollections" of the Black Sea Mutiny were published in Viet Nam and the Soviet Union.[25] Ton's article was ostensibly written in response to a request from the Soviet magazine *Sovietskii Moriak* (Soviet sailor). But I suggest that the real impetus for the publication was mounting pressure, perhaps by the CPSU or from unsuspecting people within the DLD, to finally recall the glorious episode with the Red Flag in the Black Sea in more detail. After all, the story not only connected the Bolshevik and Vietnamese Revolutions at a very early point, but also potentially represented one of the finest examples of revolutionary proletarian internationalism, a concept so central to the communist movement.

A story of such iconographic value, which "bestowed honor on the Vietnamese working class and on our people,"[26] could no longer be avoided. Ton Duc Thang was forced to explain a story that by now was no longer his. It is not clear whether Ton himself authored the lengthy article in 1957, or what kind of research was undertaken in its preparation, or to what degree Ton involved himself in all that work. In any case, the resulting "recollections" proved to be of astonishing timidity.

To summarize the article in broad strokes: Ton Duc Thang recalled how he was forced to leave Sai Gon incognito after the shipyard/vocational school strike, and how "a life on the sea" began then, eventually leading him to the French navy. (This is the fictional narrative device, discussed earlier, to erase Ton's navy recruitment in 1916.) Slowly, by reading newspapers and through the explanations of friends and coworkers, Ton learned to appreciate the historic novelty of the October Revolution and the promise it held for the oppressed of the world. When his warship was ordered into the Black Sea, the French sailors and he would not allow Soviet Russia to be attacked. Therefore the mutiny was staged, Ton Duc Thang was assigned to hoist the Red Flag, and the ship's commanders had to agree to leave the Black Sea. Everything was over within hours, and Ton regretted that he had no opportunity to join the Soviet Revolution and learn from it in preparation for a revolution in Viet Nam. The article related the mutiny to the Russian October Revolution and to proletarian internationalism, which could only be achieved in connection with the USSR. (Disparaging remarks about the Second Internationale appeared only in the Vietnamese version, not in the Russian article.) Ton Duc Thang then briefly recounted his revolutionary career after 1919, including his imprisonment, during which his belief in the Soviet Union figured prominently. He thanked the October Revolution and the USSR for creating the conditions under which Vietnamese independence was won. His article ended in a verbose, servile praise of socialism, the communist world, the Soviet Union, and its people, whom Ton had the good fortune to meet and to whom he could convey the deepest appreciations of the Vietnamese people.

Regarding the "recollections" of the mutiny and the Red Flag in particular, Ton Duc Thang inserted a disclaimer into the article: "Since then [1919], this Red Flag and the image of the mutiny of the sailors on the warship *Paris* have been deeply engraved in my soul. Thirty-eight years have passed, and my weak memory can no longer recall all of the names, other times, or the circumstances of that mutiny."[27]

Having thus allowed for the possibility of erroneous "memories," Ton proceeded to describe a mutiny with surprising details regarding its time and location. He not only claimed to have been on the French warship *Paris,* but also had the event occur *after* the initial wave of navy mutinies: It was "in the summer of 1919." The officers would not tell the crew the purpose of their voyage into the Black Sea.

> But we knew anyhow. They just could not conceal from us the news of the upheavals on the shores of France. They could not conceal the revolts of the French army and navy at Sevastopol and Odessa. They could not even conceal the widespread militant movement against the interventionist war.

The crew thus had prior knowledge of the large-scale unrest in the Black Sea and in France, which had occurred between April and June 1919. Later in the article, the timing of the incident on the *Paris* at some point after the core mutinies is reconfirmed. When the Red Flag flew above the vessel, and the crew threatened to turn the ship over to the revolutionaries unless it immediately departed for France, the commanders had to give in: "They knew that they were unable to resist the 'orders' of [the mutinous crew], just like so many other ships *had not been able* to resist."[28] Ton Duc Thang thus portrayed an isolated incident in the aftermath of the main Black Sea Mutiny of April 1919.

Where did Ton have the mutiny take place? A comparison of his published account with the map of the Black Sea and the waterways connecting it with the Aegean Sea shows that the mutiny on the *Paris* was placed in the very south of the Black Sea near Constantinople and the Bosporus Strait.

> The sky had grown dark, and the ship had almost passed the Dardanelles Strait. The atmosphere on board was seething. A number of men rallied the sailors for a meeting to oppose the commanders. They told me: "Before the meeting, go out and hoist the red flag! That way the warships of the Red Army know that we are friends, not enemies." I liked it a lot that I was able to personally do the job. It was now almost morning, and the warship entered the Black Sea.[29]

A warship like the *Paris* could conceivably pass through the Dardanelles, the Sea of Marmara, and the Bosporus in the course of one night.

Immediately thereafter, Ton Duc Thang raised the Red Flag, the crew's meeting began, the commanders came running out on deck, only to be confronted with the sailors' serious threats and demands. The commanders were forced to comply. "And so, *after a few hours adrift in the Black Sea,*" Ton continued in his article, "the warship *Paris* had to turn its bow around and steam out to the Mediterranean Sea."[30] But even under full steam, not adrift, a few hours would have taken the ship from the Bosporus nowhere near the Crimea and the northern, Soviet shores of the Black Sea. Finally, Ton Duc Thang himself stressed the

Western Black Sea and eastern Aegean Sea

unbridgeable geographic distance between his experiences and the Bolshevik Revolution. Hoisting the Red Flag on the *Paris,* he thought:

> Dear Russian friends! *Our ship is still far from you, and you have not yet seen this red flag.* But we salute you with this banner in the Black Sea. This red flag carries my hope that the warship would sail into your harbor. And then I'd go on shore, have the good fortune to take part in the revolution, and learn from it in order for me to return to my own country and make a revolution.[31]

In sum, Ton Duc Thang's published "recollections" in 1957 described a serious but isolated revolt in the aftermath of the Black Sea Mutiny, that is in June 1919 or later. The incident occurred on the *Paris* in the southern Black Sea, just beyond the Bosporus. After only a few hours, the warship left the Black Sea.

Ton's article was a far cry from his previous versions of the story, in which he participated in protests at Sevastopol during the high tide of the mutinies, fraternized with the people, and was in contact with André Marty. In 1957, his "recollections" lacked these bold assertions and instead exhibited an astonishing defensiveness. Ton only took part in an incident long after the main event and had no contact at all with the revolutionary masses. Not surprisingly, André Marty, who had been expelled from the FCP in a Stalinist power struggle in 1952 and had died in 1956, was no longer mentioned. But the account of 1957 had one important, new ingredient—Ton Duc Thang hoisted a Red Flag.

Curiously, the article revealed its author's familiarity with the historical *Paris* of 1919. The armed cruiser sailed from France to Constantinople in the Bosporus Strait around mid-May.[32] At Constantinople, the main base of a French navy division, the *Paris* became the flagship of the division commander. By then the French withdrawal from the Black Sea was well under way, and the *Paris* was to be relieved by the *Provence* around 13 June and return to France. But at Toulon, news of the impending departure for Constantinople triggered the *Provence*'s armed mutiny on 10 June. On 11 June, the *Voltaire* (at Bizerte) was instead assigned to relieve the *Paris;* but that ship, too, exploded in revolt. At Constantinople on 16 June, with no relief in sight, the *Paris* reported "lively impatience" on board. But no further incidents apparently took place; certainly, neither were a Red Flag nor a voyage further into the Black Sea reported.

The time of summer 1919 and the location in the Black Sea just beyond Constantinople of the *Paris's* revolt in Ton Duc Thang's article thus fit, if only roughly, with those of the historical *Paris*. In addition, it is also noteworthy that the crew of the *Paris* was in contact with André Marty. The mutinous officer was held in a Constantinople jail adjacent to the French embassy from the end of April. On 11 June, Marty's first court-martial took place on the *Paris*. Through secret contacts in prison, Marty managed to alert the crew of his trial. Sailors thus packed the courtroom when Marty was brought before the judges. In a two-hour-long flaming indictment of the French counterrevolutionary intervention, Marty succeeded in inciting the crew of the *Paris*. What Marty later called "excellent repercussions" might well have been the "lively impatience" reported a few days later.[33]

If the events on the *Paris* in June 1919 and the details of Ton Duc Thang's article of 1957 are in general, rough congruence, could Ton not have been on the *Paris?* Did not his earlier claim to have met André Marty mean that Ton witnessed Marty's court-martial? Did not Ton's story of his part in the Black Sea Mutiny denote his involvement in the unrest of the *Paris's* crew? After all, as previously discussed, were not Vietnamese seamen stationed at the Constantinople navy base during that time? These possibilities, however, only lead to another dead end: the register of the *Paris* proves that Ton was not among its crew.[34]

A SYNTHESIS: THE BLACK SEA STORY, 1919–57

We can now ascertain that Ton Duc Thang was not involved in the Black Sea Mutiny of 1919. Instead, the evidence points to the following scenario:

Ton Duc Thang participated in, or at least closely witnessed, the strikes, protests, and mutinies of Toulon in June 1919. During the previous years of working at the arsenal, he had undergone a process of politicization and radicalization. His experiences of organized mass action in the workshops of the port and in the streets of the city now became a defining moment in his life. In particular, his close association with the protesting common people, workers, and sailors of Toulon deeply impressed and profoundly affected him. Indeed, it was this memory of *being part of* a revolutionary movement that led him on the path to organizing the nascent working class once he returned to Sai Gon. Stories of the recent mutinies in the Black Sea abounded in Toulon and acted as further stimuli for public antiwar protests. Ton Duc Thang might have heard about the dramatic April days at Sevastopol, when the sailors of up to ten French warships rose up in revolt and briefly fraternized with the people of that port city. Or he might have heard of the mutinous officer André Marty, and about the unrest on the *Paris* at Constantinople after Marty's first court-martial on board that warship.

In Sai Gon, Ton used his experiences overseas as personal credentials to attract an entourage of impressionable young workers, with whom he hoped to build the nucleus of a labor union network. It was here that a little lie was born: for greater effect, Ton Duc Thang transposed his involvement in organized protest from Toulon to Sevastopol, where, as he knew, similar incidents had taken place, involving both ships and streets, sailors and local population, mutinies and mass protest. Unlike in Toulon, however, his activism in Sevastopol could claim an immediate connection to the great Russian October Revolution and so acquired an internationalist character. With this story of much greater symbolic significance, Ton established his authority as a promising leader of radical anticolonialism and social revolution. A militant mechanic in France thus became a navy mutineer in the Bolshevik Revolution. Ton Duc Thang's story of the Black Sea Mutiny followed him through his early political career, that is his membership in Thanh Nien, his long incarceration on Con Lon, and his admission into the party. It functioned as an impressive letter of introduction and yet was told in a modest way.

At the meeting in Vo Nhai in 1947, the party appropriated Ton's story when it came to the attention of the ICP leadership at the most opportune moment. The Vietnamese Revolution was at its lowest point, embattled and totally isolated, but the recent creation of Cominform signaled a policy shift in the communist world that bode well for the DRVN. The Black Sea tale became an imagined ancestry of Vietnamese communism. Transmitted only abroad, it was ideally suited to underscore the revolutionary nature of the party-led independent country and to appeal for reciprocal internationalist help, which the DRVN, this declared adherent to the leftist camp in the new bipolar Cold War order, so desperately needed.

Except for the possible addition of the alleged contacts with André Marty, the version propagated by the party from late 1947 to about 1950 essentially conformed with Ton's account. Ton Duc Thang still participated in the revolt at Sevastopol inconspicuously as one among thousands of equally determined, mutinous sailors, and the degree of his involvement and motivations were more implied than explained. Ton still recognized himself in a tale that emphasized his internationalist association with the "Soviet" people over any individual heroic act. He was probably even comfortable with the utility it had for the party.

All this changed around 1951. With newfound military strength after the end of its geographic and diplomatic isolation, the DRVN became more decidedly "red." As the most telling sign of this development, the ICP reconstituted itself openly as the Vietnamese Labor Party. The story of the Black Sea Mutiny now had to symbolize the *proletarian* internationalist nature of Vietnamese communism. Thus, the episode was greatly embellished by the addition of the Red Flag, hoisted by Ton Duc Thang. What had once been Ton's little lie became the party's Big Lie.

With this propagandistic move, the story was spinning out of control. Ton dissociated himself from the tale as much as possible. For once, he resented being portrayed as a revolutionary hero of great personal distinction, and the party's boastfully parading this image around went against his modesty and aversion to self-aggrandizement. But more was at stake. After all, Ton Duc Thang had not been in the Black Sea. Thus far, however, he had been safe, because his experiences of the organized mass actions in Toulon were enough to sustain his vague descriptions of the mutiny at Sevastopol, where Ton—narratively hidden among the other mutineers—had been so happily mingling with the Soviets.

The Red Flag individualized Ton Duc Thang in the story and exposed him from the safe anonymity of the mutinous crowds. After all, the three instances in 1919 in which red flags had flown over French warships—all at Sevastopol—were widely celebrated and known in detail. In trying to clarify Ton's class consciousness, the Red Flag instead *over*-clarified his tale with respect to time, location, motives, circumstances, individuals involved, et cetera—all to a degree Ton Duc Thang, who was only able to take recourse to his memories of Toulon, had no way of re-creating. Anything he would say about the Black Sea from now on carried the very real danger of embarrassing refutation, particularly in the international arena of communist party-to-party relations. Consequently, after the propagation of the Red Flag, Ton reacted evasively when asked about the story, feigned poor memory, or simply refused to talk about the past, an act of self-defense commonly misinterpreted as modesty. Such a strategy worked for several years. But in 1957, he could no longer avoid explaining "his" heroic act in the Black Sea.

Ton Duc Thang's dilemma was obvious. On the one hand, he would expose neither his little lie nor the party's Big Lie. Therefore, the event in his "recollections" had to have two essentials: (1) it had to take place in the Black Sea, and (2) the Red Flag had to be included. On the other hand, Sevastopol was the only logical place for an episode with these two basic ingredients and, in fact, the location of Ton's earlier, safer account. But now Sevastopol was blocked off by the Red Flag, too dangerously well-known and out of reach of his memory.

I can imagine the nightmare:

Ton Duc Thang mingles with the revolutionary crowds in the streets of Sevastopol, among French sailors giddy with the knowledge of the enormity of their mutinous act, and among Russian workers cheering and applauding, yet enobled by their historic revolutionary tasks. Sailors' caps and workers' hats are tossed in the air, strangers embrace, joyous people dance in circles, another group, fists raised, proudly sings the Internationale. *Ton Duc Thang, the Vietnamese, feels accepted, he, the colonized* indigène, *is invited to join in, patted on the shoulder, pulled here and there. He hears half sentences, moves on, a woman's laughter, move on!, a trumpet blaring momentarily from a window, moving on, moving, so elated, so light, so one with the Revolution, so happily one with the masses, so inconspicuously one within the crowd . . .*

Someone forces a Red Flag in his hand. Everybody stops dead in their tracks. Silence. The crowd around Ton turns toward him. Reserved, expectant faces. People move back, form a passageway toward which he is pushed. He runs a gauntlet in slow motion. Murmuring. Nervous whispers. He reaches the upper deck of the French warship. The crowd recedes and encircles him at a distance. He is exposed in the center of the ring. Surrounded by a wall of stares, Ton Duc Thang stands alone in front of the towering flagpole. "Hoist the flag!" His leaden hands. "HOIST THE RED FLAG!!"

Ton Duc Thang extracted himself from the dilemma in a move as desperate as it was brilliant. Some diligent research must have been conducted to find the *Paris,* which roughly fit Ton's purposes. With the *Paris,* he could shift his incident from April, Sevastopol time, to June, Toulon/Constantinople time, thus turning it into a faraway, isolated, and belated mutiny that few people knew about and fewer probably even cared to check out. He downplayed the affair as much as possible, assigning himself a rather passive role. Sailors told him to raise the Red Flag. Ton did so at daybreak. That was it. There were no heroic struggles with guards or officers, no cheers, no singing of the *Internationale*.

Once the Red Flag had been dealt with, Ton dispensed with his other obligation, namely to place the mutiny in the Black Sea, as fast as possible: he only dipped his toes into Black Sea waters, so to say, just beyond the Bosporus and as far away from the Bolshevik Revolution as possible. Ton Duc Thang's great discomfort speaks from his "recollections." He felt awkward in the Black Sea now, realizing that it was strange, unremembered territory. The whole incident was over very quickly. Within hours, the *Paris* steamed away. Ton's narrative relief is apparent when the warship sails out of embarrassing waters and turns toward Toulon, the familiar place he really recalled.

In this manner, Ton Duc Thang succeeded in saving his story from exposure as a lie. He salvaged all that was possible from the wreckage caused by the Red Flag. But this could only be achieved at the cost of jettisoning the one element of the story that was dearest to him: his close association with the revolutionary Soviet masses. We have to reread his melancholic monologue, when he raises the Red Flag on the *Paris,* in precisely this context.

> *Cac ban Nga oi!* (Dear Russian friends!) Our ship is still far from you, and you have not yet seen this red flag. But we salute you with this banner in the Black Sea. This red flag carries my hope that the warship would sail into your harbor. And then I'd go on shore and have the good fortune to take part in the revolution . . .

But the Red Flag itself had cut him off from the October Revolution. His memory could no longer carry him inconspicuously and safely from Toulon to Sevastopol. Now, revolutionary masses there no longer welcomed him into their midst. What awaited him was a lone, alien, unrelentingly empty flagpole. Whipped up by a storm of questions, calm waters had turned into high, forbidding waves in the Black Sea. On the *Paris,* Ton Duc Thang barely made it into the sea's southern-most stretches. Even there he could only linger for a short moment. From afar, over the howling winds that threatened to blow his cover, he called out to his cherished Russian friends. *CAC BAN NGA OI!* For more than thirty-five years he had been with them in his impressive account, in his own mind. And taking part in that way in the October Revolution had indeed been his "good fortune." His career, his public persona, and even his self-image were intimately tied to this ancestral relationship. So many, many people had joined him over the years on his exciting imaginary voyages back to 1919, back to Sevastopol, back to the origins of communism. How he wished that he could "sail into [his friends'] harbor," "go on shore," and be with the October Revolution one more time.

But the story of the Black Sea had moved away from the late colonial moment, past the revolutionary moment, and, at accelerating speed, on to the post-recognition moment. There, his story was sent spinning out of control. Ton Duc Thang returned to it one last time to prevent it from fatality. Briefly, tale and author were reunited. But Ton could only save the story by disavowing his imaginary friends in Sevastopol. Ton Duc Thang's article in 1957 was his good-bye to them. Never would he return to Sevastopol, never remember again. In closure, he bid a final farewell to the sweet illusions of the Black Sea Mutiny and, thus, to his own imagined revolutionary ancestry. When the *Paris,* Red Flag fluttering above, steamed back through the Bosporus and toward France, Ton Duc Thang, sad and yet relieved, turned his back on the Black Sea and faced his memories. Toulon recalled him, and he recalled Toulon.

IMAGINATIONS AFTER 1957

Vietnamese communism, on the other hand, was not ready to let go of its imagined ancestry in the Russian October Revolution. The one sensible version that, given Ton's dilemma, had been able to save the story made no sense at all to those who believed in the "Sevastopol connection" of the Soviet and Vietnamese Revolutions. The story of the Red Flag in the Black Sea had produced a powerful and self-affirming image that took on a life of its own as one of the defining origin myths of the Communist Party. Once the revised story no longer fully supported the image, then the story had to be wrong, while the image remained the Truth.[35] To these people, Ton Duc Thang's article was puzzling and inexplicable. Did Ton not realize that his article was missing the essential point of the personal relationship between a Vietnamese internationalist and the October Revolution? But the inserted disclaimer showed the way out: just as Ha Huy Giap had taken Ton's evasiveness for modesty, the author's failing memory was now blamed for the story's not reconfirming the Truth. And so Ton's "recollections" were deemed unreliable after so many years, or they were altogether ignored.

It needs to be stressed that Ton Duc Thang's 1957 article was the last time Ton himself would go on record about the mutiny. Yet, it was also the first instance in which the story of the Black Sea was widely propagated within Viet Nam. From then on, the tale became a regular component of the popular imagination of the Vietnamese Revolution. Yet, curiously, not a single one of the many subsequent publications extolling Ton's heroic act in the Black Sea engaged his "recollections" in any serious manner. If the article was considered at all, certain aspects of Ton's account were manipulated until they fit the desired result, namely that Ton Duc Thang raised the Red Flag during the high tide of the mutiny on Soviet shores. For example, Ton's official party biography of 1982, the subject of chapter 6, had him hoist the flag on the *France* at Sevastopol; portions of his "recollections" were in fact quoted, but the parts that did not fit were simply left out.

In 1988, at the Symposium on President Ton Duc Thang in Long Xuyen, a participating historical witness was even more brazen in his manipulations. Nguyen Van Hoan had been a fellow prisoner of Ton's on Con Lon during the 1930s. He probably remembered vaguely how, more than fifty years before, Ton told him and other inmates the story of the Black Sea, and how they had all been very impressed by Ton's revolutionary credentials. In 1988, however, in his long and very detailed "memoirs," he presented as genuine recollections of Ton's storytelling what in actuality were portions from André Marty's description of the mutiny on the *France*—at points plagiarized word for word! Nguyen Van Hoan "recalled" how Ton talked about having been a mechanic on the *France* while *at Toulon,* from where the ship sailed in March 1919. Ignoring the fact, stated by Marty on the very page from which he plagiarized, that the *France* had last been in a French port on 9 October 1916, when Ton had not even arrived from Sai Gon, he simply inserted a flag-raising Ton Duc Thang into Marty's account.[36] And—voilà!—if Nguyen Van Hoan "remembered" how, in the 1930s, Ton Duc Thang "in his own words" had talked about raising a Red Flag on the *France,* then the 1957 article had to be wrong. The Truth won yet another victory over the story.

As a final example, let us look at the reasoning of Nguyen Thanh, a veteran party historian at the Ha Noi Museum of the Revolution. In his report to the symposium in 1988, Nguyen Thanh made specific mention of Ton Duc Thang's poor memory and also arrived at the conclusion that Ton must have hoisted a Red Flag on the *France* on 20 April 1919. He briefly mentioned the 1957 article, but labeled it a "news report of the Vietnamese News Agency." Having thus avoided dealing with Ton's authorship of the disconcerting account, he was free to dismiss it: "Among France's flotilla in the Black Sea was no ship called *Paris*. Then, of course, there was no revolt on the *Paris,* and Uncle Ton did not participate [in a mutiny] on any ship called *Paris."* Looking only toward Sevastopol—that is, the Truth—Nguyen Thanh did not have to face the *Paris.*[37]

After 1957, so powerful a symbol was the Red Flag in the Black Sea, so cherished as an ancestry of Vietnamese communism, that authors of many articles and books and speakers at many commemorative events let their imaginations run free. They dealt in great detail with Ton's participation in the revolt, yet disregarded basic facts of the mutiny and, at points, blatantly contradicted one another. Ton Duc Thang served on the *France,* the *Paris,* or the *Waldeck-Rousseau;* in some accounts, beginning in 1916, or in 1918, and in others in 1919; the ships are sometimes shelling Kherson, or Sevastopol, or Odessa. And always it is Ton Duc Thang who hoists the Red Flag, invoking gripping images of Soviet films, of Sergei Eisenstein's *Potemkin:*

Charging up toward the flagpole, beneath the smoking chimney, on top of this rolling colossus of iron and steel, revolutionary convulsions below him on deck—determination written on his face, aware of the forces of history that now lead his strong worker's hands, the red flag surging higher and higher—the climax: a black-and-white zoom in on the cloth in the storm, enveloped by smoke, before a pale new sun . . .

At the symposium in 1988, Nguyen Thanh noted with misgivings that multiple versions of the story were making the rounds. But his acknowledged agenda, namely to use this unique gathering to settle the subject of the Black Sea Mutiny finally and conclusively,[38] missed the point. Historical accuracy was not the issue. The hodgepodge of versions, the jumble of voices and scenes served an end in and of itself. It actually did not matter at all to people that they were telling different versions of the story. The details, false or not, only served to make the tale sound plausible, but they were not meant to focus a blurred picture. What counted was the sheer pleasure felt in the act of recalling or rehearing the story of the Red Flag in the Black Sea. The account of Ton Duc Thang helping Soviet Russia and beating imperialism in popular lore told of the origin of Vietnamese communism. Retelling it over and over again, and in so many versions and with so many details, were acts of proud and joyful self-affirmation.

Besides in speeches, articles, and books,[39] the Red Flag in the Black Sea has appeared in various other forms. The contrast between Ton Duc Thang's heroic act in the Black Sea as one of the most potent images of revolutionary Viet Nam and the lack of historical evidence for such an event created a strong demand to make the moment visually and experientially accessible. For example, in honor of its most prominent alumnus, Cao Thang vocational school in Ho Chi Minh City, the former École des mécaniciens asiatiques de Saïgon, has declared 20 April a school holiday. On that day in 1919, the Red Flag was hoisted on the *France* at Sevastopol, supposedly by Ton Duc Thang. Photos in the school museum of Cao Thang show that on each 20 April, students perform a stage play of the Black Sea event in the school's courtyard. In the reenactment of this heroic moment, students thus symbolically link up with an imagined ancestry of their own school, to be found in Ton's proletarian internationalism.

Paintings of the Red Flag flying over a French warship hang in prominent places at several commemorative sites connected to Ton: the Ton Duc Thang Museum, the Hall of Tradition of Ba Son shipyard, and the school museum of Cao Thang vocational school, all in Ho Chi Minh City, the museum of An Giang province in Long Xuyen, and the nearby exhibit hall at Ton's birthplace in My Hoa Hung. Additionally, the museum in Long Xuyen boasts a sculpture depicting a young man resolutely raising a Red Flag, which in turn embraces the man.

Finally, a state-sponsored movie about Ton Duc Thang's adult life, directed by Huy Thanh and strangely entitled *To Quoc: Tieng Ga Trua* (Fatherland: The cockcrow at noon), was produced in 1996 for TV; scenes of Ton's sojourn in France were filmed in Paris and at a French port, Fécamp. I was unable to view the film in time for this book, but one can expect the Red Flag in the Black Sea to play an important role.[40]

In the Soviet Union, too, the Red Flag and Ton Duc Thang's show of pro-Soviet proletarian internationalism in the Black Sea have had an impact on the popular imagination. Most important, in November 1967, the fiftieth anniversary of the October Revolution, the Supreme Soviet in Moscow awarded Ton Duc Thang the Lenin Order, the highest order of the USSR. The reason for awarding the order, bestowed on Ton at a ceremony in Ha Noi, was Ton's "contribution to the struggle to defend the Soviet government during the civil war."[41] Over the years, several Soviet articles have praised Ton's role in the Black Sea Mutiny, and shortly after Ton's death in 1980, a street in Odessa was named after him.[42]

ONCE THE STORY WAS PROPAGATED in Viet Nam after 1957, Ton Duc Thang came to embody one of the most powerful origin myths of the Vietnamese Revolution. His heroic deed of proletarian internationalism in 1919 symbolized the one ancestry of Vietnamese communism with which all revolutionaries could easily identify. Therefore, northern authors and the party leadership in Ha Noi have usually highlighted the Black Sea episode in biographies of Ton Duc Thang. But just as Ton himself had not been able to stay in control of his amazing tale, so was the central party unable to keep control of it later. As subsequent chapters will demonstrate, especially southern revolutionaries could imagine additional and at times controversial ancestries of Vietnamese communism through Ton Duc Thang.

As for Ton himself, he no longer "remembered" the Black Sea after 1957. For him, this story of the ancestry of Vietnamese proletarian internationalism *abroad* had come to a close. At about the same time, however, around 1957, he began telling a new story that proved to be not very different from the one of the Black Sea. It was another tale of origins and credentials, an account of the ancestry of Vietnamese proletarian internationalism *in Viet Nam.* It was the story of his decisive involvement in the shipyard workers' strike of 1925 at Ba Son, the arsenal of Sai Gon.

PART II

Contestations

CHAPTER 4

Striking Images: Ba Son in the Post-Partition Moment

JUST NORTHEAST OF THE CENTER of Viet Nam's southern metropole Ho Chi Minh City,[1] a military shipyard lies on the bank of the Sai Gon River, a little downstream from the mouth of the Thi Nghe canal but upstream from the city's commercial port. During the period of colonial occupation, roughly from 1864 to 1954, the French referred to the terrain simply by its function, an arsenal, while the Vietnamese called (and still call) it Ba Son.[2] Since the term "Ba Son" carries no meaning in Vietnamese, the author Le Minh offers several hypotheses about its origin: "Maybe this segment of the river had plenty of fish, and the French often went there to catch them. [Vietnamese] pronounced *poisson* [French for 'fish'] Ba Son. Or there was a basin[3] at the site. *Bassin* . . . was pronounced by us Ba Son."[4]

As early as the first half of the nineteenth century, the Nguyen court had warships built at the mouth of the Thi Nghe canal, that is in the immediate vicinity of what later became Ba Son.[5] After Sai Gon-Gia Dinh had been occupied and secured by the French in the early 1860s, one of the first strategic objectives was to establish an arsenal capable of repairing ships for France's growing military and commercial endeavors in the region. Based on plans formalized on 28 April 1863, the "Arsenal de Saïgon" was built in 1864 in the favorable location next to the basin.[6]

The ship repair yard was the first mechanized factory of Sai Gon and the first French industrial enterprise in its colonial possession. Its workforce of ethnic Vietnamese and Chinese constituted the very "first group of industrial workers" in the country.[7] Expanding quickly with France's growing military power in Asia and with the developing regional and intercontinental trade, Ba Son soon added its own river craft construction capabilities. With technological advances, the demand for "indigenous" skilled labor was rising, and plans for a vocational school for mechanics were first made around 1880.[8] In 1897, the École des

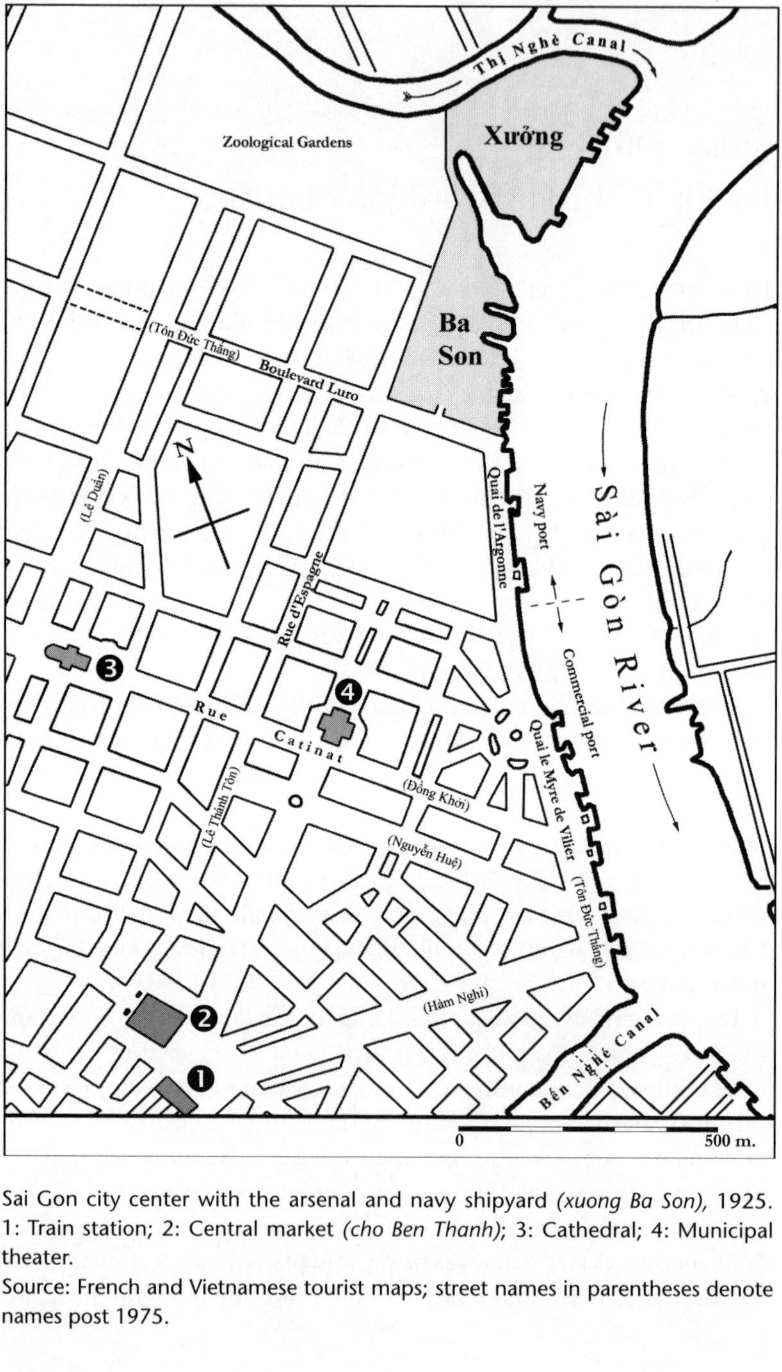

Sai Gon city center with the arsenal and navy shipyard *(xuong Ba Son),* 1925. 1: Train station; 2: Central market *(cho Ben Thanh)*; 3: Cathedral; 4: Municipal theater.

Source: French and Vietnamese tourist maps; street names in parentheses denote names post 1975.

mécaniciens asiatiques de Saïgon was founded and became closely affiliated with the arsenal.[9]

During World War I, tens of thousands of Vietnamese went to France to work and fight for their colonial rulers. Many of these men worked in weaponry and other industries or, like Ton Duc Thang, in arsenals of the French navy,[10] where they acquired professional skills. After the war, colonial authorities prepared to employ these specialized workers in Indochina's shipping industry and in the arsenals, where skilled labor was again in high demand.[11] However, these Vietnamese workers received more than just vocational training in France: similar to Ton, they also gained experiences among the well-organized and politically active French working class, where they observed unionization, bargaining, and various ways of using labor as a weapon.

Back home, the returnees infused their new self-assurance and awareness into the tiny, concentrated working-class milieu. Furthermore, radical anticapitalist and anti-imperialist ideas in print or by word of mouth soon began trickling into Indochina, mainly via France. Somewhat more moderate, the (yet-unfulfilled) vision of a republican, independent China under nationalist leadership also had strong appeal in Indochina, in particular among ethnic Chinese traders and workers, but also for the anticolonialist cause in general. Finally, France's postwar colonial policy, with its unprecedented influx of private capital and accelerated development of industry aimed at the best possible utilization of the colony, transformed both the country's economy and society. Colonial exploitation and injustices worsened and were felt by larger segments of society. A formerly small urban and rural proletariat grew to numbers significant enough to assume political roles. Vietnamese workers of the early 1920s, therefore, were quite different from those of prewar times. Cochinchina's major military-industrial plant, Ba Son, likely had its share of these men: sensitive to injustices on their jobs, capable of situating themselves within a broader sociopolitical context, and willing to fight for their interests in due time.

In the summer of 1925, a strike erupted at the arsenal. It was the first major labor conflict at the shipyard, but certainly not its last: for example, in May 1926, a daylong sympathy strike was staged for a recently incarcerated, prominent anticolonialist intellectual, Nguyen An Ninh.[12] And in the mid-1930s, during waves of political and labor unrest shaking Indochina, the workers of the arsenal in Sai Gon were again among those who struck. Yet, no event became more closely associated with Ba Son in Vietnamese public perception than the strike of 1925. Communist historiography usually describes as the strike's main feature an underlying *political, internationalist* motivation, namely the immobilization of a French warship bound for China to help suppress anti-imperialist protests. It is also said to have been the first *organized* strike in Indochina: led by a secret labor union (the subject of the following chapter) headed by Ton Duc Thang, it had enough funds and cohesion to sustain an alleged covert "slowdown strike" after the open walkout had ended. Some accounts even give the strike the function of a turning point marking the end of a period of few, feeble, and spontaneous strikes and the beginning of a time when the Vietnamese working class assumed a leading political role with powerful, organized labor actions.

Ton Duc Thang was central to how the events of 1925 at the arsenal came to be represented in postcolonial Vietnamese historical accounts. Around 1957, at just about the same time he publicly "remembered"—for what would prove to be the final instance—the ill-fated story of the Red Flag in the Black Sea and was forced to dissociate himself from his imagined participation in mass action during the October Revolution, Ton told the communist revolutionary-turned-historian Tran Van Giau[13] of his crucial, yet clandestine role in organizing the strike at the Sai Gon arsenal in 1925. Tran Van Giau complemented his own ongoing documentary research into the strike with the information provided by Ton and another historical witness and, between 1957 and 1961, published an increasingly detailed, dramatic, and celebratory version of the walkout at Ba Son, a version still authoritative in Vietnamese historiography today.[14] Before turning to the late 1950s' account by Ton Duc Thang and Tran Van Giau, however, let us first consider available contemporary evidence regarding the strike.

THE INTERNATIONAL ENVIRONMENT IN 1925

In the spring and summer months of 1925, just before the strike at the arsenal broke out, the French in Indochina received alarming news reports about events abroad that seemed to have a direct impact on worldwide French power and authority. Three developments in particular shaped the larger context within which the *colon* public as well as various anticolonial Vietnamese groups perceived and interpreted the strike at Ba Son: the war between French troops and Riffian rebels in Morocco, anti-imperialist protests, strikes, and boycotts in China, and the uprising against French mandatory authority in Syria.

In 1921, an anti-Spanish rebellion broke out in Morocco, which had been divided into Spanish and French "protectorates" a few years before.[15] By 1924, after major battlefield victories over Spanish troops, the rebel leader, Mohamed ben Abd el Krim, became the personification of anticolonial and independence aspirations far beyond the Islamic world. Given the grave Spanish setbacks in the Rif region, France's government saw its own Moroccan interests threatened and, although Abd el Krim repeatedly sought a modus vivendi, provoked war with the rebels. Unexpectedly, however, Abd el Krim's forces at first gained the upper hand and, in July 1925, inflicted severe losses on French colonial troops.[16] A stunned public could not foresee that the uprising was soon doomed to fail.[17] In the weeks right before the strike broke out at Ba Son, daily alarming dispatches in French colonial papers reported on the "bandit" Abd el Krim and his "aggression," which Marshal Pétain, the French commander in Morocco, described as "the overwhelming rush of the barbarians" against the "work of civilization."[18]

About the same time, similar deeply unsettling news reached Sai Gon from Syria. After World War I and the demise of the Ottoman Empire, a government of Syrian independence had been formed, but in 1920 the newly formed League of Nations imposed a mandate status on Syria and gave France mandatory authority.[19] The French leadership lost no time disposing of the Syrian government, and serious challenges to its authority came only in 1925. When the French arrested several nationalist leaders in July 1925 during bogus negotiations, an armed insurrection broke out. In their first engagement with Syrian nationalist forces on 1 August, French troops suffered a stunning and widely reported defeat.[20]

But in the summer of 1925, further threats to France's power and prestige arose much closer to Indochina. Just to the north in China, Canton had become the power base of the Nationalist government led by the Guomindang under Sun Zhongshan (Sun Yat-sen). Sun's republican government sought to revise the Chinese-Western unequal treaties, which had, among other provisions, established extraterritorial concessions for the imperialist powers in Chinese treaty ports. These demands found a mass basis in China's rapidly expanding urban working class.

Sun's death in March 1925 temporarily brought the GMD's left wing to power. Among rightist *colons* in Indochina, the impression that the GMD was ruled by increasingly radical, "Bolshevik" elements was furthered by the formation of the communist-led All-China General Labor Union in Canton in May 1925 and by the outbreak of huge anti-imperialist protests, strikes, and boycotts particularly in southern China—the so-called May Thirtieth Movement. On that day, 30 May, British concessional police in Shanghai had shot dead eleven students during mass demonstrations. The massacre triggered numerous, mainly anti-British and anti-Japanese, strikes and protests, which quickly spread to other urban centers. Led by an informal student-worker's alliance, it took on a powerful anti-imperialist thrust. Japan, Britain, Italy, and the United States reinforced their occupying troops in Shanghai, and twenty-six foreign warships lay in the harbor, among them the armored cruiser *Jules Ferry,* flagship of the French Forces navales d'Extrême-Orient.[21] Later in June, when British and French concessional guards in Canton fired from Shamian Island on a demonstration and killed fifty-two people, nationalist agitation and public anger reached new heights: the famous Hong Kong-Canton General Strike began. Its boycott of British goods would last for fifteen months.

The events in China in the spring and summer of 1925 made headline news around the globe. For the first time in many decades, imperialist interests were directly confronted in China. In addition to monitoring developments in Morocco and Syria, newspapers in Indochina carried daily dispatches from China on their front pages and joined other pro-colonialist Western media in a campaign of demonizing the "reds" or "Bolsheviks" in Canton. In contrast, just like European and Japanese labor organizations that began campaigns of financial support for the Chinese strikes,[22] ethnic Chinese in Indochina ("Huaqiao" in Chinese, "Hoa Kieu" in Vietnamese) as well as Vietnamese anti-colonialists closely followed the events, and Hoa Kieu probably also forwarded large sums to workers in China.[23]

Thus, merely days before the workers at the Sai Gon arsenal went on strike, a feeling prevailed that crises of huge dimensions, maybe even wars, were imminent throughout the colonized world. *L'Asie française,* for example, predicted in its July edition that one was "on the eve of a war of the races."

THE STRIKE AT BA SON IN THE LOCAL MEDIA

By coincidence, the strike at Ba Son happened not only at a time when uprisings in Morocco, China, and Syria created a sense of peril and uncertainty for the future of "French" Indochina, but also at a moment when domestic politics in Cochinchina suddenly heated up and public discourse became more restive, polemic, and divisive.

In Cochinchina, the *colon* establishment had formed an inner circle of particularly powerful, reactionary, and corrupt men: Governor Maurice Cognacq; Ernest Outrey, Cochinchina's deputy in the French Chambre des Députés; the president of Sai Gon's Chamber of Commerce, de la Pommeraye; and Henry de Lachevrotière, the vice president of Cochinchina's Colonial Council and editor of the leading colonial newspaper, *L'Impartial.*[24] Occupying positions of influence, making full use of the security apparatus, and with lackeys strategically placed throughout the administration, these men ruled over Cochinchina as if it were their private domain. Opposition at that time came mostly from reformist elements, like the so-called Constitutionalist Party, a small group of Vietnamese bourgeois who advocated equal treatment and better educational and business opportunities for Vietnamese within the realm of "French-Vietnamese collaboration." Colonial abuses were the main target for their criticism, not colonialism as such.

However, beginning in about 1924, the political landscape in Sai Gon became more and more restive. Opposition grew more vocal in the Colonial Council, where some Constitutionalists as well as more progressive Frenchmen, like the young lawyer Paul Monin, had managed to gain a few seats. Further, numerous French language newspapers were established and became the medium to voice reformist ideas for the small but active Vietnamese intelligentsia. Constantly harassed by the notorious French secret police, the Sûreté, kept under strict censorship, and watched with suspicion by the *colons,* the newspapers' life spans were not always long, but they posed the first challenge to the French colonial establishment since the end of the war. The most famous of these papers was Nguyen An Ninh's *La Cloche fêlée,* which was published from late 1923 to mid-1924.[25] In 1924, the young French author André Malraux came to Indochina and, appalled by the injustices and abuses of power in the colony, decided to publish a critical newspaper.[26] In cooperation with Paul Monin, he founded *L'Indochine* in June 1925. It soon became *the* liberal opposition paper and government watchdog in Cochinchina. Through *L'Indochine,* Malraux and Monin advocated an enlightened Franco-Vietnamese collaboration. In addition, the two relentlessly targeted the *colon* establishment, especially Henry de Lachevrotière and his *L'Impartial,* and ultimately Governor Cognacq, the person pulling the strings of corruption from behind his cover of colonial office. From mid-June until mid-August, *L'Indochine* and *L'Impartial* fought each other in bitter editorial battles.

Two of the scandals that Monin and Malraux exposed during *L'Indochine*'s short existence should be briefly mentioned: First, they proved in early July that the colonial government had illegally funded *L'Impartial* and other pro-government newspapers with huge amounts of official subscriptions in an effort to control the colonial press. Second, in mid-July, they brought to light an attempt of the government to conduct fraudulent auctions of large stretches of land south of Sai Gon.[27] The publicity that *L'Indochine* gave this scheme made the Cognacq government back down, but it remained an embarrassing matter.

Just when this attempted fraud by highest officials was publicized and became the object of gossip in Sai Gon, the interim governor general Monguillot came to visit the city on 30 July. To make things worse for the reactionaries, the French Painlevé government, a coalition of leftist parties, announced on the very same day that Alexandre Varenne would become the next governor general of Indochina. Varenne was to be the first socialist on such a high post in France's entire colonial empire. The news shocked the rightist *colon* society of Indochina, which in its hysteria about anything that smacked of change saw it as an assault against their privileged position and as an attempt to impose a tighter metropolitan control over the colony—the eternal fear of the colonialist species.[28] With their corrupt rule exposed and challenged, Monguillot in Sai Gon, and Varenne's governorship looming, the *colon* leaders desperately sought to distract attention away from themselves—just one week before the strike at Ba Son broke out. The government-controlled press thus started a campaign of distortions and lies against allegedly anti-French, Bolshevik elements represented by Malraux and

Monin. Only days before the labor action at the arsenal, Cognacq's cronies set up an "anti-Bolshevik committee" and loudly, if unsuccessfully, demanded the arrest of the "communist" Monin. In addition, during the same days, the Cochinchinese government quietly decided to muzzle *L'Indochine.*[29]

BESIDES *L'INDOCHINE* AND *L'IMPARTIAL,* colonial newspapers that covered the strike at Ba Son in some detail were *L'Écho annamite,* the organ of the Constitutionalist Party, *Progrès annamite,* published by the vice president of the Colonial Council, Le Quang Trinh, and *L'Avenir du Tonkin* from Ha Noi, another ultraconservative paper.[30] When looking at colonial newspapers, we must consider that although Cochinchina in the mid-1920s had a lively media scene, the papers worked under government restrictions, including a censor's approval prior to publication. But the press was also an elite organ with a narrow perspective.[31] It remained largely within its rather self-absorbed world of Sai Gon's intelligentsia and petty bourgeoisie. With these provisos, what did newspapers report about the events that led to the strike at Ba Son?

Workers at the arsenal were paid twice a month, on or around the fourth and the eighteenth. On paydays, labor ceased at 5 P.M. and not at 5:30 P.M. as on normal workdays. During the thirty minutes thus gained, workers got their *fiches de travail* and received their wages.[32] This rule was altered by a new director of the arsenal, one engineer Courthial, who ordered that work was not to end until 5:15 P.M. on paydays. Strong discontent among the workforce was the result. On Saturday, 18 July 1925, the first payday under the new regulation, around five hundred workers at the arsenal left their jobs in protest at exactly 5 P.M., disobeying the new orders.[33] Waiting in front of the payroll office, some workers were shouting, but general discipline was kept, and by 5:15 wages were received in an orderly way. The workers also protested against other "chicanery," as *L'Écho annamite* put it:

> Workforce reductions by brutal dismissal, without prior notification and valid motive, of old servants, before they had time to find another bread-winning job; refusal to pay the workers for hours during which electricity failures had compelled them to halt, failures not due to those poor workers who could do nothing about them, but due to the Compagnie des Eaux et Électricité de l'Indochine.[34]

In the patronizing tone typical for the Constitutionalists, the same article expressed hope that Courthial would show some "friendly consideration" for his "native subordinates," concluding that "it is with honey, not vinegar, that one catches flies." During the following fortnight, discontent continued to grow among Ba Son's workforce, and plans were allegedly made for a general strike.[35] Some negotiations between the management and workers' delegates took place, but came to no conclusion.

On 4 August 1925, at about 7:30 A.M., the French armored cruiser *Jules Michelet* arrived in Sai Gon. Soon entangled in the brewing labor conflict at the arsenal, it would not depart until 29 November 1925. It had left France on 15 June, sailed via Djibouti, India, and Singapore, and was to stay in Sai Gon for only a few days. What was the warship's mission in Asia? With the Forces navales d'Extrême-Orient at that time equipped with one armored cruiser, the *Michelet* was to proceed from Sai Gon to China for the *regular* relief of the *Jules Ferry,* its sister ship. Originally, the *Ferry* would have left China in July, but due to the widespread unrest, it was made to wait in Hong Kong until the *Michelet's* arrival. The *Jules Ferry* finally left China in early September and handed over command to the *Jules Michelet* in Sai Gon before returning to France.[36]

In the city's media, the visit of the *Jules Michelet* had not been announced in advance. But almost immediately *L'Impartial,* which was at the forefront of alarmist reporting on developments in China, wrote that urgent repairs could prolong the ship's sojourn if the situation in China were not to deteriorate.[37] Coincidentally, Tuesday, 4 August, was also the next payday at the arsenal after 18 July, when the workers had first protested. Wages again were not paid until 5:15 P.M., in line with Courthial's new orders. Unlike on 18 July, however, work was *not* stopped prior to that time. With imperious satisfaction, *L'Impartial,* ever suspiciously on the lookout for the least sign of anticolonial activities, reported no "incidents and complaints."[38] But things were not to remain calm for long.

On the following morning, Wednesday, 5 August, work was to begin as usual at 6:30 A.M. However, except for the *capelans majors, capelans,* colonial supervisors, and office workers, who appeared in full, none of the roughly 720 workers entered Ba Son. Instead, the men, described as being noticeably calm, gathered on the boulevard Luro in two large groups, one on its intersection with the rue d'Espagne and the other at the riverside where the quai de l'Argonne leads into the boulevard. The gatherings thus covered the two approaches to Ba Son's main gate, and whoever was bound for the arsenal ran into the workers. At about 7 A.M., everybody left the area without having voiced any protests or demands.[39] The strike was under way.

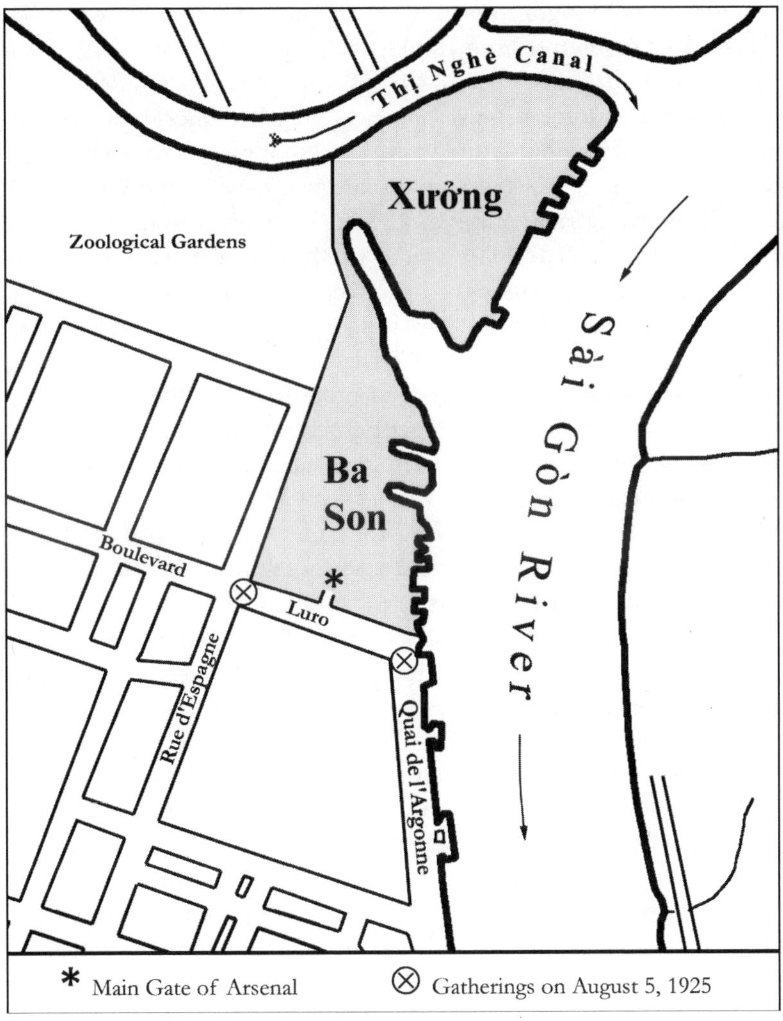

The Sai Gon arsenal *(xuong Ba Son)*, 1925

On the following mornings, 6 and 7 August, smaller, orderly gatherings took place in front of Ba Son just before 6:30 A.M., and again no worker entered the arsenal, and no demonstrations were held. Finally, on Saturday, 8 August, the fourth day of the strike, no one showed up at all.[40] On all those days, only foremen and office clerks worked as usual. No contacts were established between the striking workers and Ba Son's management during these first days of the walkout. No demands were brought forward from the side of the workmen.

The round of interpretations and speculations about the strike's goals was opened on the afternoon of the first strike day by a peculiar article in Malraux and Monin's *L'Indochine.* Headlined "An Important Strike in Saigon," an anonymous letter was printed that must have come from among the striking workforce, and that must have been written right after the morning's gatherings at Ba Son.[41] The letter to the editors of *L'Indochine* announced that the workers of the arsenal had gone on strike and asked that their "rationales be judged with the greatest impartiality."[42] It recounted Courthial's new rules for working hours on paydays, and how the anger resulting from this decision had manifested itself on 18 July. Plans were made for a general strike, of which the director had been informed. Yet, "instead of rectifying his error," the workers were again not paid until 5:15 P.M. on 4 August, the next payday. "This morning, none of them came to work. They assembled around the Arsenal at 6:30 A.M. and left after the director had gone through." A second reason for the strike was that when a power failure had occurred at Ba Son, Courthial sent the workers home and reduced their wages, as if they were responsible for the mishap. "And such a reduction of the workforce since his arrival!" Malraux and Monin were finally asked to write an article based on the letter. But the two editors simply printed the letter, adding: "What article could be more accurate than this very letter?"

A rather different story appeared on the same afternoon, 5 August, in *L'Impartial,* the mouthpiece of the reactionary *colons* in Cochinchina. The author recounted what "a well-informed friend" told him about the events of the morning: how foremen and clerks went to work and how the workers gathered outside Ba Son, only to leave soon after. "They had surely come to work," but were apprehended by "instigators who had ordered them not to go back to their jobs." The article then described the reason for the workers' discontent: Courthial's ruling to extend work on paydays by fifteen minutes. On 18 July, however, Courthial's order had been ignored. With its typical arrogance, *L'Impartial* stated that Courthial punished nobody, as a "gesture of conciliation," and ordered "five or six intelligent natives" to present their complaints. But their proposal to start work on paydays fifteen minutes earlier to be able to stop at 5 P.M. had been rejected to "protect the prestige" of the authorities, who refused "to tolerate the act of insubordination." Another grievance of the workers was the laying off of a lot of workers, "for budgetary reasons," and Courthial's order then was "the drop of water that made the bucket overflow." But the delegates agreed that this conflict was to be solved peacefully, and the next payday on 4 August, indeed, passed without incident. Since the strike had thus come as a surprise, *L'Impartial* assumed foul play:

> It is certain that instigators and outside advice have influenced the decision of the workers. . . . The arrival of the *Jules Michelet,* which has to undergo serious repairs quickly, seems to have been the appropriate time to stage that strike. People know that the *Jules Michelet* must sail to China to help defend the international concessions. A sudden strike at this point deprives the Europeans in China of a means of action. . . . We have no idea who is behind that movement, but it is surely instigated by hidden influences.

The author hoped that the instigators would be prevented from further agitating "this *petite* working population which, when not stirred up by bad shepherds, only wants to earn a peaceful living."[43]

A *L'Impartial* editorial on the following day, 6 August, the second strike day, voiced even stronger convictions of a conspiracy. By now, the workers' grievances were no longer specified but only mentioned in passing as mere "futile reasons." The workers wanted to work, the article claimed again, for they had shown up in front of the arsenal on the morning of 5 August. Yet, under orders of instigators, 800 "disciplined" men, "who for so long have been earning an honest living in our great Far Eastern military shipyard, did not dare" to pass through the gate. By a "strange coincidence," the strike broke out when similar conflicts occurred in Hong Kong, Shanghai, and in the Dutch Indies. Therefore, "without a doubt, a foreign influence" was involved, and the article lost no time implying who represented it in Sai Gon:

> The organ of the Malraux-Monin pair published a significant letter on the strike yesterday. And still there are people who deny the unhealthy deeds undertaken in this country. Fearing responsibility

> on the all too well-known principle "Don't rock the boat!," certain people stubbornly keep their eyes closed. This is an "ostrich policy."... We, however, will fearlessly live up to our responsibilities.

The article concluded that there was "alarming news" from China and that Indochina was particularly targeted by the events there. And just when a warship bound for China needed urgent repairs, the strike continued.[44]

Opposition to the conspiracy charges of *L'Impartial* came from *L'Indochine.* On the same day *L'Impartial* published its second editorial, 6 August, *L'Indochine* printed another anonymous letter to the editor, obviously from the same spokesperson for the Ba Son worker who had written the previous one. It stated that *L'Impartial's* article about the strike had not been impartial at all; rather, "someone primitive" had painted a "naive picture" of the event. The letter noted sarcastically that the "friend," to whom *L'Impartial's* editor had referred, must have forgotten to tell him about the power failure on 16 July, when wages had been reduced as if the workmen were responsible for the mishap. It asked bitterly: "What factory director in France would have the courage to undertake such a wage reduction with his employees? For God's sake, you gentlemen who are 'sane' among the Sai Gon population, answer me."

Regarding the allegations that the strike had to do with Chinese events, the letter denied any "outside advice." The whole matter had been planned in the arsenal in view of the new director. The "dark intention" of delaying the repairs of the *Jules Michelet* "has never crossed the minds of our fellow citizens. It was *L'Impartial* who first suggested this idea to them. What would it say if they carried it out now? What a mania of the press . . . to mix politics into such an incident!"

Finally, in a postscript, the letter reported that secret agents had appeared in front of the arsenal. It predicted gloomily that "the discontented [workers] will probably be pacified by force or by violence."[45] And with this not only the letter ended, but also Malraux and Monin's reporting on the strike at Ba Son, even though *L'Indochine* appeared for another week before it was forced to cease publication. The paper's rather muted reaction to the events in the shipyard might be explained with a general disregard of working-class problems at that time and with its preoccupation with "big" issues like the corrupt rule of the governor.

Cautious sympathy for the strike's reasons was expressed by the self-styled "representatives of the native population," the Constitutionalists, and, surprisingly critical, given his portrayal as a mere marionette of the *colon* establishment, Le Quang Trinh. *L'Écho annamite* had criticized Courthial's insensitivities already in July. It stated on 6 August that the strike showed the discontent over the new working-hour rules Courthial had "preferred to cling to, instead of reversing his unpopular decision." But now, according to information Le Quang Trinh had received, the workers were determined to stay off the job until their grievances had somehow been satisfied. Le Quang Trinh, in an editorial on 14 August in *Le Progrès annamite,* was even more openly critical: "The discontent created by Mr. Courthial's decision seems to us to be somewhat justified." It is noteworthy that he closely followed the arguments of the letters in *L'Indochine.* Le Quang Trinh claimed that he had intervened on behalf of the "native" employees of the arsenal when their wages were reduced after the power failure:

> We were overheard. This will not prevent us now to protest energetically against the inopportune—not to say draconian—measures of a director, who, despite his undeniable merits and his technical know-how, seems to have rather little knowledge of our fellow citizens' mentality.[46]

By 8 August, the fourth day of the strike, no apparent direct contact had been made between Ba Son's management and its striking workforce. Instead, the director now issued a warning to the workers, to be conveyed by the *capelans,* that the arsenal would be closed if they did not return unconditionally to the premises on Monday, 10 August. *L'Impartial* complacently "hoped" the workers, who are "exploited by hidden and unscrupulous instigators, will not want to plunge their wives and children into misery."[47]

On 10 August, however, no laborer showed up for work. An order signed by the interim governor general and by the commander of the navy of Indochina, Douguet, was then posted throughout the shipyard: the arsenal was to be closed for the time being until the workers, through the mediation of the *capelans,* asked for its reopening and the resumption of work. By 10:30 A.M. the lockout had begun. *L'Impartial,* again, could not refrain from indulging in its self-righteousness. Barely hiding intimidations, it wondered "whether the workers will prefer to listen to the sage advice" of their "benevolent" superiors, or "blindly follow instigators, who, for reasons yet unknown to their victims," will make them lose their own and their families' livelihood.[48]

On Tuesday, 11 August, the seventh strike day and the second day of the lockout, four *capelans* came to Ba Son, identified themselves as workers' delegates, and presented Courthial with two conditions under which the workers were willing to return to their jobs: (1) no sanctions would be taken against them, and (2) payment would be made for the workdays lost during the strike. Courthial allegedly refused these demands vehemently. He insisted that the arsenal would not reopen until at least half of the workforce had shown up for work. After "long discussions," as news reports indicated, the two parties signed the following document, dated 11 August:

> The Director of the Arsenal orders all the *capelans,* especially Nguyen Van Ke, native colonial supervisor, Tran Van Canh, *capelan major,* Nguyen Van Nguon, *capelan major,* Tran Van Doc, *capelan,* to have all the workers of the Arsenal resume work at the given day and time, with at least half of their personnel.

The four delegates then promised to try to have at least half the workers resume their jobs by the following day. The reopening of Ba Son, however, was tied to an ultimatum: if the workers had not returned in numbers sufficient to assure operations of the shipyard within the following five days, that is by Monday, 17 August, the arsenal was to be closed again. It did not come to that: on 12 August, the day after the document was signed, about 250 of 720 workers entered Ba Son again to resume work. On 13 August, there were around 350, and on Friday, 14 August, approximately 550 workers had returned to Ba Son. By 17 August, Ba Son's workforce was once again complete.[49]

When the news about the settlement between Courthial and the four representatives broke on 11 August and Ba Son's workers began to return to the arsenal on the following days, there was a certain relief among the media: the Constitutionalists above all else wanted peace and quiet in the colony in order to be presentable to the French, and the *colons* just wanted the arsenal to operate. For some, however, this was not enough.

On 15 August, *L'Impartial*'s counterpart in Ha Noi, *L'Avenir du Tonkin,* published a front-page editorial of its director Dandolo about "The Strike at the Arsenal in Sai Gon" that would prove to be the most inciting article written in Indochina on the subject. Dandolo told his readers that the recent strike in Sai Gon had been well organized to paralyze the *Jules Michelet.* The mission of the *Michelet* was then presented in alarming terms: the cruiser was desperately needed in China, and the situation in Canton was especially critical. Initially, *L'Avenir du Tonkin* claimed, it had welcomed the way in which the government had dealt with the strike; its reaction to the lockout had been a "Bravo!" But then it had received news of the negotiations of 11 August, where "those Gentlemen" had the nerve to demand payment for strike days and no sanctions. Although they had been rebuffed, it remained that, by negotiating, a government had stooped to the level of the workers. To Dandolo, "the scandal [was] excessive." He connected the "shameful" negotiations in Sai Gon with the metropolitan leftist government's wish for silence, while the problems in Morocco, Syria, and China mounted. Dandolo's main point was that "instigators" were at work in Indochina, but some people tended to downplay the danger. He concluded, "Indochina has to be defended. We shall not tire of repeating it."[50]

In a direct reaction to this agitation, authorities in Sai Gon released an official communiqué, around 17 August, that newspapers published soon after. About the strike at Ba Son, the communiqué recounted the lockout, the petition of the *capelans* to reopen the arsenal, and the five-day ultimatum to the personnel to resume work in sufficient numbers. It came to the conclusion that "an inquiry revealed that nothing suggested outside influences." As to the action's impact on the *Michelet,* the communiqué asserted:

> Contrary to erroneous and tendentious accounts published by certain organs of the Indochinese press, the strike at the arsenal has in no way affected the movements of the *Jules Michelet,* whose engine damage was already discovered upon its departure from Djibouti. It could sail at reduced speed with its two other engines. It will depart for Hong Kong on the 22nd. The necessary repairs are impossible in Saigon—in the arsenal and in private enterprises—since they require an inspection in a dry dock. *Jules Michelet*'s dimensions do not permit use of the dock in Saigon.[51]

Yet, contrary to the communiqué's prediction, within a few days the *Michelet* did in fact enter the premises of the Sai Gon arsenal, and repairs on its engine commenced. What accounted for this reversal of the navy's earlier decision to undertake the shipyard work at Hong Kong? Local government documents from 1925 provide some evidence and will have to be considered next. But before turning to these nonpublic sources, let us first conclude the local media's reporting on events at Ba Son.

By mid-August, André Malraux and Paul Monin had been forced to cease publication of *L'Indochine,* for Sai Gon's printing presses were no longer willing to accept their business—usually after having been visited by Sûreté agents. With their biggest adversary thus silenced, and once the workers had returned in full force and repairs had begun on the warship, the pro-government media turned their attention elsewhere. Their more moderate competitors followed suit. The *Michelet* appeared only sporadically in the news: when its military band gave public concerts, when its highest-ranking officers joined the *colon* establishment at opulent balls, or when, on 10 September, the *Jules Ferry* arrived in Sai Gon from Hong Kong. On the following day, the China-bound patrol boat *Marne* joined the *Jules Ferry* and the *Jules Michelet* for a grand display of French naval power, which was proudly covered by the media.[52] The transfer of command over France's Far Eastern fleet from the *Jules Ferry* to the *Jules Michelet* took place soon after. By November, newspapers announced the approaching completion of repairs on the *Michelet.* There was no suggestion—surely to have been taken up by *L'Impartial* and its ilk, given the slightest chance—that a "slowdown strike," outright sabotage, or similar actions by the shipyard workers had prolonged the ship's repairs; indeed, as we will see below, work on the cruiser concluded *ahead* of the schedule laid out by the authorities. After conducting trial runs in the vicinity of Sai Gon-Cape Saint Jacques, the *Jules Michelet* finally left Sai Gon for China on 29 November 1925.[53]

THE STRIKE AT BA SON IN GOVERNMENT SOURCES

Internal official documents largely supported the newspapers' portrayal of the sequence of events at Ba Son, although they sharply disagreed with the alarmist interpretations that *L'Impartial* and others had advanced. We will focus here on three documents directly related to the labor conflict at the arsenal: a report of the interim governor general Monguillot to the Colonial Ministry, communications—back in

France—between several ministries regarding the strike's impact on the *Michelet,* and an account by Sai Gon's senior public prosecutor to the new governor general shortly after Alexandre Varenne had arrived in the colony.

ON 10 SEPTEMBER 1925, the interim governor general Monguillot in Sai Gon sent a "Report on the Strike of the Arsenal" to the minister of colonies in Paris.[54] The letter provides the first available official interpretation of what took place. Evidently, it was prepared in reaction to highest level concerns about the public debates and the alarmist campaigns of the Right the strike at the Ba Son shipyard had caused. This is shown by the governor general's overall conclusion that the event had been exaggerated "out of proportion," and that there was no evidence to substantiate the "hypothesis of outside influence."

Monguillot begins with Courthial's measures to "improve the performance" of Ba Son. A "better utilization" of personnel led to dismissals of some "native" secretaries and workers and created initial annoyance. The discontent grew after Courthial's order adding fifteen minutes to work time on paydays, leading to the protest on 18 July. Due to "the impossibility to recognize the instigators," Courthial "pretended to consider the event to be the result of an error on the part of the workers," but made it clear that another similar incident "would be considered a grave violation of discipline." Rejecting the workers' demand to withdraw the controversial order, he "informed the personnel that any worker or *capelan* who quit work before 5:15 P.M. on the next payday would be dismissed for four days. Although showing profound discontent, the workers promised to conform with the order of the management."

On the next payday, 4 August, work ceased "without incident" at 5:15 P.M. On the same day, the report of 10 September continues, the *Jules Michelet* arrived with "serious engine damage" that needed repair. Monguillot writes:

> Without having been a direct cause of the strike, the arrival of *Michelet* at Saigon seems to have accelerated [its] outbreak. . . . [T]he following morning . . . the workers came in rather great numbers to the accessways of the Arsenal . . . [and] retreated around seven o'clock without having made any pronouncements. Only the overseers and the *capelans* returned in full to the workshops. The situa-

> tion remained the same on August 6, 7, and 8. To provoke the resumption of work, the Director informed his personnel that he would demand the closure of the Arsenal on August 10 if by that date the workers had not returned in sufficient numbers to assure services.

After the lockout had indeed begun, a "radical measure they had not anticipated," the overseers and *capelans* demanded Ba Son be reopened and promised to make sure that at least half the workforce would return. By 13 August, there were already 323 men willing to work. On the same day, the *Jules Michelet* received orders to sail to Hong Kong for its repairs. Monguillot believes that "[t]his news could have been the cause of the significant return of workers" on 14 August: 557 men came back to work. By the seventeenth, all personnel had returned.

According to Sûreté information, the account continues, the main instigator was a certain Nguyen Van Bay, called Bay Cop, who had not returned to the arsenal since the strike. He was charged with "obstruction of the freedom of work." Other investigations were under way. Again Monguillot emphasizes there never was any rally or disturbance of "public order," nor was any "proper fact" found to "confirm the hypothesis the strike of the Arsenal may have been caused by outside influences." He concludes that "this event has to be reduced to its just proportions" and deserved no "exaggerated importance." The strike seemed to have been the manifestation of a "passing discontent" at Courthial's measures—a disaffection "skillfully exploited by some instigators" who would soon face "severe sanctions."[55]

Two things should be noted. Monguillot's did not disclose the electricity outage and subsequent wage reductions to the Colonial Ministry in Paris, an indication the colonial government considered Courthial's decision problematic. Because it might provide justification for the workers' protest, it was omitted lest it weaken the appeasing tenor of the report. And Monguillot, like all newspaper accounts, mentioned no demands being raised during the strike, nor any management concessions granted.

IN LATE OCTOBER, back in Paris, the French ministers of colonies and foreign affairs made the absence in the French concessions in China of the protection of a cruiser the object of remonstrances to the minister of the navy: not only had the *Jules Ferry* sailed for France in early

September, but also the *Jules Michelet* remained in Sai Gon. Therefore, there was an obvious need for a second armored cruiser in the Far East. In a letter dated 7 November, the minister of the navy answered his colleagues that it was "purely accidental and entirely temporary" that the *Michelet* was not in China.[56] Damages during its voyage had forced it to stop in Sai Gon for repairs due to last until mid-December. For reinforcements, the letter cautioned, the patrol boat *Marne* had already arrived in China; another gunboat was on its way. Heavier ships were unavailable without depleting European forces. In any case, lighter craft were more useful for "our operations in China," for they alone could ply the rivers.[57] Finally, the minister lectured, a cruiser operated in China mostly through its landing corps, to be brought by lighter boats to "sensitive" spots. Forty marines from the *Michelet* had already been sent to Canton; sixty more served on various patrol boats. If a larger corps was needed, it could be better obtained from nearby Indochina, not from an additional cruiser. In any case, with the May Thirtieth Movement largely aimed against Britain and Japan, there was no urgency for French military actions.

ON 26 NOVEMBER 1925, the senior public prosecutor at the Sai Gon court of appeals, J. Colonna, sent a report to Governor General Varenne—with a copy for the minister of colonies—about "the affair named 'Strike of the Arsenal' that had inflamed . . . the Indochinese press as well as certain journals of the Metropole."[58] By then, as we will see below, the strike had become the object of politicized reporting in French and Chinese papers.

Colonna writes that on 5 September, navy commander Douguet, who was in charge of the arsenal, filed a suit against the worker Nguyen Van Bay for "obstruction of the freedom of work" and "incitement of personnel to go on strike." Colonna commissioned the public prosecutor of Sai Gon with the complaint. An investigation was concluded on 23 September. Colonna believed at that point that,

> although the Sûreté's inquiry could not establish sufficient evidence against the arrested individuals, I called in the investigating judge to obtain [an even more] complete explanation, because of rumors which had been readily spread about this strike (communist menaces, an action of the [GMD] of Canton, a movement unleashed to delay the departure of the cruiser *Michelet,* etc.).

Colonna continues his 26 November report by listing "facts and ascertainments" from the investigating judge's dossier: Courthial changed the working hours on paydays on 7 July, and the protests of 18 July, when workers defied the new rule, thus occurred on the first payday following that order. On 22 July, a petition of the overseers and *capelans* demanded in the name of all "native" workers the return to the 5 P.M. rule. In response, Courthial on 28 July informed an overseer, two *capelans,* and two workers, "chosen by the management to represent the personnel," that Commander Douguet had rejected their petition. The overseer then requested that, on paydays, the morning shift should begin fifteen minutes earlier to allow the workday to end at 5 P.M. after all. (This modification, Colonna adds, was adopted as of 1 October 1925). When the navy commander's decision was posted in every workshop, the delegates informed Courthial on 30 July that only the *capelans,* but not the workers, planned to obey the order. Therefore, on 3 August, Courthial urged the workers to conform with the new regulation on the following day, the next payday after the incident of 18 July. Indeed, on 4 August, the new rule was obeyed when work stopped at 5:15 P.M.

Colonna then details the workers' gatherings on 5 August and on the mornings thereafter, the lockout on 10 August, the promise of overseers and *capelans majors* on 11 August to assure the resumption of work with half of the workforce if the arsenal reopened, and the rising number of returning workers until, by 17 August, all personnel were back on the job. Concluding that "it is therefore established that the workers went on strike . . . to obtain the preservation of work's end at 5 P.M. on paydays," Colonna writes:

> There is reason to state that this strike . . . cannot be considered to be a result of Bolshevik menaces, all the more because preliminary investigations of the Sûreté and a judicial inquiry discovered no action of any kind of influence upon the workers. Furthermore, the strike neither delayed nor rendered impossible the departure of the *Jules Michelet,* . . . which arrived on August 4, and was scheduled to leave on the 13th. Orders to carry out the repairs at Sai Gon did not arrive from Paris until August 27.

Colonna's report of 26 November further emphasizes that "neither the investigation nor the hearing have revealed any attempt at the liberty of work," citing a Sûreté report of 22 August:

> Against those individuals, except for Bay, no concrete act of violence or threats against workers who wanted to continue or resume work were brought up. Furthermore, no noisy demonstration took place, public order was never disturbed, [and] the police did not have to intervene.

Concerning Bay and the events on 5 August, when the arsenal's gates had just been opened, Colonna quotes from the same Sûreté report:

> For a quarter of an hour, this Bay Cop circulated on a bicycle among the workers' groups, exhorting them not to take up work and threatening to punch those who would enter [the arsenal]. Workers who were already won for the strike helped him in this coercion of the hesitating, and only the *capelans* passed through the gate.

For Colonna, however, there was insufficient proof to charge Bay. Only some hearsay implicated Bay, but "no precise testimony" and "no complaint could be gathered from the workers' side." Colonna thus could not but quash the case, and the investigating judge rendered a ruling to that effect on 26 November.[59]

There is, again, neither any indication of demands being voiced during the strike, nor of any attempt to slow down the *Michelet*'s repairs, which were finished by the time the report was written. What Colonna does mention, though, complete with a date (30 July), is that Courthial was informed about the workers' plans to oppose his recent order—well prior to 4 August when the *Michelet* arrived. As with Monguillot's, this document reflects concerns the alarmist campaign of some *colons* must have caused within the colonial and metropolitan bureaucracies. Because of the public accusations and agitation, the report states, extraordinary scrutiny went into repeated legal inquiries. Colonna wanted to show that everything conceivable had been done to uncover possible conspiracies or instigators behind the strike, and that he would have pressed charges if the results of the investigations had permitted him to do so. They had not.

THESE WERE ALL THE AVAILABLE contemporary primary sources on the strike, and the following summary picture of its major aspects emerges from them.

Early in July 1925, Ba Son's new director angered the workers with some arbitrary, insensitive measures; a number of workers were fired, an old rule for working hours on paydays was altered to the disadvantage of the workers, and after an electricity failure stopped all operations in the arsenal on one day, wages were reduced accordingly. On 18 July, workers ignored the new orders and voiced their discontent in an organized protest. During the following two and a half weeks until the strike, a sort of power struggle occurred between the workers and Ba Son's management. Workers' delegates demanded a return to the old working-hour rule and, when this was rejected, offered an alternative solution to the problem.

Again rebuffed by a haughty director, they specifically informed him on 30 July—six days before the walkout, and without knowing that the *Michelet* would soon arrive—of plans for a strike. The director in turn threatened sanctions if his orders were again ignored on the next payday. On 4 August, workers grudgingly conformed with the new rule; there were definitely no protests.

When the *Jules Michelet* arrived—alone and unannounced—in Sai Gon on 4 August, first reports that it needed repairs appeared on the same afternoon in newspapers. All during the strike, the *Michelet* lay on the Sai Gon River; it was unclear if and when repairs would have to be conducted. In fact, it had no such orders yet. A political strike to paralyze the ship would logically have been staged *after,* not *before,* its docking inside Ba Son, and *after,* not *before,* commencement of repair work. However, the *Michelet's* arrival on a mission seemingly pivotal to the French and its presumed need for their labor might well at that point have provided the workers with an unexpected but welcome extra leverage against the management of Ba Son and strengthened an already existing resolve to go on strike. Support for the May Thirtieth Movement by delaying the ship might thus have been a by-product of the strike plans, but we can rule out proletarian internationalism as a veritable driving force behind the strike at Ba Son.

No demands were put forward during the strike. During the initial gatherings on the morning of 5 August, there were no demonstrations or speeches. Furthermore, no further contact existed for six days between Ba Son's management and the workers. No delegates came out to convey claims. Finally, the letter in *L'Indochine* spoke specifically of the strikers' rationales, not demands; the opposite side no longer needed to be told what the grievances were. The gatherings on 5 August assured full participation in the strike. But the reasons were so clear that hardly any coercion was needed, as is indicated by the French inability to produce viable evidence against alleged bullies. Instead, an eerie calm prevailed, and workers went home in an orderly way "after the director had gone through."[60]

Authorities in Sai Gon felt their "prestige" challenged and reacted harshly. The Sûreté made some arrests and looked for instigators, who were threatened with dire consequences for their deeds. Most important, a stubborn management did not think of negotiating at all. Instead, it imposed a lockout on Ba Son's workforce.

Thus, the initiative to resume work came from the side of the workers, or at least from the *capelans*. For the first time since the outbreak of the strike, workers' delegates appeared. Thereby, they implicitly agreed to play to the tune of the management and acknowledged the greater effectiveness of the lockout over the strike. In that very instance, only one day after the lockout, they had lost the contest of wills: the specific demands they brought forward now could only be defensive in nature; they did not relate to the strike anymore but to the lockout, and their goal was not the satisfaction of their initial grievances but only an assurance of some kind of safe passage back to work.

At the end of negotiations on 11 August, the *capelans* had to accept an unconditional resumption of work. Adding insult to injury, Courthial even gave them a humiliating five-day ultimatum to bring back the workers in sufficient numbers to assure the arsenal's operations. Between 12 and 17 August, all the workers returned to Ba Son; they had not achieved anything. An alternative working-hour rule initially requested by the workers in July was adopted in October, but it in fact was only a modification of Courthial's new orders.

With two of its three engines intact, the *Michelet* could have sailed on if its mission had indeed been urgent. In fact, the strike at Ba Son probably caused the initial decision to leave Sai Gon around 20 August for repairs in Hong Kong. By then, the arsenal was operating again, however, and plans were changed once more in the light of the instability in China. On 27 August, the *Michelet* received approval from France to undergo repairs in Sai Gon,[61] which officials expected to last until late November or mid-December. In fact, work concluded slightly ahead of schedule.

In sum, the walkout at Ba Son was a protest in reaction to earlier developments at the arsenal, with demands that had clearly been voiced weeks before and needed no repeating, only Courthial's fulfillment.

Despite the workers' courage and unity[62]—sustained for a whole week—a lockout defeated the strike, which ended with no tangible achievements and subsequently had no apparent impact on the *Jules Michelet.*

HOW DO WE GET FROM THIS ASSESSMENT, based on available primary sources, to the highly celebratory version of the strike at Ba Son propagated in the DRVN since the late 1950s? We will remember that Ton Duc Thang—as self-ascribed strike leader in 1925—and the revolutionary-cum-historian Tran Van Giau were instrumental in 1957 in commemorating the events at the arsenal as a threefold "first": Viet Nam's first union-organized and first political strike, and the first manifestation in Viet Nam of proletarian internationalism. Furthermore, they claimed that the workers were victorious in delaying the *Michelet*'s departure for three months and in forcing colonial authorities to grant major concessions. While the next chapter will take up the issue of the union, we will concentrate here on the strike's portrayal as having been staged primarily in internationalist support of China's May Thirtieth Movement, and that it ended in a resounding success.

To be sure, already during and soon after the strike in 1925, interpretations had been forthcoming that it was an internationalist act within an anti-imperialist movement operating around the world. But these had been part of larger alarmist, diversionary campaigns, initially orchestrated by, ironically, reactionary *colon* leaders against an increasingly pesky local opposition and then readily picked up and amplified by newspapers back in France. As *L'Écho annamite* reported during the autumn, metropolitan conservative media accused the leftist French government of watching passively while Indochina was "wide open for Bolshevik propaganda." In addition, elements of the Vietnamese exile community in France, among them the papers *Le Paria* and *Viet Nam Hon,* had instrumentalized the protest of Ba Son's workers by trumpeting its alleged internationalism for the purpose of advancing an "Indochinese-Chinese cooperation against imperialism" within the context of current Parisian anticolonial politics.[63] All these observers, however, had ignored the workers' grievances and, although diametrically opposed to one another, had shared an interest in depicting anti-imperialist internationalism as the only reason for the walkout—for the Left to idealize, and for the Right to demonize.

Some thirty years later, on the other hand, Ton Duc Thang and Tran

Van Giau did not simply allege that internationalism was behind the strike in the same unsubstantiated and crudely sloganeering fashion of those observers in 1925; instead, they made that very claim in a detailed historical description of the events, based in part on the same contemporary newspaper sources I consulted as well: *L'Impartial, L'Indochine, L'Écho annamite, L'Avenir du Tonkin,* and *Cong Luan Bao,* among others.[64] Yet, whereas I concluded that Ba Son's workers protested in reaction to earlier developments internal to the arsenal and that a lockout defeated them, by contrast Ton Duc Thang and Tran Van Giau boldly asserted that the strike succeeded splendidly, that it was aimed principally against the *Michelet* and therefore, with its glorious display of proletarian internationalism, represented Viet Nam's first political labor action. We will see in the following section that they could arrive at these conclusions only by taking recourse to some historical engineering.

TON DUC THANG'S AND TRAN VAN GIAU'S ACCOUNT

Both in Vietnamese and Western historiography, practically all published accounts of the labor action at Ba Son in 1925 hark back to the initial version put forth since 1957 by Tran Van Giau.[65] His accounts thus far have offered the most extensive information and interpretations of the walkout at Ba Son. In addition to using contemporary newspaper articles, they drew on the recollections of Ton Duc Thang who, according to Tran Van Giau, "took part in organizing this important strike."[66]

Ton Duc Thang and Tran Van Giau essentially used four maneuvers to engineer the authoritative version of Viet Nam's first political strike at the Sai Gon arsenal: First, they overdramatized global and colonial challenges to French authority and, thus, the supposed urgency of the *Jules Michelet's* mission. Second, they either ignored prior events at the arsenal or transposed them from July to August to coincide with the warship's arrival. Third, they ignored the lockout and invented the strikers' victory. And fourth, they selectively used contemporary "enemy" sources as "state's evidence" while omitting historical data that would contradict their argument.

Tran Van Giau's historical contextualization first paints a picture of a politically lively year 1925. The French empire was facing military challenges and difficulties in Morocco and Syria; for reinforcements,

Vietnamese soldiers were shipped to the Near East. In Cochinchina, critical Vietnamese newspapers were thriving and public demonstrations common. Tran Van Giau mentions here the returns—one forced, the other voluntary—of the old resistance leaders Phan Boi Chau and Phan Chu Trinh to their homeland, public speeches by Nguyen An Ninh, the puppet-monarch Khai Dinh in Hue, and the role of the Vietnamese revolutionary Nguyen Ai Quoc at the Fifth Comintern congress in 1924. Of all these, however, only Phan Chu Trinh's return to Sai Gon in the early summer of 1925 could perhaps be brought into some kind of relationship to the events at Ba Son, while the other events were probably included for greater dramatic effect.[67] Most important for Tran Van Giau, the situation in China was very tense in mid-1925. Revolutionary forces were victorious in the civil war, and anti-imperialist protests and boycotts were staged in foreign concessions. Tran Van Giau quotes from newspaper interviews, in which the newly appointed, socialist governor general Varenne voiced concerns that the "Chinese and Bolshevik movements" had created a "critical situation" for Indochina, where "14,000 French *colons* and 4,500 French soldiers [faced] 20 million Annamites."[68] To protect their interests, imperialist powers, including France, sent reinforcements to their Chinese concessions:

> On the Sai Gon River lay the warships *Jules Ferry, Ma[r]ne,* [and] *Jules Michelet.* The *Jules Michelet* had just arrived in Sai Gon from France and needed *urgent* repairs to *hurry on* to China. The leaders of the Sai Gon trade union planned to somehow prevent the French warship from leaving, or at least to delay its departure to express sympathy with the Chinese revolution. The union leaders—Ton Duc Thang worked then at "Krupp" company—talked to Mai Van Ngoc and Nguyen An Ninh to ask the newspaper *Cloche fêlée* for support.[69]

But as we have already seen from the very same sources that Tran Van Giau used, in early August the *Michelet* arrived alone in Sai Gon. The meeting of the three ships occurred only in mid-September, four weeks after the strike; its transposition by the authors back to the onset of the strike added credibility to the image of French desperation. Furthermore, Nguyen An Ninh's newspaper *Cloche fêlée* was not published at the time of the strike; publication restarted only on 26 November 1925. Why would the workers ask for support from a closed newspaper? Could *Cloche fêlée* have been *L'Indochine* instead, and Mai Van Ngoc and Nguyen An Ninh stand-ins for Paul Monin and André Malraux? Given the two anonymous letters printed by *L'Indochine* at the outset of the strike, this is certainly a strong possibility. But it would suggest that in the starkly nationalist orientation of 1950s revolutionary historiography—here "us" Vietnamese, there those foreign aggressors—an image of Vietnamese radical intellectuals helping their working-class compatriots was much more palatable than that of progressive Frenchmen being outspoken supporters of Vietnamese labor activists.

Tran Van Giau adds to the tone of urgency and crisis by making selective use of his newspaper sources. He quotes from an article of *L'Impartial* where the strike at Ba Son was firmly connected to the arrival of the *Michelet* and its mission in China. The same article also claimed that a "Comintern chairman"[70] said, "today China is rising in rebellion, tomorrow it will come to be Indochina's and India's turn to rise." But Tran Van Giau fails to mention the two mitigating letters printed in *L'Indochine*—which he lists as a source—and does not point out that *L'Impartial*'s coverage of the strike was part of an alarmist campaign of distortions and slander against "Bolshevik" menaces in Indochina, where the strike at Ba Son came in handy to further fuel public hysteria. In that way he is able to marshal further "proof" that the walkout had an anti-imperialist thrust since even the workers' contemporary "enemy" acknowledged (rather than alleged) the nexus.

Ton Duc Thang's and Tran Van Giau's account about the outbreak of the strike at Ba Son mentions considerable hurdles: Sai Gon's biggest industry with "over 1,000 workers"[71] was under military command. Severe antistrike measures were in effect. An overtly political strike would have provoked swift and brutal suppression. "One had to have *economic* reasons first to incite a *political* strike to erupt." But to find a legitimate economic grievance as a front for what was really a political strike was not easy. The shipyard was the only workshop in Indochina to have an eight-hour workday. Wages were generally higher than in other enterprises, and labor itself was not as exhausting as in most workshops. Luckily, economic grievances were quickly found in the issue of work hours on paydays. An engineer, Courthial, who had just come from France, extended work hours on those days by fifteen minutes until 5:15 P.M. before wages could be picked up.

> The workers protested against Courthial on 4 August 1925, a payday; yet again, the brothers stopped work at 5 P.M. Courthial also had some workers fired. The *Michelet* moored to the docks for urgent repairs. All of the workers gathered and demanded a 20% wage increase, reinstatement of the fired workmen, and maintenance of the [old] rule for paydays. While waiting for the director's answer, all of the brothers ceased work from 4 August on.[72]

Some observations: For an argument of a primarily political strike to be convincing, it necessitated but one sequence of events: the warship's unannounced arrival must come first, of course, in order to trigger plans for anti-imperialist action. In turn, these plans must predate and lead to a strike. In reality, however, events happened in a different order: internal grievances came first, followed by failed negotiations and explicit strike threats over the course of a few weeks, only then did the *Michelet* arrive, and finally the strike broke out. The *Michelet,* still at anchorage out on the Sai Gon River, at best added leverage to the workers' demands; we have seen that it did not enter Ba Son until after the strike had been defeated. But had Ton Duc Thang and Tran Van Giau allowed for this actual sequence, their portrayal of the strike as internationalist at its core and, hence, political from the outset would have collapsed. So they rearranged the events in a more fitting order.

The obvious result of their re-sequencing was a dramatic contraction of time. Events that had actually taken place over weeks all happened in a few frantic hours on 4 August: the warship's arrival, the immediate decision by Ton Duc Thang and his comrades to paralyze it, their rush to secure the support of *La Cloche fêlée* (the unmentionable *L'Indochine*?), and their search for and then "quickly finding" economic strike reasons for the workers. These "over 1,000" men then needed, of course, to be told about these reasons before they might leave for home at the end of the workday at 5:15 P.M., and while all this must have been going on in a great hurry, the *Michelet* did the strike planners the incredible favor of mooring in Ba Son and becoming "paralyzable" in the first place. Yet it all somehow succeeded by 5 P.M.: the workers demonstrated against the director's new policies, raised demands, and went on strike.

Even more seriously, Ton's and Tran Van Giau's re-sequencing reduced the workers' grievances to mere pretexts or secondary motives and, by alleging a clandestine, ideologically more advanced leadership with an anti-imperialist agenda, deprived them of agency. Courthial's firings, the account implied, occurred during 4 August, not as the sudden, unreasonable acts of early July. The wrongful wage reductions after the power outage of mid-July were not mentioned, despite the historical sources at Tran Van Giau's disposal. And were the remarkably courageous and organized protests on 18 July and during the following fortnight against these injustices and the longer work hours on paydays not justified and noteworthy enough? Inconveniently having taken place *before* the *Michelet*'s arrival, these grievances stood in the way of the authors' ambition to recast the strike into the first Vietnamese manifestation of proletarian internationalism. Instead, they were transposed and compressed into 4 August, immediately *after* the warship's appearance, when (and only when) an argument for the supposedly "real," political goals of the strike could be advanced.

As to the strike itself, Ton Duc Thang and Tran Van Giau recounted the initial early morning meetings outside the arsenal, the appearance of workers' representatives after a few days, and finally the navy commander's threats of a lockout, only to go on as follows:

> [But] the deputies were not intimidated by the colonialists' threats. They again insisted on the fulfillment of the workers' original claims and even demanded in addition that all strike days be paid. . . . Threats did not work. The Westerners were forced to give in. The workmen received a 10% wage increase. The strike came to a victorious end. It would encourage workers in other places to fight. . . . The workers of Ba Son returned to work only to initiate a slowdown strike. The repair of the *Michelet* dragged on until 28 November; only then could it weigh anchor to sail north.[73]

Ton Duc Thang and Tran Van Giau must have believed that for Viet Nam's first political strike to be fully significant, it also had to have been successful. Why else would they have suppressed the lockout, invented demands of 20 percent higher wages as well as an ultimate 10 percent increase, and turned defeat into resounding victory?[74] We have seen that there is neither any evidence that the "Westerners were forced to give in," nor that they agreed to a 10 percent pay hike. Why would all contemporary observers have ignored a demand for higher wages if it had indeed been voiced? For *L'Impartial,* it would have been welcome ammunition for its pretended outrage. In reports of the administration, which was chronically under tight budgetary restraint, it would have surfaced. And whoever wrote the letters in *L'Indochine* would have mentioned the demand—especially if the letters were to distract from a *Michelet* connection. Likewise, nobody would have been able to keep a 10 percent pay hike concession on the part of the Ba Son directorate secret for long. For reactionaries like de Lachevrotière and Dandolo, it would have fitted perfectly into their campaign against a government that was "selling out *colons* and French interests in Indochina." But our historical sources remain silent on these issues, and we can confidently dismiss a wage increase as the authors' invention. Lastly, regarding the slowdown strike—undetected by all sources—it would have had no delaying effect on the *Michelet;* we will remember that French authorities even expected normal repairs to take until mid-December.

Finally, Ton Duc Thang and Tran Van Giau not only credit Ton's secret labor union and the workers' steadfastness for the strike's "victory," but they also report on large-scale financial support from among sympathetic Sai Gon citizens to enable Ba Son's workforce to sustain a longer strike. According to their account, "all the offices and workshops in Sai Gon-Cho Lon started a big fund-raising campaign. . . . The several 10,000 workers of Sai Gon-Cho Lon in particular supported Ba Son and regarded its fight as everyone's. The unanimity of a majority of the workmen during that struggle was very obvious."[75]

These are the essential points laid out by Ton Duc Thang and Tran Van Giau in their version of the strike at Ba Son. But the historian Tran Van Giau adds one final, supposedly authoritative, voice as further "proof" that the event was Viet Nam's first political strike: after all, at the Sixth World Congress of the Communist Internationale in Moscow in the summer of 1928, the "delegate from Indochina" mentioned the strike of August 1925 in his report to the congress, saying that "workers of Ba Son could not bear to repair the ship *Jules Michelet* that French imperialism meant to send to terrorize the Chinese people."[76] But what was the significance of this Comintern congress in 1928? According to Huynh Kim Khanh,

> the Comintern called for a new "revolutionary purity" involving a "proletarianization" of Communist parties and an adoption of "class-against-class" tactics vis-à-vis the bourgeoisie. . . . This ultra-leftist revolutionary line was accompanied by a new perception of

> the role of revolutionary movements in the colonies. In a radical departure from the previous Eurocentrism and inattention to the colonies, the Sixth World Congress assigned the colonies an important place in the world revolutionary movement. . . . It was the duty of the proletariat of the world to give effective aid to the struggle of the colonial peoples.[77]

In this context, it becomes clear why the walkout of 1925 at Ba Son assumed such a symbolic role in the report of the Indochina delegate to the congress. He wanted to highlight all those three newly adopted, main policy lines of the Comintern: the strike thus became an example of *internationalism* that was both *colonial* and *proletarian.* It was thereby used as credentials for the Vietnamese revolutionary movement within Comintern, showing that its people presumably were in tune with the World Revolution.

DISPUTES OVER STRIKING IMAGES

Some thirty years after the sixth Comintern congress, in the very different historical environment of the late 1950s, why, we might ask at this point, did Ton Duc Thang and Tran Van Giau, too, reinterpret and misrepresent the events at the Sai Gon arsenal as Viet Nam's first political strike? Let us first turn to Ton Duc Thang, who had undoubtedly witnessed the walkout in 1925 and might even have been involved in it behind the scenes.

Ton told Tran Van Giau about his secret labor union and the strike's events sometime in 1957 and early 1958, right about the same time when he was no longer able to avoid publishing his "recollections" of how he had raised the Red Flag in the Black Sea. The story of the Black Sea had established an imagined ancestry of proletarian internationalism for Vietnamese communism, which dated all the way back to the October Revolution. But the party's addition of the Red Flag exposed Ton Duc Thang among the revolutionary masses at Sevastopol. Eventually he was forced to dissociate himself irrevocably from his imaginary comrades in the Soviet Revolution. Constantinople became his fallback option since Sevastopol was now out of reach and Toulon could not be acknowledged. No longer could he return to the one part of his tale that had always been dearest to him: having been one among many other proletarian internationalists at a historic moment.

There are strong parallels between the Black Sea Mutiny of April 1919 and Ton's version of the strike at Ba Son in August 1925. The prime motive of the revolt in the Black Sea was internationalist support for a revolutionary movement. However, material and political objectives were pursued at the same time. Further, as Philippe Masson makes the point, the revolt should more accurately be called a "mutiny-strike," for the mass of the sailors did not seek to gain command of the ships but simply refused their services as long as certain demands were not met.[78]

It is thus quite likely that Ton Duc Thang in 1957 grafted onto the strike at Ba Son what he had just so painfully lost in the salvage operation of the *Paris*. In his exaggerated version of the walkout, modeled on core features of the Black Sea Mutiny, he could immediately retrieve his political credentials from the Soviet Revolution and (re-)establish—in Viet Nam—an imagined ancestry of proletarian internationalism. Ton resurrected an impressive story where he, the clandestine union leader, was intimately involved in a historic revolutionary act. Involved not through heroic exploits and individual exposure (which were unbefitting his unassuming personality) but yet again by being one with brave and steadfast masses. The Red Flag had just cost him this cherished personal connection in Sevastopol. But in Sai Gon in his union-led strike—made ever more meaningful with ultimate "victory"—he almost seamlessly reinhabited his revolutionary persona from the glorious times in the Black Sea. With these striking images of internationalist anti-imperialism at Ba Son, he could slip back into the identity he had always been most comfortable with: mysteriously influential yet simply inconspicuous.

Much later, in a rendition of the strike at Ba Son published in 1987, Tran Van Giau indicated his awareness of the powerful allusion to the Black Sea in Ton Duc Thang's recollections of Ba Son in 1957. "The strike of August 1925 was not just a normal strike," he wrote, "but was truly a heroic act by which the Vietnamese working class and the people of Sai Gon in fact set an example of proletarian internationalism and continued Ton Duc Thang's spirit of the Black Sea."[79]

IF TON'S INVOLVEMENT in the historical engineering of the walkout was reactive and restorative—to regain what the Red Flag had taken away—Tran Van Giau's interest was active and creative. For the historian, the strike at the arsenal in 1925 became a cornerstone of a major historical argument he was intending to make: that there was an independent development of a Vietnamese working class already in the early 1920s. To this end Tran Van Giau not only accepted Ton Duc Thang's version of events, although at odds with his historical evidence, but also selectively used and even manipulated his sources to make his account fit with its intended meaning. How, then, did Tran Van Giau contextualize the events at Ba Son and portray them as proof of the importance of a distinct workers' movement in that period?

Tran Van Giau saw the post-World War I years from 1919 to 1926 marked in particular by a "patriotic-democratic" opposition in Cochinchina. In a "legal movement," elements of the Vietnamese middle class, intelligentsia, artisans, students, and workers demanded political reforms, equal treatment with *colons,* and economic opportunities. But within these developments, he stresses, workers constituted a social force of their own. At times they found common ground with "patriotic petty bourgeois" activists and provided the majority at public demonstrations, but their ultimate objectives differed. Thus, instead of joining petty bourgeois groups, workers formed their own organization: Ton Duc Thang's clandestine union. During the heyday of the legal movement in the years 1924–26, a number of strikes broke out, "of which the most organized, the most class conscious, and the most internationalist minded was . . . at Ba Son." Under the repressive colonial system, Tran Van Giau argues, the "arrest of the *Jules Michelet"* proved that the workers' movement "was of a political nature at an early point."[80] After a French crackdown began in 1926 and the petty bourgeois opposition largely collapsed, workers remained steadfast and incorruptible, and their politicization and organizational division from other social groups soon enabled them to become the leading core of a more radical struggle against colonialism in a "democratic and national-revolutionary movement."

The strike at the Sai Gon military shipyard itself signifies for Tran Van Giau the end of a phase of "spontaneous" movements among the Vietnamese working class and the beginning of a period of relative organization. He concedes that the walkout still was in many ways spontaneous as it lacked the leadership of a broadly based trade union or of a genuine workers' party. On the other hand, a level of organization was evident in the appearance of workers' representatives at Ba

Son, in gatherings of mutual encouragement, and in a division of labor where some people collected contributions, others distributed the aid, and others prevented scabs from working. Tran Van Giau also notes the solidarity of the workers, as well as the role of Ton's union, which laid the foundation for trade unionism in the entire country. In this sense, the walkout of 1925 was not only the culmination of one development, but also a link between two different stages in the history of the Vietnamese working class: it showed characteristics of both.

In consequence, Tran Van Giau passionately argues against those (whom he does not identify) who underestimated the importance of the workers' movement as a distinct social force and its impact on political developments during the mid-1920s. His criticism is indication of an ongoing and fierce debate within the historical sciences of the DRVN in the late 1950s and early 1960s, a debate that apparently focused on the role of the working class before the creation of communist organizations. Referring to the strike at the Sai Gon arsenal in 1925, he criticizes his colleagues: "Many historians have ample reason to pay good attention to the legal movement in Cochinchina, especially in Sai Gon. Yet thus far, very few have taken note of workers' activities . . . in that year (1925)."[81] Even when some of his opponents did consider Ba Son's labor struggles, they obviously not only doubted the political character of the strike, but also did not see the event embedded within a broader movement. As Tran Van Giau angrily charges:

> There are people who suspect that, if . . . the workers of Ba Son indeed struck to prevent the warship *Michelet* from sailing to China, then this occurred only "randomly" and "by chance" [i.e., spontaneously]. [They argue that] one should not exaggerate a small and temporary event. We think that in this situation and time, the said events were big and not small. And even if [the strike at Ba Son and similar events] were still small, then they were . . . developing small matters worthier of attention than big things already antiquated and decaying. . . . Although the international contacts and the internationalist spirit of Vietnamese workers had just begun and still lacked organization, they were very big and new nonetheless, for they were taking root and sprouting.[82]

To illustrate his colleagues' supposed skewed priorities, Tran Van Giau refers to the ill-fated newspaper *Jeune Annam:* it was shut down right after its first release in March 1926, and its publisher, Lam Hiep Chau, and the celebrated Nguyen An Ninh were arrested at the same time. These colonial acts of repression triggered large protests, including school "boycott-strikes." Tran Van Giau sarcastically notes:

> There is something we regard as strange, i.e., even after the August Revolution and the resistance [war against the French], people still often want to talk more about a newspaper that was only published once than about dozens of vigorous strikes occurring ca. 1919–1925, and people pay more attention to a school strike than to the struggle of several thousand Ba Son workers to paralyze the warship *Michelet* at Sai Gon.[83]

Without doubt, Tran Van Giau's attacks were aimed mainly at Tran Huy Lieu, the DRVN's foremost historian, who, like Tran Van Giau, had been a leading anticolonial activist during the 1920s, '30s, and '40s.[84] By the late 1950s, Tran Huy Lieu had already written veritable landmarks of Vietnamese historiography: a three-volume *History of 80 Years against the French,* and a twelve-volume *Historical Reference Materials [on] the Modern Vietnamese Revolution*. The point of view Tran Van Giau assailed so vehemently might well be represented in the following quote from Tran Huy Lieu:

> An incontestable fact is that in a colony like Viet Nam, the working class was not generated by indigenous capitalism. But if anybody believes that the Vietnamese working class came into being before the Vietnamese bourgeoisie, he still has some deeper research to do. . . . From 1920 to 1925, even though struggles appeared *sporadically* in some places where workers were concentrated, most of them were *singular, spontaneous,* and lacking unity and organization. At that time, demands and fighting slogans mostly belonged to the economic realm and did not yet have a political character. A very small number of workers among the progressive ranks which were influenced by movements from outside, or a few *isolated* organizations do not permit to say that this was a workers' movement.

Even for 1925–28, the period between the walkout at Ba Son and the establishment of communist organizations, Tran Huy Lieu did not believe that workers constituted a separate social force;[85] whereas Tran Van Giau, as we have seen, put a distinct labor movement at the core of a new "democratic and national-revolutionary" anticolonialism during those years.

In Sai Gon in 1925, the newspaper *Dong Phap Thoi Bao,* where Tran

Huy Lieu was working as a young editor, had barely mentioned the strike at Ba Son.[86] And in all of his later historical studies and memoirs, Tran Huy Lieu never mentioned the strike and dealt with pre-1929 labor only in passing.[87] Instead he wrote extensively about what he had once been part of: Sai Gon's intelligentsia of the mid-1920s with its journalist circles and elite discussion groups, and the changing alliances and associations among anticolonial middle class progressives and entrepreneurs. Against those priorities Tran Van Giau's arguments clashed head-on.

Thus, just as Ton Duc Thang used the doctored version of the strike at Ba Son to recoup his lost revolutionary identity, Tran Van Giau exploited it as argumentative ammunition in an attack on another Vietnamese historiographical school represented by Tran Huy Lieu. He utilized the strike at the Sai Gon arsenal in the summer of 1925 to support his emphasis of the working class's distinct and important role in Vietnamese anticolonialism of the 1920s—at least as far as the south of Viet Nam was concerned!

FINALLY, THEREFORE, we must take into account that Tran Van Giau and his historical witnesses, Ton Duc Thang among them, were all southerners exiled in the north. At the time their engineered account was published, hopes for a quick reunification of the partitioned country were dashed. At Geneva in 1954, the 17th parallel had been established as a temporary cease-fire line to disentangle revolutionary and French-controlled military forces. All-Vietnamese elections were to produce a unified government for the entire country by 1956. But soon the United States, hostile to the Geneva Accords from the start, muscled their way into southern Viet Nam and replaced France as Western overlords. With strong U.S. encouragement, expecting electoral defeat to Ho Chi Minh's DRVN, the Sai Gon-based government of Ngo Dinh Diem, now calling itself the Republic of Viet Nam (RVN), prevented the elections from taking place. After years of fighting to overcome the French-imposed artificial division of Viet Nam, the dream of an independent, unified country remained unfulfilled once again because of another Western intervention.

What had begun as a temporary relocation to the north now became a northern exile of unknown duration for many southern revolutionaries. Feelings of being overlooked and marginalized by northerners, of not fitting in, were widespread among them. In addition, many southerners were impatient with the priority of the DRVN of first consolidating the party-led state in the northern half of the country after the costly years of war against the French. They resented the party's wait-and-see attitude toward the regime of Ngo Dinh Diem, which, wholly financed and armed by the United States, was unleashing a suppression campaign against remaining revolutionaries in the south. In April 1959, János Radványi, then a Hungarian diplomat (who defected to the United States in 1967), took part in an official state visit to the DRVN. He reported the following scene at a large ceremonial occasion in the garden of the presidential palace in Ha Noi:

> In one corner of the tent, clustered together and talking among themselves, were the South Vietnamese living in Hanoi. Apparently, the Northern leadership regarded them rather like poor relations—to be tolerated but virtually ignored. At any rate, no one seemed to pay much attention to them. . . . [Radványi] started a conversation with one of the South Vietnamese, Nguyen Huu Tho . . . [who] flatly stated that the situation in South Vietnam was ripe for revolutionary guerrilla activity . . . But still the guerrillas must stay their hand, he concluded with heavy sarcasm, because Hanoi contended the time was not right for action.

Radványi also writes that Prime Minister Pham Van Dong acknowledged these differences between northern and southern party members and "discoursed at length on the worries caused by South Vietnamese guerrilla leaders residing in Hanoi."[88]

In the light of these regional tensions, the Sai Gon shipyard workers' strike of 1925, as propagated by southerners in Ha Noi in the late 1950s, was not just an attack on a rival historiographical school that disagreed on matters of historical emphasis and analysis. Even more, it was an early attempt to give revolutionary credit to the south. This regionalist argument identified the origins of proletarian internationalism in Viet Nam as having appeared in the strike at Ba Son, led by Ton Duc Thang's secret labor union. Therefore, it insisted, a distinct, organized, and politicized Vietnamese labor movement appeared first in the south in 1925, years before a northern counterpart was created by Ha Noi-based communist organizations. Ironically, the portrayal of Sai Gon workers as politically advanced prior to their northern comrades came at the cost of denying them the real agency they had so clearly exhibited in the protests against Courthial in July 1925.

Unlike the Black Sea story, however, Ton Duc Thang's and Tran Van Giau's Ba Son tale was not embraced by all revolutionaries. The transplanting of proletarian internationalism from Sevastopol into Vietnamese soil instead met with some historiographical resistance. In the *post-partition moment* of the late 1950s, Ton and Tran Van Giau created an ancestry of Vietnamese proletarian internationalism that would be imagined mainly by southerners and largely rejected by northerners. To be sure, the historiographical dispute over the strike at Ba Son and the role of the southern labor movement was couched in prerequisite Marxist terminology and still rather muted overall. Nonetheless, it carried seeds of sharp regional divisions within Vietnamese communism, where southerners came to feel increasingly displaced and treated condescendingly as less accomplished in the common endeavor of national and social liberation. From then on, Ton's imagined ancestries became part of a distinctly southern revolutionary identity. Freed of wartime pressures to close ranks once the Revolution triumphed over the Americans and the RVN in 1975 and reunited the country, this identity of southern revolutionaries was bound to (re-)surface and assert itself more forcefully. In the following chapter, these regional tensions will be traced in vigorous post-unification debates over the correct assessment of Ton Duc Thang's secret labor union.

POSTSCRIPT: In 1995 I sent copies of my core archival and documentary evidence regarding the strike to the Ton Duc Thang Museum in Sai Gon and to the historical department of Ba Son military shipyard.[89] Even earlier, in a workshop held in Ha Noi in May 1992, I shared my findings on the walkout with a number of historians who had published on the events in 1925.[90] In recent years, however, versions of the strike at Ba Son continued to be published in Viet Nam that closely adhere to Ton Duc Thang's and Tran Van Giau's account. Among the authors of these recent publications were some of those with whom I had shared my data, including the Ba Son shipyard itself.[91] Not one of them used any of the documents I had provided, or, for that matter, analyzed or questioned them. In fact, no one even mentioned the existence of these sources that so fundamentally challenge the veracity of Ton Duc Thang's and Tran Van Giau's creation of striking images.

CHAPTER 5

The Secret Labor Union in the Post-Unification Moment

UNTIL 1983, the DRVN and its successor state, the Socialist Republic of Viet Nam (SRVN), celebrated 20 July as Labor Union Day, commemorating the unification of several labor organizations under the General Labor Confederation of Viet Nam on that day in 1946. In a directive of June 1983, however, the politburo of the Vietnamese Communist Party (VNCP) decided, "in order to conform with the realities of the revolutionary history of the Vietnamese labor unions, . . . that the founding day of the Vietnamese Labor Union is July 28, 1929, when the Congress for the Foundation of the General Red Labor Union of Bac Ky [Tonkin] convened under the leadership of the Communist Party of Indochina."[1] Not surprisingly, given that it came from the VNCP politburo, this decision was adopted a few months later in 1983 by the Fifth All-Vietnamese Labor Union Congress. The General Red Labor Union of Tonkin was thus officially recognized as the ultimate precursor and the earliest organizational root for the present Viet Nam Federation of Trade Unions (VFTU),[2] and since 1984, the Socialist Republic of Viet Nam has celebrated 28 July (1929) as the Founding Day of the Vietnamese Labor Union.

Some five years after these changes, however, in August 1988, at the "Symposium on President Ton Duc Thang in Commemoration of the Centennial of His Birth" in Long Xuyen, An Giang, the politburo decision of 1983 came under strong criticism. Symposium participants were discussing the so-called "secret labor union" that Ton Duc Thang supposedly founded and led in the early 1920s in Sai Gon. To many of these symposium participants, the claim that this union was the first such organization in Viet Nam seemed undeniable, and its influence on the development of the Vietnamese working class appeared crucial. In consequence, they called for—indeed, demanded—not only a revision of the politburo ruling that had favored 28 July 1929, but also the official recognition that Ton's much earlier founding of the secret labor union constituted the real birth of Vietnamese unionism. The symposium, which was attended mostly by cadres who were engaged in the fields of cultural work, information, and propaganda, and by historians with VNCP affiliations, marked the argumentative and emotional climax of a historiographical debate that already had been smoldering for some years and that had, in fact, originated in the late 1950s in connection with Ton Duc Thang's and Tran Van Giau's first historical account of the strike at Ba Son.

This chapter will trace the debate on Ton Duc Thang's secret labor union over time, identify some of its issues, and discuss the arguments put forward. On the surface, the controversy centered on whether Ton's organization could be considered to have been the country's first union, what a correct historical assessment of its role in Vietnamese labor history should be, and whether such an evaluation warranted a change in the celebration of Labor Union Day. But my analysis intends to show further that, beyond these arguments, an undercurrent of quite different concerns and tensions existed that, however, either remained unaddressed or was hidden within the historiographical discourse. A closer reading of key texts of the debate on the secret labor union will show that, after the Revolution had achieved final military victory in 1975, regional identities played an ever more pronounced role in the construction of historical imaginations in Viet Nam.

ACCOUNTS OF THE SECRET LABOR UNION

Regardless of the side they took in the debate, Vietnamese historians and information cadres all readily acknowledged that Ton Duc Thang had been the person who singularly gave life and meaning to the labor union. Indeed, without a proper appreciation of Ton's alleged activities prior to the union's founding (and, to some extent, also of those after its dissolution), the controversy would have made no sense. By the time of the symposium, it was an established "fact" that Ton had worked as a mechanic during the 1910s and had gathered extensive experience of organized labor actions while working among the French proletariat in the arsenal of Toulon. His celebrated hoisting of the Red Flag in the Black Sea Mutiny was proof of his proletarian internationalism and advanced class consciousness. After his return to Sai Gon, possibly in late 1920, he therefore began organizing the secret labor union.

What do we know about the union, or rather, on what historical information was its historiography during the controversy of the 1980s grounded? Undoubtedly, the most authoritative account of the secret labor union of Sai Gon was given by the historian Tran Van Giau in 1958, a text to which all later publications frequently refer and from which they liberally quote. It should be noted, though, that Tran Van Giau's description was entirely based on an interview with Ton Duc Thang that took place on 7 February 1958.[3] Nobody has ever found a single written document pertaining to the organization. My own archival searches turned up nothing, not even reports of the usually extremely well informed French secret police. The Sûreté had been very successful in the 1920s in infiltrating associations and monitoring activities deemed potentially or actually threatening to French colonial dominion over Indochina. Yet, a large clandestine union that at its height in 1925 supposedly organized the strike at Ba Son and had several hundred members somehow managed to remain entirely undetected.

Furthermore, we have already seen in chapter 1 and in the person of the octogenarian worker Duong Quang Dong how unreliable other "recollections" of an alleged union member turned out to be. With his initial postwar claim of association in the 1920s with the revolutionary hero Ton Duc Thang came a measure of local fame and privilege for Duong Quang Dong. And the more frequent public recognition produced embellishments in Duong Quang Dong's story, the more it prevented historians from challenging his inaccuracies. In the end, we are left with Ton Duc Thang's detailed portrayal of his union, which, self-interested as it may be, cannot be verified.

ACCORDING TO TON'S RECOLLECTIONS, writes Tran Van Giau, many Vietnamese workers returning to Sai Gon from metropolitan service after World War I (of whom he was one) had become politicized through radical French labor politics and unionist actions. Although many other Vietnamese returnees from France had no clear political convictions—some "backward" ones even praised the French—to be sure, some workers had become anti-imperialists in Europe, and through their influence a consciousness was sprouting that workers ought to unite and organize. Thus, in 1920 or 1921, Ton began organizing a secret labor union in Sai Gon-Cho Lon, "the first in Viet Nam."[4]

Its goals were mutual aid, the defense of workers' rights, and "to oppose imperialism and capitalism." Union cells were established over time in all major industrial and commercial enterprises of the city or, if lacking sufficient numbers for a workplace cell, in neighborhoods. Ton Duc Thang was the head of a five-person Executive Committee. By 1925, the union had more than three hundred members, making it, in Tran Van Giau's analysis, "the biggest and most active secret organization in Viet Nam" of its time.[5]

Was this union, if it indeed existed, really Viet Nam's first? According to archival sources and published accounts, there were quite a number of ethnic Chinese unions in Cho Lon, Sai Gon's predominantly Chinese section. These unions or guilds might have been founded before the 1920s. For 1926/27, French sources listed some seventy-three *syndicats* for Cho Lon with more than eleven thousand members and close ties with the radical Chinese labor movement centered in left-wing republican Canton.[6] It is thus quite likely that unionism *in Viet Nam* began among ethnic Chinese workers, while Ton's might have been the first ethnic Vietnamese union. This distinction, I suppose, could have been deliberately blurred by Vietnamese historians after independence in order to create a Vietnamese working-class legacy.[7]

How did Ton Duc Thang go about organizing the secret labor union? In 1958, in his interview with Tran Van Giau, he specified early labor union activities:

> The union had no written statutes. . . . It was up to each member to pay dues, normally not exceeding a day's wage per month. The union had no headquarters. . . . Usually, monthly meetings were held [in private homes] on the city's outskirts, using banquets of ancestral offerings as a cover. The union had cells at the power stations of Sai Gon and Cho Quan, at Ba Son, at FACI [Forges, Ateliers et Chantiers d'Indochine Co.], and where there were [too] few members [for a work cell], [men from various shops] formed units within their residential areas. Its field of activity was restricted to Sai Gon-Cho Lon.[8]

Copies of radical French newspapers, such as *L'Humanité* and *La Vie ouvrière,* organs of the French Communist Party and of the Confédération Générale du Travail, which were smuggled into Cochinchina by Vietnamese sailors, circulated among the union members. Martial arts practices and rowboat outings on the Sai Gon River were other activities of members, affording them cover for their meetings. The union took part in all open demonstrations in Sai Gon at that time but kept strict secrecy vis-à-vis other progressive organizations, like those of Nguyen An Ninh. "We stood outside his newspaper office," recalled Ton Duc Thang, "but cheered him on [only by] looking inside."[9] However, there was one interesting exception: Ton himself served as the union's liaison with trade unions of ethnic Chinese workers in Cho Lon to ensure mutual (financial) support during times of labor protests. Until 1924/25, however, Ton's secret labor union was too weak for organizing actions on and of its own. Its organizing and propagating activities began in the period just before the strike at Ba Son. Then, the union became "the biggest and most active secret organization" in Indochina.

According to Ton Duc Thang, the union's leadership was organized in an Executive Committee and comprised as "Chairman: Ton Duc Thang (mechanic at Cho Quan power station); Vice-Chairman: Nguyen Van Can (locksmith at FACI); Secretary: Manh (painter at Cho Quan power station); Treasurer: Sam (turner at Sai Gon power station)."[10] Most likely, the full name of the treasurer was Dang Van Sam. In the big Sûreté crackdown on the Cochinchinese resistance in 1929, after the botched intra-VRYL murder case of the rue Barbier, Ton Duc Thang was arrested along with Dang Van Sam and Nguyen Van Can. A certain Manh remained at large. Nguyen Van Can's court case was quashed, but Ton Duc Thang and Dang Van Sam received sentences of twenty and ten years of forced labor. Ton and Dang had worked together in the early 1920s, when they ran a car-repair shop in Phu Nhuan, Dang's home on the northern outskirts of Sai Gon. On this last point, another source elaborates that, upon his return from Europe, Ton refused to work as a mechanic for French-run enterprises and instead opened an auto-repair shop with fellow workers. Such a legal enterprise provided some jobs but also secretly served as a center for long-term planning and communications with other workplaces during the initial years of the union's existence.[11]

The high point of the union's activism came with its alleged organization of the famous strike at the Ba Son navy shipyard. Chapter 4 has already shown how Ton Duc Thang and Tran Van Giau exaggerated the events of the summer of 1925: in their engineered version, a French warship arrived in Sai Gon to undergo "urgent" repairs at Ba Son to be able to reinforce Western forces in China, where a huge anti-imperialist movement of strikes and boycotts was targeting foreign concessions. Ton's union immediately decided to support the Chinese anti-imperialists by delaying the warship's departure as long as possible. Under the pretext of economic demands, Ba Son's workforce staged what has since commonly been seen as Viet Nam's first political and internationalist strike. When threats of a lockout had no effect because the strike received union-raised financial support from all over Sai Gon, Ba Son's management had to give in to the demands. The union, however, was said to have slowed down the repairs so much that the warship left Sai Gon only at the end of November 1925. To recap further, this "successful" strike marked for Tran Van Giau a turning point for the Vietnamese working class, which was now a social force of its own: its actions were no longer spontaneous and solely economically motivated but were now organized, union-led, conscious, and politically motivated. The working class, however, still lacked the guidance of a Communist Party.

Tran Van Giau reports, finally, that in late 1926, cadres of the proto-communist Vietnamese Revolutionary Youth League (VRYL), who had come to Sai Gon from Guangzhou to build a Cochinchinese branch of the VRYL, established contact with the secret labor union. Ton Duc Thang and probably quite a few other union members then joined the VRYL, and the secret labor union of Sai Gon-Cho Lon ceased to exist.[12] Ton Duc Thang and some of his comrades of the former union would come to serve in leading positions of the VRYL's Sai Gon and Cochinchina committees.

FOR MORE THAN TWENTY YEARS, Tran Van Giau's account remained the only description of Ton Duc Thang's secret labor union and its activities. It was, for example, notably absent from the "(First Draft) History of the Vietnamese Workers' and Labor Union Movement," published in 1974 in Ha Noi by the official Research Commission for Vietnamese Labor Union History. While celebrating Ton Duc Thang's act of internationalism in the Black Sea and the "successful" strike at Ba Son in 1925 as the first political strike of Vietnamese workers, the book made no mention of Ton's secret labor union and its alleged leadership role in the strike at Ba Son.[13]

Instead it argued that workers' organizations before 1928 were only mutual aid associations modeled on the deeply rooted solidarity culture of peasant life, from which, after all, most workers had come. Nguyen Ai Quoc's booklet *Duong Kach Menh* had introduced concrete ideas of unionizing tasks "for the first time" in 1927. The so-called proletarianization drive of the VRYL then promptly put these directives into action in 1928. Consequently, the "first," still scattered labor unions had appeared in late 1928 in Tonkin and Annam and, at the same time, had been the "first labor unions under the influence of a revolutionary labor union ideology." In other words, an advanced ideology was the necessary precondition for the initial formation of "real"—revolutionary—unions. The workers movement was therefore only then prepared to pass from a period of "spontaneous" to a period of "conscious" actions, a direct contradiction of Tran Van Giau, who, after all, had made the strike at Ba Son in 1925 the symbolic turning point of this particular transformation.

Once the official labor union history of 1974 had moved the emergence of a conscious labor movement from 1925 to 1928, it made a further and critical distinction between "red" and "yellow" unions. The color red, I suggest, marked the adherence to the Third (Communist) Internationale, while yellow meant adhering to the Second (Socialist) Internationale. The official history laid out a clear—politically correct, so to say—sequence in which unions would appear: a revolutionary ideology transformed a directionless workers' movement to becoming conscious and forming first revolutionary unions. But for this process to be complete, such revolutionary unions had to come under the proper organizational guidance; they had to become red, communist-led. Which revolutionary organization, then, was identified to have undertaken this crucial final step? The book argued that it was the so-called Communist Party of Indochina, an ideologically more "advanced" faction that had split from the VRYL in 1929 and was based mainly in Tonkin. It was this regional faction that finally transformed the first revolutionary unions into "red" labor unions with a clear communist-revolutionary outlook. Once "red," these labor unions were then quickly united by the Communist Party of Indochina on 28 July 1929, when the General Red Labor Union of Bac Ky [Tonkin] was created. The book concluded its argumentation with an authoritative quote from Le Duan, the party's general secretary: "In Viet Nam, in contrast to developed capitalist countries, it was the vanguard party of the working class that founded labor unions to organize, educate, and mobilize workers."[14]

With this publication in 1974, the DLD wished to reconfirm its orthodox view of Vietnamese labor history vis-à-vis Tran Van Giau's version. Not that Tran Van Giau had ever been an iconoclastic or very idiosyncratic historian. His account, however, of a labor union active in the *early* 1920s and supposedly bringing the labor movement to new heights all by itself—*prior* to the introduction in Viet Nam of a revolutionary ideology and Communist Party—had violated the orthodox and mechanistic master script the party imposed on the past: all major developmental steps in the steadily forward-moving revolutionary history could only have been brought about by the vanguard party. Therefore, in 1974, there was just a short nod toward then-president Ton Duc Thang for his Black Sea deed, but his alleged secret labor union could not, and therefore *did* not, exist in a period that could not have produced anything but mutual aid associations. By its very silence about Tran Van Giau's earlier account of Ton Duc Thang's labor organization, the book sought to set the record straight.

And so, between these two poles of competing historical narratives (both of which nevertheless remained within the framework of Marxist-Leninist historical analysis), the stage was finally set for the historiographical controversy about Ton Duc Thang's secret labor union. It took a certain changed historical environment, however, to allow such a debate to take place. During the years of all-out warfare with American forces and their Vietnamese allies, the Revolution would not have tolerated divisions of the sort that eventually emerged in the 1980s. Before detailing the debate over the secret labor union, we therefore need to consider briefly the years immediately after the Revolution's military victory in 1975, the post-unification moment.

AFTER HAVING SHARED with Tran Van Giau in 1957 and 1958 his accounts of the clandestine Sai Gon union and the strike at Ba Son, Ton Duc Thang never again took any discernible part in furthering or amending those imagined ancestries of Vietnamese communism that had become closely tied to his biography. We can speculate that Ton was simply content with having re-created in the strike at Ba Son his aura of personal mystique from the days when he still had wielded control over his fantastic Black Sea tale. It was the mystique of a seasoned and successful revolutionary who had been centrally yet inconspicuously involved in events of great historic import. Perhaps he had learned from the disastrous Red Flag episode that it was unwise to provide too much detail.

In the fifteen years of all-engulfing warfare in Viet Nam, between the resumption of armed revolutionary struggle in the south in 1960 and the headlong flight of the last Americans and the unconditional surrender of the Sai Gon government in 1975 that marked the Revolution's ultimate triumph, Ton Duc Thang had served as the DRVN's vice president and, after Ho Chi Minh's death in 1969, as the country's president. Although possessing practically no intraparty influence, he was the Revolution's public face in a dual symbolic function: as the rare genuine proletarian within the leadership, he represented the party's social revolutionary project, and as Ho's "close battle friend" from the south,[15] he personified its moral claim to waging war for the south's liberation, national unity, and independence from foreign domination.

In 1975, these revolutionary ideals, so bitterly fought over in the carnage of a most devastating conflict of not only Vietnamese or even Indochinese but also of global proportions, seemed finally within reach. President Ton Duc Thang was in his late eighties when he returned to Sai Gon for the victory parade (and a brief visit to Ba Son); it was forty-six years since he had last been in the city as a free man. Soon after, now a frail figurehead leader of his country, he presided over the formalizations of the Revolution's goals: in 1976, south and north were officially united, the Democratic Republic of Viet Nam became the Socialist Republic of Viet Nam, and the Vietnamese Workers' Party absorbed southern revolutionary parties and organizations and renamed itself the Vietnamese Communist Party. Sai Gon was officially called Ho Chi Minh City.

But the takeover of the south, the "liberation" that so very many had died for and many more supportive of the Revolution had long wished for, was undertaken by the party in a heavy-handed and unyielding manner. Promises had been made before and immediately after the historic victory over the southern state and its U.S. overlord. These had been promises of magnanimous reconciliation, dialogue, and collaboration among all patriotic Vietnamese to rebuild the utterly destroyed homeland, but they were soon broken: Thousands of former functionaries and military personnel of the Sai Gon regime were indefinitely imprisoned in so-called "reeducation" camps. Many southern families, whose allegiance to the party was deemed suspect, became victims of massive discrimination in schooling, housing, and employment, and often of forced relocation from the cities to reclaim for farming remote rural areas ravaged by warfare. Furthermore, even the Revolution's southern partisans felt as if their liberated homeland had been conquered as they suffered suspicion, condescension, and marginalization at the hands of their northern comrades. More often than not, local cadres were subordinated to, or were replaced by, northern Party apparatchiks, and southern revolutionary organizations were disbanded or neutralized through absorption into larger, "national" counterparts controlled from and by Ha Noi.

We have seen in chapter 4 how regional tensions within the Revolution's ranks had already existed in the post-partition moment of the later 1950s. But subsequent warfare had demanded solidarity and outward unity. Now, after national unification, regional divisions were able to resurface amid the rising frustrations of southern revolutionaries. They were denied the leading role in governing the south that they thought they had rightfully earned in the national revolutionary struggle. Even more, in their rush toward rapid socialist transformation of the southern economy, northerners seemed to ignore the local expertise of their southern comrades and to brush aside their cautions that unification needed a much more measured pace. And perhaps worst of all, it appeared that soon after victory, southern contributions to the revolutionary struggle and its final triumph were systematically downplayed, denigrated, and even silenced. In the end, many southern revolutionaries felt disillusioned, bitter and betrayed.[16] The debate over a correct historical evaluation of Ton Duc Thang's secret labor union that ensued in the 1980s must be read against the background of these postwar developments.

THE EARLY DEBATE OVER THE UNION

In his ninety-second year of life, Ton Duc Thang passed away in March 1980. In the same year, a brief but telling passage in a book on "The Propagation of Marxism-Leninism and the First Communist Organizations in [Sai Gon]" pertained to Ton Duc Thang's clandestine union and the strike at Ba Son. The authors of the "Commission for the Research of Party History of Ho Chi Minh City"—Luu Phuong Thanh being one of them—closely adhered to Tran Van Giau's earlier account from the 1950s. Some marked variances, however, should be emphasized. First, besides his experiences with French labor politics, Ton Duc Thang's founding of the union was now said to have also been influenced by the Russian October Revolution (which Ton had supposedly defended in the Black Sea). Second, the organization was for the first time called the "secret *red* labor union." Third, no more mention was made of the ethnic Chinese trade unions with which Ton Duc Thang claimed to have cooperated. And fourth and most important, for the first time the union was identified as "the first labor union in Viet Nam."[17]

These four points were, of course, not made accidentally: the union's proclamation as the first *in Viet Nam* necessitated the omission of the Hoa Kieu unions of Cho Lon. And, aware of the labor history of 1974, the authors tried to placate orthodox arguments and bolstered their claim by a reference to influences of the sacrosanct October Revolution on Ton Duc Thang, as well as by attaching the label "red" to the secret labor union.

In 1982, the official VNCP biography of Ton Duc Thang was published by the Central Commission for the Research of Party History in Ha Noi (this book will be the subject of chapter 6). More details about Ton's activities in the early 1920s were given, albeit without revealing the sources of this information. The authors claimed that, after his return to Sai Gon, Ton had rejected a French employment offer at the École des mécaniciens asiatiques that had been intended to "bribe" him and keep him under surveillance. Instead, he and some friends opened a car-repair shop in the suburb of Phu Nhuan to provide jobs and vocational training for some unemployed comrades and to have a basis for Ton's union organizing activities. After the strike at Ba Son—retold in his own and Tran Van Giau's glorifying version—Ton Duc Thang supposedly also began establishing union cells outside Sai Gon-Cho Lon. Unlike the party historians of its subdivision in Ho Chi Minh City in 1980, however, the Central Commission for the Research of Party History was neither willing to call the union "red" nor "the first." On the other hand, in their eulogy of the recently deceased president Ton Duc Thang, the authors could not ignore his claims altogether—as the official labor history had done in 1974—that he had indeed led a secret labor union.[18]

The next account of Ton's secret labor union and the Ba Son walk-out appeared in 1984. Soon after the politburo decision (and its subsequent adoption by the Fifth All-Vietnamese Labor Union Congress) in 1983 recognizing 28 July 1929 as the Founding Day of the Vietnamese Labor Union, a booklet by the Propaganda Commission of the Viet Nam Federation of Trade Unions (VFTU) sought to popularize the importance of 28 July 1929. Summing up prior events in Vietnamese labor history, the booklet ostensibly described the Ba Son strike in 1925 in accordance with Ton Duc Thang's and Tran Van Giau's version as successful and the first political and internationalist strike of the country's working-class movement. The union's significance, however, compared with earlier descriptions of Ton's secret labor union of Sai Gon-Cho Lon, was drastically downplayed: "The labor union of Ba Son existed and was active only for a number of years, and only in the confines of Ba Son, without tendencies to develop any further."[19]

Unlike in 1974, the proponents of an orthodox interpretation of Viet Nam's labor history obviously could no longer afford to simply ignore publications—now slowly growing in number—on the secret labor union. Instead, they grudgingly acknowledged its existence but immediately settled for a sloppily argued, negative assessment that possibly was even worse in a tactical sense. For the VFTU's hitherto unheard of—and yet official—historical evaluation of Ton Duc Thang's organization as temporary, static, and "confined to Ba Son" must have exacerbated the frustrations of a number of people and heated up a historiographical debate that would come into full swing at the symposium in Long Xuyen in 1988.[20]

In opening shots prior to the symposium, in 1987, Tran Van Giau and Luu Phuong Thanh used new publications of theirs to reiterate and even go beyond their earlier stances on Ton's association. In a telling departure from his 1958 book, Tran Van Giau, who had thus far been the only one to mention Ton Duc Thang's liaison and cooperation with Hoa Kieu trade unions in Cho Lon, now dropped this information altogether. Thus "ethnically" (but not ethically) free to take sides, he concluded: "In Viet Nam, the first labor union came into being in Sai Gon in 1921." He also rejected the orthodox views of his opponents when he argued, again, that "this was no longer a mutual aid or friendship association since, apart from [these] goals, its objective was also to fight capitalism and imperialism." And less cautious than in 1958 about claims for the union's activities, he now wrote simply that it organized "many struggles."[21]

In his new book, Luu Phuong Thanh repeatedly referred to the union in the same way he had in 1980: it had been leading "many of the city's workers' struggles" as a "secret red labor union." Now, however, Luu primarily focused on Ton Duc Thang. After relating how, for example, Ton had arranged rowboat outings on the Sai Gon River for his comrades to read safely the progressive newspapers smuggled into Cochinchina from France, Luu declared him the "first Vietnamese working-class leader." Ton was the "earliest propagator of Uncle Ho [Chi Minh]'s progressive thinking among the Vietnamese working class," who "prepared the earth in the city to make [Uncle Ho's revolutionary] seed quickly sprout, grow, flower, and bear fruit." And thanks to the full incorporation of Ton's union into the Cochinchinese branch of the VRYL in 1927, Luu argued, "the VRYL in Sai Gon was not solely comprised of petty bourgeois like in [Annam and Tonkin], but mostly of workers."[22]

At this point, a few comments seem in order. What can be made of this last, rather cutting remark of Luu Phuong Thanh about which VRYL branch was the more proletarian and thus purer in its revolutionary class makeup? I would argue that shortly before the symposium, the issue of the union's correct historical assessment had already become so charged that underlying stresses were clearly revealed. The historiographical debate now began to resonate with overtones of regional tensions, namely animosities between northerners and southerners.

After all, the southerner Tran Van Giau in 1958 and the official labor union history, published in Ha Noi in 1974, had defined the issue from opposing sides. Ha Noi had avoided mentioning the southern union and linked the founding of Vietnamese unionism to the appearance (in the north) of a "vanguard party." Then again, the argument of the southern VNCP branch in Ho Chi Minh City in 1980 that the "secret *red* labor union," organized in Sai Gon, was the "first" in Viet Nam had been ignored by the Central Party History Commission in Ha Noi in its 1982 biography of Ton Duc Thang. Instead, in 1983 the VNCP politburo and the VFTU—both Ha Noi-based—had moved the national Labor Union Day celebrations to the date of the founding congress (in Ha Noi) of the General Red Labor Union of the North (Tonkin). This 1929 congress had convened under the guidance of the Communist

Party of Indochina, the northern faction after the disintegration of the VRYL. It had at that same time aggressively worked against the southern "Annam Communism" faction of the ex-VRYL,[23] where—no surprise here—many former members of Ton Duc Thang's secret labor union were active. In short, from a date with which everybody could have identified (the creation in 1946 of a *national* labor umbrella organization), Labor Union Day had now been moved—by decree from Ha Noi that smelled of retroactively "taking sides"—to a date smack in the middle of a bitter inner communist regional rivalry. And adding insult to injury, then, a VFTU publication from Ha Noi in 1984, which propagated the "northern" date of 1929, seemingly distorted and drastically downplayed the historical significance of the earlier southern labor union.

By the time the symposium began, the impression that northern viewpoints and organizations always, and often insensitively, prevailed over southern perspectives and associations with regard to Viet Nam's labor history must have appeared irrefutable. At the "Symposium on President Ton Duc Thang," attended in large part by cadres from the south of Viet Nam, the debate about the secret labor union of Sai Gon was consequently put high on the agenda, with hopes that a seemingly skewed picture could be revised and rectified.[24]

AT THE SYMPOSIUM

The symposium on the occasion of Ton Duc Thang's centennial took place in Long Xuyen in conjunction with the solemn inauguration of the so-called Commemorative Area for Ton Duc Thang in nearby My Hoa Hung village. It included his childhood home—freshly renovated as a shrine to the deceased president—and, about fifty meters away, a newly built museum devoted to Ton's life. (Chapter 7 will analyze the commemorative area in detail.) Both the conference and the shrine at Ton's birthplace were conceived and brought about by southern culture cadres of the party and clearly bore the signature of an influential, but soon to be ill-fated southern VNCP faction, the Club of Former Resistance Fighters (hereafter CFRF, Vietn., Cau Lac Bo Nhung Nguoi Khang Chien Cu). First organized in 1986 by former southern guerrilla leaders as an association to give voice to veterans' interests, it soon articulated the simmering postwar grievances over the

Revolution's unconciliatory policies in the south and the continued subordination of southern revolutionaries to northern party people. According to Zachary Abuza,

> The CFRF saw itself as a loyal opposition to the party. This was the first and only attempt to create an organized pressure group within the VNC[P]. Founded in Ho Chi Minh City, its branches spread throughout the south. At its inception, the CFRF claimed 4,000 members and quickly grew to 10,000 by 1988, most of whom were party members. The club was tolerated for several years but only because of the stature of its members.[25]

Not surprisingly, one of the club's founders was Tran Van Giau, who by then had sought for some thirty years to document southern revolutionary ancestries—for example in the 1925 strike at the Sai Gon arsenal and in Ton's secret labor union. Other prominent founders and affiliates were General Tran Van Tra, the highest-ranking military leader of the National Liberation Front (NLF, the southern guerrilla organization between 1960 and 1975), whose work on the contributions of the NLF to the Revolution's triumph Ha Noi had banned immediately after its publication in 1982, Tran Bach Dang, the famous underground party leader of Sai Gon during the anti-American resistance, and Huynh Van Tieng, who, we will remember from chapter 2, had fought with Ton Duc Thang in the early months of the southern anti-French resistance in 1945 and accompanied Ton to France (and to the meeting with André Marty) in the following year. The period in which the CFRF was most influential and highly outspoken in its criticism of the course the Revolution had taken since 1975 was from spring 1988 to spring 1989. Thereafter, however, the VNCP leadership in Ha Noi grew increasingly concerned over the intraparty (and regional) challenge the club posed. Deeply alarmed by the rising turmoil in the disintegrating socialist camp over the remainder of 1989—from the massive prodemocracy demonstrations on Beijing's Tiananmen Square, the democratization policies in Poland and Hungary, to the popular revolts in East Germany, Czechoslovakia, Romania, and Bulgaria—it lashed out against the CFRF, and by spring 1990 the club was banned outright and some of its leaders arrested or put under lengthy house arrests.[26]

The August 1988 symposium on Ton Duc Thang in Long Xuyen, therefore, took place exactly at the height of the CFRF's strength, influence, and confidence. Many of the conference's southern participants were club members, and neither the ensuing debate about Ton's secret labor union nor the commemorative project at Ton's nearby birthplace can be interpreted in isolation from their larger political and regional contexts.

WHAT, THEN, WERE THE MAJOR ARGUMENTS put forward at the symposium with regard to Ton Duc Thang's Sai Gon labor union?

In his paper, unambiguously titled "The Historical Truth Should Be Given Back to the History of the Creation of the Vietnamese Labor Union," Vu Lan, a social scientist from southern Hau Giang province, especially targeted the politburo decision of 1983 and the VFTU pamphlet of 1984 that had so drastically downplayed the importance of Ton Duc Thang's secret labor union. Commemoration days could easily be changed again, he argued. After all, even the Founding Day of the Communist Party had once been celebrated on 6 January before being moved to 2 February 1930. Concerning the VFTU version of the "Ba Son union," Vu Lan was flabbergasted. How could one praise the triumph of the political and internationalist strike of the Ba Son workers, a strike brought about by years of diligent union organizing under most difficult conditions, and then go on to state that "the Ba Son labor union had no tendency for further development"? To Vu Lan, these arguments contradicted each other so blatantly that he insinuated that the authors might have been forced to bend their views to conform with directives from above.

After an excursion into the histories of labor unions abroad and a cursory discussion of developments in Viet Nam up to the 1920s, Vu Lan rejected the idea that labor unions could be created only after a "leading party" came into existence. He concluded that "the birth of [Ton Duc Thang's] labor union in 1920 [as well as its subsequent contributions to Vietnamese unionism] fully combined the necessary elements and criteria according to the theories of the teachers of the international communist workers' movement. It did so in such a correct way that it deserves to be called the founding day of the Vietnamese labor union." With the next All-Vietnamese Labor Union Congress soon to come, Vu Lan called for a revision of the decision favoring 28 July 1929. He could, however, not come up with any concrete alternative date.[27]

Phan Van Nhan, chair of the Research Commission for Party History of Long An Province, sounded a message of equal urgency. He briefly recapitulated all the literature pertinent to the union, recalled Ton Duc Thang's alleged exploits in the Black Sea and his experiences with radical French labor unionism, and recounted major labor protests in Cochinchina during the early 1920s, which he freely associated with Ton's secret labor union. All these historical events, Phan Van Nhan concluded, had a direct relationship to Ton's revolutionary activities and happened long before the birth of the red labor union in Tonkin in 1929. Therefore, the symposium should lobby the VNCP to reconsider its earlier decision and to recognize Ton's labor union as the first such organization in the country, with Ton Duc Thang as the first leader of a revolutionary union.[28]

It fell to Dang Hoa, a historian at the Museum of the Vietnamese Revolution in Ha Noi, to defend the northern perspective. He readily conceded that the secret labor union of Sai Gon was Viet Nam's first labor union. But to Dang Hoa the real question was what position Ton's union occupied in the history of the organization of the Vietnamese working class. In that respect, he cautioned, the total lack of written documents on the union prevented any quick resolution of the issue. So far, all the information about the union had come from recollections, but no one had ever really validated such evidence. Wishful thinking and emotions, he observed, possibly with regard to Vu Lan's and Phan Van Nhan's symposium papers (and historical witnesses of Duong Quang Dong's caliber), which were rich in emotions but poor in substance, were all too often presented as facts but lacked actual proof.

Regarding claims that Ton Duc Thang's experiences of French labor politics led to his founding of the secret labor union later in Sai Gon, Dang Hoa's analysis of the French Socialist Party (FSP) and the General Labor Confederation (CGT) during Ton's sojourn in France suggested that both organizations had made serious ideological mistakes and showed signs of "right deviationist opportunism" among their leadership. Therefore, Dang Hoa indicated, more despite than because of his experiences in France, Ton Duc Thang showed his untiring commitment to organizing the workers of Sai Gon.

Furthermore, reminiscent of arguments already put forward in the official labor history in 1974, one had to distinguish between "red" and "yellow" unions, and unions could only turn "red" under the leadership of a Communist Party. In any case, concluded Dang Hoa, before final conclusions about the secret labor union could be drawn, more time and wider input were needed from "researchers in the whole country"—an indication of how defensive and outnumbered Dang Hoa felt amid the regional tensions at the conference.[29]

Next one up was Luu Phuong Thanh, the author in 1980 and 1987 of the two important contributions to the earlier debate about the union. His report to the symposium was basically a repetition of his article published a year earlier. Two differences should be noted, though. First, he had now dropped the attribute "red" and only referred to Ton's organization as the "secret labor union." I suggest that Luu realized that insisting on the word "red" would only weaken his stance in the historiographical debate now that his opponents had built their case around a distinction between "red" and "yellow" unions. Second, in response to Dang Hoa, he insisted that, despite the absence of a vanguard party, the working class under the leadership of Ton's union never had reformist or opportunist ideas, but rather showed communist tendencies and pro-Soviet leanings.[30]

In a much sharper response to Dang Hoa, To Thanh Tam of the An Giang Propaganda Commission dismissed any notion of an FCP or CGT influence on Ton Duc Thang. Ton's real-life experiences alone, from the workshops of Sai Gon to the Black Sea Mutiny, had already taught him the value of uniting. And even though Ton's union was founded before the Communist Party, To Thanh Tam argued, it never showed any "right deviationist opportunism." In fact, the conformity of the secret labor union's practice with the theories of Nguyen Ai Quoc's booklet *Duong Kach Menh* was remarkable. The union prepared the earth for the revolutionary seed of Nguyen Ai Quoc's ideas and thus conformed to the "laws" of workers' organizations: mutual aid groups would turn into economic and then political organizations, and finally the leading party would be born from them—not the other way around![31]

Tran Bach Dang emphatically seconded To Thanh Tam's points. In his "personal opinion," that, he made a point of saying, he put "in parentheses," he proposed to scrap 28 July 1929 as Labor Union Day in favor of an official, countrywide commemoration of Ton Duc Thang's "red labor union." In the developmental process of the workers' and communist movements of the world, Tran Bach Dang argued, it was *normal* that labor unions were the cradle of communist parties. Indeed, if Vietnamese unions had been founded by a party decision, as the northern orthodoxy had been claiming since 1974, it would constitute nothing less than a deviation from the historical truth![32]

In other words, what To Thanh Tam termed the "formalistic logic"—whether a union had come into being before or after the founding of a Communist Party—was roundly rejected. How could one close one's eyes before historical realities? asked To Thanh Tam. And in clear reference to the ongoing Doi Moi reforms in Viet Nam, patterned on the Soviet Union under Mikhail Gorbachev, he suggested "historical thinking also must have the necessary perestroika." An organization's *practice* had to be the measure for its historical assessment, and "whether an organization was 'red' or 'yellow' was not for its leading party to determine."[33]

We have already observed how north-south rivalries were being played out in this debate. Now, with To Thanh Tam's openly challenging statement, a second dimension of hidden tensions has become fully apparent. After years, northern historiography had finally conceded that Ton Duc Thang's secret labor union had in fact been Viet Nam's first labor union, even before the founding of a Communist Party. But then the north had regrouped, so to say, and now it was arguing that only "red" labor unions—becoming "red," of course, only under the leadership of the vanguard party—occupied a worthy (revolutionary) position in the history of the Vietnamese working class to justify national commemoration on a Labor Union Day. In other words, the VNCP still held the keys, and a shift away from 28 July 1929, toward a recognition of Ton Duc Thang's secret labor union as the earliest manifestation of Viet Nam's present unionism was as unlikely as ever. At this point, with To Thanh Tam's anger expressing itself in his outburst that this "is not for its leading party to determine," the historiographical controversy about Ton Duc Thang's union had turned into nothing less than a veritable challenge to the right of the VNCP to impose its orthodox exegesis of the past onto the nation's historical memory.

A POSTSCRIPT TO THE DEBATE, which had effectively been stifled with the banning of the CFRF in 1990: In 1992, the historians Dang Hoa, Do Quang Hung, and Pham Xanh dismissively told me in Ha Noi that they regarded the so-called "secret labor union" of Ton Duc Thang to have been nothing more than a social "club." On the other hand, when I met To Thanh Tam in Long Xuyen, he still hoped, albeit with a good measure of frustration, that Ton's union would eventually be officially recognized. When I mentioned there was no clear founding day for Ton's union—its beginnings variously dated sometime late in 1920 or early 1921—he told me that 4 August (1925), the alleged outbreak of the strike at Ba Son upon the *Jules Michelet's* arrival in Sai Gon, would be a good choice to celebrate Labor Union Day.

What I have tried to show in this chapter is that underneath a historiographical debate on the proper historical assessment of a secret labor union in Sai Gon, a hidden agenda of regional and ideological-political concerns had been at work. In a certain sense, the right of the Vietnamese south to reclaim its identity was demanded, just as much as the right of the VNCP to define a national discourse of and about the past was challenged. I would even argue that in this post-unification moment, these deeper concerns over how to "unfix" history and how the north had always taken the credit were actually the stronger driving forces of the debate than its obvious historiographical subject, Ton Duc Thang's so-called "secret labor union." In other words, the debate was less over the ancestry of the Vietnamese working-class movement itself and more over who (or which identities) could *claim* ancestry to this historical process. What is quite surprising, however, is that this was not just a case of what Phan Huy Le rightfully criticizes as the "politicization of history,"[34] of talking about the past in order to talk about the present, but a complex process in which deeply embedded identities, complexes, and memories were triggered and—inextricably intertwined—transcended the present, the past, and the historical imagination.

PART III

Commemorations

CHAPTER 6

Telling Life: Ton Duc Thang's Official Biography in the Posthumous Moment

ON 30 MARCH 1980, Ton Duc Thang died in Ha Noi at the age of ninety-one after a period of steady physical decline.[1] He was buried at Mai Dich state cemetery outside Ha Noi with its hierarchically ordered layout, where—absent Ho Chi Minh's remains, which are exhibited in a mausoleum—he received the most prominent burial site. Since then, how has Viet Nam remembered its second president? As chapters 4 and 5 have argued, already during Ton's lifetime, certain episodes of his biography became contested and utilized in veiled disagreements between broadly regionally defined factions of the party. Similar tensions manifested themselves after Ton's death in commemorative projects around the country, of which the two most significant ones will be the subjects of chapters 6 and 7. In the new historical contexts and dramatically changing political-cultural environments of the 1980s, differences in biographical accentuations and various interpretations of the meaning of Ton's life were reflective of, and contributed to, much larger intraparty debates. In a sense, the celebration of the life of an accomplished, unassailable revolutionary became a safe ersatz arena for contests about nothing less than the ancestries, the spirit, and the future direction of the Vietnamese Revolution.

WITHIN THE SUBSTANTIAL BODY of biographical writing on Ton Duc Thang, clustered either in the years immediately following his death in 1980 or around Ton's centennial anniversary in 1988, one text stands out: *Comrade Ton Duc Thang, an Exemplary Staunch Communist Fighter,* published in 1982 by the Central Commission for the Research of Party History of the Vietnamese Communist Party.[2] Because of its production so close to the central VNCP leadership, this booklet undoubtedly was meant as Ton's official, party-sanctioned biography. It represents most clearly the commemorative concerns emanating from the northern core of communist state power, and this chapter will closely examine some of the text's features: its discursive and, in a broad sense, aesthetic makeup, its built-in agenda of Telling Life, and its historical-political functions. That an official biography is highly didactic and prone to hagiography can be assumed to be a foregone conclusion. But how, more precisely, does this particular pamphlet work? For Ton Duc Thang's biographers, what made his life telling?

Beyond the specific text, an examination of its generic form will show that official biographies inherently contain complex mixtures of seemingly contradictory textual movements of appropriation and exclusion, containment and expansion. These phenomena are inseparable from the underlying paradigm of Marxian historical materialism after which such biographical writings are patterned. The notion of a highly deterministic historical process that moves in steady progression according to scientific laws is therefore predictable, and the claims of a revolutionary vanguard party as its most progressive human force might provide a certain kind of comfort, or self-flattery, for those who see themselves belonging to the leading camp. Yet, more important, a control of the present is to some degree dependent on the control of, or at least dominance over, the exegesis of history. Therefore, people who define themselves as the historical vanguard are trapped in a never-ending legitimizing, indeed de- and re-legitimizing, process, a historiographical Sisyphean labor, of fitting the past, including their own and their ancestry's, to this very paradigm. In other words, the custodians of a teleological historical model of predictability are engaged in a constant battle against the unpredictability of history, against the unsettling impermanence of historical truth. Ton's official party biography is a product of this perpetual self-legitimizing task and part of a more expansive genre of prescriptive texts—like, for example, communist prison memoirs and Ho Chi Minh stories—that aim to "correctly" decode the past of Vietnamese communism.

WHEN TON DUC THANG'S official biography was published in 1982, the Revolution's momentum from the military triumph of 1975 and rapid unification had almost completely evaporated. The rush toward socialist transformation in the south had resulted in the near-collapse of the southern economy, and hundreds of thousands of southern refugees left the country. Instead of the long yearned-for peace, Viet Nam found itself engaged in a low-level border conflict with an aggressively xenophobic Kampuchea under the genocidal Pol Pot regime. The United States, deeply shaken by its defeat in Viet Nam, imposed a punishing economic embargo that exacerbated the already staggering legacies of an immensely destructive war. Relations with China, which had slowly deteriorated since the early 1970s, completely collapsed when Viet Nam invaded Kampuchea in late 1978, deposed the Chinese-backed Pol Pot, and installed a pro-Vietnamese Khmer government. In February 1979, China invaded northern Viet Nam in retaliation, and only a spirited but costly Vietnamese defense forced a Chinese withdrawal in March.

By the time of Ton Duc Thang's death in 1980, and only five years after the Revolution's ultimate victory, Viet Nam experienced widespread economic malaise and poverty, popular discontent, and international isolation that forced the country to rely almost completely on the support of the Soviet Union. It was a stunning turnaround, brought about equally by the destructions and disruptions of the decades-long revolutionary wars, by postwar political and economic ineptitude of an aging VNCP leadership, and by great military and diplomatic pressures from outside. We need to keep this historical context of the posthumous moment in mind as we undertake an analysis of Ton Duc Thang's official biography.

AFTER A SHORT PREFACE by the publishing house Su That (The Truth), Ton Duc Thang's official biography of 1982 opens with a reprint of "President Ho Chi Minh's congratulations upon conferring the Order of the Gold Star to comrade Ton Duc Thang" on 20 August 1958. In this short address, Ho congratulated Ton on the occasion of his seventieth birthday and praised Ton's long revolutionary activities. After listing the posts that Ton held at that time, Ho declared him "a model of revolutionary morality: all his life industrious, frugal, and incorruptible; a lifelong service with all his heart and strength to the revolution and the people."[3] There is no better biographical introduction than this highly symbolic scene, when the most esteemed national leader gave the highest decoration of the state to Ton as its very first recipient.

The initial chapter of the actual biography, "The Vigorous Youth of the Worker Ton Duc Thang," is ten pages long and covers forty-one years, until 1929. Fully one-third of this chapter is devoted to the events in the Black Sea, while the strike at Ba Son receives less than half that attention. The second chapter, "Seventeen Years in Prison, yet Still Upholding a Staunch Revolutionary Spirit," is slightly longer than the first and deals with Ton's incarceration until 1945. The third, about the period from 1945 to 1980, "Devoted to Serve the Causes of Resistance and of Building Socialism," is about twenty-three pages long, of which the last three talk about the details of President Ton's state funeral. Comparatively overemphasized in proportion to the years covered, the last passages were written in either the most polemic language (regarding China, with which Viet Nam was then in a state of hostilities) or the most protocol-like style (about the funeral).

The booklet ends with a conclusion confirming the strong didactic purposes of this Telling Life. Here the biography makes it clear it understands itself not as a literary form but as a genuinely historical text conveying facts with concrete and prescribed lessons to be learned about the past. The conclusion starts with a long quotation from a "special communiqué" of leading party and state organs of 30 March 1980,[4] extolling Ton Duc Thang's merits. Almost all the rest of the conclusion adheres closely to the main address given by Truong Chinh at the memorial service for Ton on 3 April 1980,[5] without being identified as such. Finally, the booklet erupts in exclamations of pride in Ton Duc Thang on the part of the party, the Vietnamese working class, and the nation.

One can expect a book written by a collective of the Central Commission for the Research of Party History to have been carefully composed and closely screened before publication lest it misrepresent the then-valid political line. The biography's language thus closely adhered to official party terminology. For example, the book's title itself was drawn from descriptions of Ton used in communiqués in the days after his death,[6] and Ho's 1958 characterization of Ton appears almost unchanged, but without acknowledgment, in the publisher's 1982 preface: Ton maintained "the morality of a revolutionary: industrious and frugal, incorruptible, modest, and plain." Furthermore, the booklet is about *comrade* Ton Duc Thang, and even the third person singular form used is *dong chi* (comrade), one of several options in Vietnamese for "he." The biography never deviates from this somewhat official mode of reference to Ton. Close adherence to official terminology is also apparent in characterizations of Ton Duc Thang, evaluations of his role and importance in a given episode, and descriptions of events that took place not long before the book was written in 1982 and that were therefore still sensitive issues: the ongoing tensions with China and the growing diplomatic and economic isolation of Viet Nam, which called for frequent, strongly reassuring invocations of the friendship with the USSR and the two "brother countries" Laos and Kampuchea.[7]

What were possible motivations for this booklet's publication? Of course, one obvious reason was the preservation of the memory of the widely venerated "Uncle Ton," who had died not long before. But the preface also states:

> The Vietnamese Revolution has been able to gain great achievements, but coming tasks will still be very difficult and will demand that everybody must fight as strongly as possible to fulfill the noble cause that our party has pointed out. . . . With the goal of disseminating communists' revolutionary, fighting examples among . . . the readers of our country, especially among our young friends, we publish [this] book.

Thus, various motives for the writing of this biography can be discerned: it aimed at (a) the Communist Party and its followers, who could take pride in a comrade whose exemplary life has been recorded as an honor to the party; at (b) the average Vietnamese, who had to be prepared for the coming, mainly economic, hardships by reminding them how past difficulties were overcome in a successful process personified by Ton Duc Thang; and at (c) Vietnamese youths, who needed guidance and encouragement to be part of a socialist society, and to whom Ton's example might be an inspiration. Additionally, Vietnamese youths were particularly targeted by the biography's emphasis on Ton's special concern for children and adolescents. Pertinent passages are placed right before the paragraphs about Ton's death and funeral; their location near the end of the text highlights their importance to the reader and can be seen as Ton Duc Thang's testament.

HOW, THEN, DID THE OFFICIAL BIOGRAPHY portray Ton Duc Thang's life? We will focus here on a number of aspects: Ton's "origins," his professional training, his sojourn in France and the Black Sea Mutiny, the strike at Ba Son, his arrest and imprisonment, and his post-1945 career.

As will be discussed in the following chapter on his birthplace, Ton was born in August 1888 into a family of prosperous peasants. Well into the 1980s, however, such a higher rural class background was suspect and could never be acknowledged. Therefore, most sources, including the party biography, identified Ton's family as "toiling" or "poor peasants."[8] In 1969, a short official biography released upon his election to the presidency of the DRVN even stated that he came from a "workers' family."[9] In the light of Ton's presidential role as a personification of the communist-led state, it was the party's aspiration to be identified clearly with the oppressed laboring classes, the historically assigned avant-garde of humanity.

The official biography connected the child Ton Duc Thang to Vietnamese anticolonialism. Seven leaders of southern uprisings of the nineteenth century were named, and the "revolutionary tradition of the *nation"* supposedly "had a good influence on his thoughts and sentiments."[10] Here, in a curious maneuver, the child was drawn into a presumably long-established cultural-spiritual current of a higher order; his biographers placed him securely within an imagined historical, "national" continuum that transcended class distinctions and, in some way, diminished their socio-historical relevance. Ton's "origins," which fueled his later development, thus lay in the remarkable confluence of national spiritual heritage and membership in the exploited classes. And so, practically right from the cradle, Ton embarked on a career of a flawless revolutionary, a picture reiterated throughout the biography: in whatever circumstances he found himself, Ton drew the right analyses; whatever progressive current (anticolonialism, anti-feudalism, anticapitalism, anti-interventionism, etc.) was around, he picked it up in due time; whatever kind of correct action (mobilization, protest, show of class consciousness, internationalist solidarity, compassion, etc.) was opportune, Ton engaged in it. This instinct for purest revolutionary conduct, presented from the beginning of his biography, attested to the teleological notion that "correct" consciousness and actions can be scientifically applied to corresponding stages of the historical process. For Ton, always doing the right thing was one kind of origin.

Although most of the accounts differed in details about Ton's vocational training and his first jobs in Sai Gon from 1906 to 1915,[11] Ton's biographers generally agreed that his exposure to the city and to a worker's life was an initiation into anticolonialism and into early forms of organized protest. As one biography put it, "early on, the working-class life trained his patriotic enthusiasm."[12] The statements Ton made in 1957 about that period of his life were usually taken as the evidentiary basis for these views. In that account, as a student of the École des mécaniciens asiatiques, he led a student and shipyard workers' strike against colonial exploitation in 1912. Forced to flee the country in disguise, he worked on merchant vessels and ended up on a French warship in the Black Sea. But as I have argued in chapter 1, Ton did not enter the vocational school until 1915, and he became a navy recruit in 1916. The episode of 1912 was merely a heroic version of 1916, a narrative device to erase the 1916 scene of wartime service recruitment.

By the time of Ton's official party biography, however, new evidence confirming his 1915 enrollment at the École des mécaniciens asiatiques and his recruitment in 1916 had surfaced that was clearly at odds with Ton's earlier statements. We will briefly recall how party biographers reacted: the official biography simply ignored the incompatibility of 1912 and 1916 and instead left both dates intact as two discrete yet parallel events, artificially fitted together by the invention of Ton's looping "return" to Sai Gon in 1915. But further adjustments had to be made: Ton's activism in 1912 would preclude a *re*enrollment at the vocational school in 1915, and so the authors made Ton lead the "strike of 1912" from outside. The ease with which party historians manipulated their data is testimony to the demands of their historiographical Sisyphean labor to align their tale again and again to the ever-heroic, ever-advancing historical model.

Once having acknowledged the navy recruitment in 1916, albeit as a "forced" one, the party account of Ton's life proceeded to give special prominence to the Black Sea Mutiny. But we know from chapters 1–3 that Ton Duc Thang had not been in the Black Sea; for greater effect, he merely transposed his experiences of mass unrest in Toulon in June 1919 to the navy mutinies at Sevastopol in April 1919. By adding the Red Flag to the story around 1951, however, party propagandists overclarified the tale to a degree that Ton was unable to sustain with his memories from Toulon. Pressed for "recollections" in 1957, he was forced to retreat from Sevastopol and place himself on the *Paris* at Constantinople in the summer of 1919, adding only the minimum requirements of the story to his adjusted version; that is, he hoisted the Red Flag and had the *Paris* briefly enter the Black Sea. But saving his story from exposure as a lie came at the terribly high price of cutting the direct link between the alleged show of Vietnamese proletarian internationalism and the Russian October Revolution.

Like all other biographical accounts that appeared after 1957, Ton's party biography of 1982 was unwilling to forego the imagined ancestry of Vietnamese communism in the October Revolution. In order to arrive at the Truth—the radical Vietnamese Ton Duc Thang lent proletarian internationalist support to young Soviet Russia by raising the Red Flag in Sevastopol—the historiographical Sisyphus resorted to similar manipulations of the kind observed in the 1912/1916 episode. In direct contradiction to Ton's "recollections," the biography insisted on placing Ton on board the *France* in the very center of the April revolts. The Truth was justification enough to simply cast aside an authoritative yet conflicting version. Equally ignored was Ton's claim that "his" ship had immediately left the Black Sea. The party's version of 1982 instead invented a scene loosely following the historical *France:* after the initial mutiny with the Red Flag, there was a friendship meeting between the sailors and the people of Sevastopol, and only after several days did the sailors "decide" to part and sail back out of the Black Sea.

To be sure, the official biography did not totally ignore Ton's article of 1957. Some portions were in fact incorporated into the party's version of the mutinies, but again in an engineered fashion that would not upset the larger Truth of Ton's heroic act. Here, the biography's use of Ton's monologue under the Red Flag on the *Paris* is instructive. We will recall the crucial first lines: "Dear Russian friends! Our ship is *still far from you,* and *you have not yet seen* this red flag. But we salute you with this banner in the Black Sea. This red flag carries my hope that the warship would sail into your harbor . . ." Ton bemoaned the gulf the Red Flag had opened between him and the October Revolution. He was at a necessary, safe distance from Sevastopol, but, at the same time, distancing himself from his imaginary Soviet friends pained him. In regard to the *France,* however, which anchored in Sevastopol harbor during the mutinies, in full view of the "Russian friends," Ton's initial sentences made no more sense. And so the biography simply silenced Ton at that point, having him begin his direct speech as follows: "We salute you friends with the red flag being raised in the Black Sea. This red flag carries my yearnings that the cruiser would moor [to remain] in Russia . . ."[13]

Chapter 4 about the strike at the Ba Son arsenal in Sai Gon showed that the commonly propagated version of the labor dispute, which we find in Ton Duc Thang's official biography as well, exaggerated the event and finagled key evidence: The walkout at Ba Son in 1925 was not motivated by internationalism, nor, therefore, was it Viet Nam's first "political" strike, nor did it end in success. Instead, workers protested local injustices when, by coincidence, the "crippled" French warship arrived. The strike collapsed after the imposition of a lockout, ignored in Vietnamese historiography. For the purposes of this chapter, however, the biography's inaccuracies regarding the walkout will be of less interest than its failure to use the tale to invoke Viet Nam's connection to China.

There is much overlap between the stories of the Black Sea Mutiny and the Ba Son strike. In both instances the acting sailors or shipyard workers were said to have perceived themselves as witnesses to an aggression against a newly risen revolutionary movement. They did their share to try to hamper if not stop the opponents of their "brothers." Both events were staged against a French warship. But the Vietnamese workers' internationalist solidarity in 1925 aimed at the Chinese people of the May Thirtieth Movement. Despite the parallels with the Black Sea, and despite Ton's claim of a much more direct—indeed, directing—role in the walkout in Sai Gon, Ba Son received far less attention in the official biography than the Red Flag. Partial quotations from Ton's "recollections" of the mutiny further highlighted the event, as if he were directly talking to the Russians. For the strike at Ba Son, however, available quotes of Ton were not cited.[14]

There are two reasons for the strike's inferiority to the mutiny. First, as detailed in chapters 4 and 5, the strike at Ba Son was not uncontested and became part of an increasingly vocal southern revolutionary identity that claimed to have preceded that of the north in terms of workers' organizations and conscious labor actions. Ton's official biography, on the other hand, authored by the *Central* Party Commission for the Research of Party History, had a distinctly northern outlook. The Red Flag at Sevastopol established an ancestry of *Vietnamese* proletarian internationalism, and the official biography emphasized the episode with pride. But the strike in 1925 constructed an ancestry of proletarian internationalism *in the south of Viet Nam* and thus received significantly less attention and praise. In that sense, we can interpret Ton's 1982 party biography as a co-optation of the deceased president by the northern-dominated VNCP leadership. By highlighting Ton's contributions to *national* struggles for independence and social revolution, it attempted to freeze his official image in such a way that unauthorized, regionalist reinterpretations of his exploits could be marginalized and henceforth prevented. Yet, chapter 7 will show how southern identities continued to coalesce around Ton as the 1980s progressed.

A second reason for the downplaying of the Ba Son strike and its connection with China is that in 1982, when Ton Duc Thang's biography was published, its symbolism vis-à-vis China carried little weight; its imagery could not project reciprocity between the two sides. The internationalist assistance of 1925 at best served as proof of a Vietnamese moral superiority over the now hostile socialist neighbor. By contrast, in 1982 the picture of the flag-raising Ton acquired specific significance vis-à-vis the Soviet Union, when Viet Nam was in dire economic and diplomatic straits and entirely dependent on the USSR. Ton with the Red Flag presented Viet Nam in a less-imbalanced position. Instead, one could reinterpret dependence on the Soviet Union as mutual, and only momentarily one-sided, assistance. After the Ba Son strike in 1925, China ceased to exist in the booklet, until its reappearance in the border war of 1979. There are descriptions of Ton's trips to the Soviet bloc, but none of contacts with China. This omission was not accidental: shortly after Ton Duc Thang had died, for example, a reprint of an article from 1956 appeared about how "Uncle Ton received the Lenin [i.e., Stalin] Prize for peace and friendship among the nations." After lengthy descriptions of the ceremony in Moscow, the 1956 article was edited for the 1980 reader in the following way: "A Soviet airplane brought Uncle Ton back to the East, back to his compatriots in his country. . . .[sic] On the morning of February 1, he crossed the Chinese-Vietnamese border to return to Lang Son."[15] The transit through China was effectively and obviously (". . .") skipped.

Generally, the biography ignored all possible trouble spots in the USSR-PRC-Viet Nam triangle: the huge amount of aid both allies gave Viet Nam during its wars against France and the United States, and also the delicate subject of conflicts between pro-Chinese and pro-Soviet factions inside the VNCP. Possibly, Ton really did not play any major role in these sometimes dramatic confrontations,[16] and his role on the international stage was too closely tied to the USSR,[17] and not to China.

Yet, the peculiarity of the relationship to the USSR as portrayed time and again in Ton's biography lies in its pretension to be unselfish and personal. For example, the text cited Ton recalling in *Sovietskii Moriak* how he led a drive on Con Lon prison island against "pessimism" over the USSR's chances to survive World War II:

> I and many other comrades anxiously followed the events. Yet, we always firmly believed in final victory for the USSR. We argued simply and clearly: the people of the USSR, with their own strength and the support of the world proletariat, had smashed the imperialists' armed intervention. More than twenty years later, the USSR has become stronger and again has wide support of an international antifascist front; the USSR therefore surely wins.[18]

Unlike with China, here a reciprocal relationship emerged. Whereas Ton defended the Soviets in 1919 and emphasized his continuing concern for the USSR, the USSR in turn sustained his spirits during the traumatic prison years. Later the USSR rewarded Ton's work as chairman of the Viet Nam-USSR Friendship Association with the conferral of orders in 1956 and 1967. Thus, from the sailor with the Red Flag to the statesman with the decorated chest, the relationship seemed to be a personal one, an exchange of prizes, symbolic deeds, loyalty, support, eulogies, and kisses. In those unselfish gestures all national self-interests seemed to evaporate. Under the idyllic picture, however, lies the impersonal function of the USSR in the biography as an *über*-authority blessing his fine revolutionary life and legitimizing the party's power. By contrast, in omitting China, the biography denied the Chinese Revolution such an authority.

However, the official biography makes no bigger and more glaring omission than the one in the paragraphs about Ton's membership in the Vietnamese Revolutionary Youth League (VRYL) and his arrest. No mention is made of Ton's involvement in the intraparty killing that took place in the rue Barbier in December 1928, of which my introduction has sketched a preliminary picture. Why did the biography not touch on the episode? An answer seems obvious: the murky affair simply did not fit. It would have interrupted the linear way in which the party chose to present Ton's life, soiled an otherwise spotless revolutionary career, and disturbed Ton's image of an always nice guy with a pure heart.

Not surprisingly, few Vietnamese historians have ever mentioned the killing in the rue Barbier, if only in cryptic terms. The most detailed account, albeit with some of the actors' names changed, so far is that by Le Minh—precisely because of, not despite, the fictional label she gave her biographical approach to Ton Duc Thang.[19] The only historical source to mention the *affaire de la rue Barbier* before Ton's death was a cautiously critical Tran Huy Lieu—himself a victim of the ensuing Sûreté roundup—who, in 1957, gave few details:

> Like other petty bourgeois parties, the VRYL still had a policy of *individual terror* against those who harmed the Revolution. Thus happened in 1928 the assassination of Nguyen [sic!] Van Phat, Nam Ky Regional Committee, because of a case of depravity. . . . [It] brought a lot of harm to the party under the enemy's terror and did not have a good influence on the Revolution.[20]

Only in the latter half of the 1980s did a few more, carefully limited accounts appear. In 1986, for example, one source said in a rather gruff tone:

> The Barbier incident was an *internal* punishment of a VRYL member for a violation of discipline, by issuing the death sentence. . . . It was discovered, and some directly related people were arrested by the police. The enemy knew this was an action of a political organization, *but* to quell our organization, they used the killing to announce that it was a common criminal case without a political connection, trying to avoid reactions of the public opinion: Ngo Thiem was sentenced to death, Ton Duc Thang to life imprisonment, *etc.*[21]

Finally, in 1988, Ngo Quang Lang accentuated the incident in yet another way, making sure that Ton Duc Thang was not implicated in it too much.

> Most of the [VRYL's] Nam Ky and Sai Gon Committees' leaders were petty bourgeois intellectuals of various backgrounds, including some opportunist elements. Thus appeared in the Regional Committee a spirit of power struggle leading to a death sentence for one of its comrades for "illegitimate male-female relations." . . . Ton Duc Thang opposed the death sentence and requested that the Central Committee [in China] be asked for its opinion [but was overruled by] some Nam Ky Committee leaders. . . . The murder was discovered, but the colonial powers regarded it as a criminal case and probed no further. . . . In mid-1929 [in the competitive environment between the VRYL and breakaway factions], the colonialists discovered [the full extent of]

the affair of the rue Barbier because of a traitor. Some people . . . were arrested.[22]

It was not until 1992 that a Western-language publication dealt with the rue Barbier-VRYL-Con Lon complex.[23] In 1930, however, the trial received wide publicity. The French Left, including the *Section française du secours rouge international,* staged campaigns in favor of the defendants, trying to undermine the official propaganda of a purely criminal case. But the affair was quickly forgotten. For example, two noted French Viet Nam scholars, Chesneaux and Fall, both connected Ton's imprisonment to his participation in the Black Sea Mutiny.[24]

Even today the affair seems a delicate matter in Viet Nam. In 1982, when Ton's biography was published, it was even more so. Apart from its disturbing the linearization of Ton's life, the authors had two more reasons for ignoring Le Van Phat's murder: first, it was not a self-defensive necessity, say, to silence a traitor. Instead, it involved love and jealousy, careerism and envy, arrogance and vanity—attributes that an "exemplary revolutionary fighter" could not have. And given Tran Huy Lieu's and Ngo Quang Lang's "petty bourgeois" label for the affair—although they were anxious to avoid sticking it on Ton directly—Ton's "exemplary" working-class background and proletarian consciousness could not be maintained. Second, any hint at a division within the communist movement, at internal conflict or disharmony, was strictly banned from Ton's biography. But it was exactly this dissension—or more precisely, petty bickering—that led to the crime in the rue Barbier. The result was a disaster of large proportion for the VRYL and for the anticolonial cause in Cochinchina, a tragic, futile blunder for which Ton Duc Thang bore a certain amount of responsibility.[25]

For the post-1945 period, when Ton quickly rose to prominence, his biography changes in style: it becomes more and more a listing of a growing number of impressive positions, titles, and decorations. Chapter 2 has already provided an analysis of Ton's career after 1945. To briefly recount: Although serving in a number of high offices, politically Ton was unimportant. His strength and his role as a prominent leader of the DRVN and the SRVN lay in representational functions. Presented as Ho Chi Minh's longtime "close battle friend" and a national father figure, he had a unique symbolic value for the VNCP: no other leading cadre could convincingly represent the party's self-image of proletarian internationalism. And after the country's partition, Ton became a natural choice for the DRVN's vice presidency under Ho because of his southern origin. In domestic affairs, Ton's biographers frequently connect him with campaigns (patriotic emulation, fighting illiteracy, etc.) and positions from which he gives encouragement, advice, and compassion. In turn he receives rewards of honorary chairmanships (Labor Confederation, Children's Committee, etc.) and the Order of the Gold Star. In external affairs, we find Ton as the leader of a National Assembly delegation abroad and as chairman of several peace and friendship organizations that played a crucial role during the 1950s and 1960s in influencing world opinion. Again, in turn he is rewarded with the Lenin (i.e., Stalin) Peace Prize, the Lenin Order, and a membership in the World Peace Council.

The obvious discrepancy between the public busybody and the political nobody provoked drastic characterizations of Ton from anticommunist Viet Nam watchers. Tongas saw him as wax in the hands of the powerful, a southern Vietnamese being "tonkinisé," while for Honey he was simply "senile" and "placed on a public platform to give . . . his blessings" to each and everything.[26] For the liberal journalist Holzer, Ton's ascension to the presidency after Ho's death in 1969 was possible only because of the Vietnamese "respect of old age" and because "the decisive men" wanted to avoid exposing themselves.[27] It is impossible to refute what lies at the core of these exaggerated remarks. Ton's official biography hardly showed him actually *doing* anything; time and again Ton just made references to Ho when quoted. Symptomatically, his acceptance speech after being elected state president in 1969 did not even fill a page: he thanked several times, highlighted the honor for him, and pledged to do his utmost to "fulfill the sacred will of President Ho" and the tasks given to him.[28] Even the many articles and anecdotes about Ton published after his death and on his centennial anniversary provided no other image than that of a nice old man with a big heart. It is for these reasons that the official biography, as well as the eulogies on Ton that it quotes, were a deluge of praise for Ton's conservative, passive virtues: loyal, hardworking, steadfast, patriotic, sacrificing, devoted, modest, affectionate, incorruptible, plain, etc. They also imply what Ton Duc Thang was not: a leader, charismatic, and creative.

ON MODELS, IDEALS, AND EXAMPLES

In the official biography, the lack of a private Ton Duc Thang is striking. After a brief introduction to his childhood family (peasant parents, one brother, two sisters), the reader has to wait fifty-eight years for a private scene to resurface: in 1946 Ton met his wife and children again, whose existence had actually been unknown to the reader until then. But Ton had to leave "immediately" again, "on urgent matters of the country," and would not be reunited with his family until 1954.[29] Only one more time, after the unification of Viet Nam, does one read about a trip back to Ton's native place, described, however, in a rather formal way. Another aspect of the missing private person is the lack of feelings on an individual level. Ton Duc Thang is never afraid, he never doubts. His anger, joy, and compassion are always aimed only at impersonal masses—"the enemy," his compatriots, "the people." The biography tries to counterbalance this one-dimensional portrayal by a recurring reference to how "humble" and "close to the people" Ton was. Whenever Ton receives a reward or praise, he is quoted as saying modestly that he would accept the honor on behalf of the whole nation. And just as Ton Duc Thang has hoisted the Red Flag on the French warship, the biography cuts in with the following quote:

> I believe that no matter what patriotic Vietnamese, especially a worker—had he taken part in those historic moments in the Black Sea—would not have been able to act any differently than I, since loving the Fatherland and hating imperialism also mean loving the October Revolution and hating the opponents of the October Revolution.[30]

The only other person the biography actually names is Ho Chi Minh. This is a key to understanding Ton's official identity. He is defined in relation to this paramount symbol of the Vietnamese Revolution and hence with the Revolution itself. With Ton Duc Thang thus construed as (what Huynh Kim Khanh has coined) a "modern secular monk," the Revolution and its party became Ton's "family," giving him strength, encouragement, and feelings of security and spiritual shelter. While imprisonment is normally meant to punish by depriving the prisoner of a free interaction in a private and social environment,

Ton painted his prison term in light colors: "Because of the party, because of the ideal, we were happy all the time."[31] In working and living for the party, Ton became himself.

What then can be made of Ton Duc Thang's biography? In contributions to a book about "Self and Biography" and the "Individual and Society," Wang Gungwu has highlighted East Asia's "strong tradition of eulogistic, didactic and historical biography," and stated that, within a "strong collective tradition," the " "traditional biography was not really concerned with the individual. The emphasis was more on a person's contribution to history."[32] In a related context, David Marr has concluded that Vietnamese biographical writing in the twentieth century has not focused much on the individual, for it is the Marxist notion of a historical process that ultimately determines one's actions.[33] Both statements intersect where one also finds Ton's official biography: in the notion that a person's importance lies in its role in society, in a politico-economic setting determined by the historical process. Comrade Ton Duc Thang, an exemplary, staunch communist fighter, described a model life. This is not so much because Ton's might have been a model life; rather, his biographers of the Central Commission for the Research of Party History cast him—in a movement of *containment*—into a preexisting form.

This model has three features: a linearization and harmonization in the course of the story, the lack of a private view on the biography's subject, as I have just shown, and an inflexible, formulaic language. Ton's biography is first and most important a booklet serving didactic purposes, a feel-good book, or, in the increasingly bleak context of 1982, a feel-better book. Consequently, linear narrative strings, a clear argumentative line, and a somewhat predictable plot are needed. Any disharmony or conflict, any setback or surprising twist in the story must be avoided. The ultimate outcome is a stereotyped communist success story after which Ton Duc Thang's life has been modeled. In a second textual movement of *exclusion,* all threatening signs of individuality, spontaneity, and privacy have been banned, and all biographical deviations—the edges, mistakes, unpredictable outbursts, and contradictions that appear in a human life—are cut away lest they undermine the dominant narrative.

The figuration of Ton's life into a cast can now be made to correspond to the larger historical paradigm, in a third movement of *expansion.*

Ton Duc Thang becomes a flawless superhuman being, always in tune with the necessities of the "objective" historical setting. This model life might be conceptualized as follows: Provided by his peasant home and national heritage with patriotism, he sets out to become a worker. The working conditions further shape his consciousness, and Ton gets his first opportunities to put his anticolonial convictions into action. His experiences abroad add anticapitalism and internationalism to his thinking and to his actions. This first stage in Ton's Telling Life culminates in a symbolic *apprentice* examination: the hoisting of the Red Flag in the Black Sea, which marks the transition to the next stage. Here, as a *journeyman,* so to say, Ton Duc Thang applies his ripening skills, additional experiences, and deepening class consciousness within his native environment, in the course of which his methods become refined. He organizes, propagates, and leads among the working class of Sai Gon, and as soon as the ultimate guiding light of Marxism-Leninism appears, he is ready to join the organization that stands for the correct ideology. Different from the first transition from apprentice to journeyman, a single act in which the ripening skills were demonstrated in an extremely condensed form, Ton's model transition from journeyman to *master* takes place over a long period, a passage, a Vietnamese version of the "Long March"[34]—the years on Con Lon. As with the Black Sea, these years in captivity are highly prominent in the biographical text. Overcoming this period of extreme trial in the vicinity of death and, yet, still playing an active role for the Revolution and his fellow prisoners—as Ton's biography suggests, and as Tran Tu Binh supports[35]—make him a true candidate for a future leading position. Huynh Kim Khanh has suggested such a nexus:

> The most inhumane treatment [was] reserved for Vietnamese "politicals" in Con [Lon]. . . . The higher the rank in the ICP or Trotskyist party, the more frequent and more severe the punishment. . . . To Vietnamese, [Con Lon] is associated with dread and terror. . . . But it is also associated with nationalist heroism as a "kiln which fired and created heroes." . . . It is rumored that the number of years [in prison] . . . was one of the most important elements of the *curricula vitae* of the [VNCP] leaders; it was an important qualification for advancement in the party hierarchy.[36]

Ton Duc Thang's sixteen years in prison thus become his masterpiece, where his skills are honed, tested, and proven over a prolonged period.

From then on, Ton's presumably linear development leads directly to a long list of positions and titles.

Now that Ton Duc Thang's life has been cast—through movements of containment and exclusion—into a sanitized model corresponding—through a movement of expansion—to "objective" stages of history, the text is prepared for its fourth movement of *appropriation:* Ton is presented as an *example.* As one of only a few VNCP leaders with clean proletarian credentials and, in the iconography of the Red Flag, as the earliest Vietnamese participant in the Soviet Revolution, he provides a crucial link between the party and its ideal image: the vanguard of the working class, with its ancestry retraced to the mother of all communist revolutions, the October Revolution. By making him an example, an "exemplary, staunch communist fighter," the official biography strategically positions Ton Duc Thang to connect the party with its legitimizing historical paradigm.

WHEN VISITING THE MAUSOLEA of Ho Chi Minh and Mao Zedong, each time I only felt some unease, instead of awe, in front of those historic figures who had changed the world so much. Essentially, I realized, there is a terrible shamelessness to mausolea, a creepy kind of pornography, a hidden brutality in the exhibition.

It is no platitude that death makes all human beings equal: shed of their social roles only bodies remain, each with stories of a finished life. Death is a two-step process: the end of an active, sensuous life as well as physical decomposition. Death can only be both. Decomposition is a kind of defense mechanism of a defenseless corpse. It enables the dead to vanish where life has come to a halt, out of sight and into memory. Decomposition is the individual right to an end, to close the book, to retain a sense of uniqueness, completeness, and complexity. The preservation with the aim of exhibition violates this right, since the victims are in a peculiar way not fully dead.[37]

And so the dead-undead esteemed leaders are kept for the veneration by the living. But veneration needs objects to look up to, to submit under. The exhibited corpses, however, are not above the beholder. Rather, the implied power relations appear oddly reversed: not unlike the voiceless and defenseless sex objects of "men's magazines," the preserved Great Men are hostages of their keepers, subjected to their needs, at (and for) their disposal. In mausolea, the ceremonial exhibition and the act of viewing represent a solemn, yet violent spectacle.

Ultimately, in the project of the mausoleum we meet the historiographical Sisyphus again. Fighting the decay of the human form, the impermanence of physical texture, he is, at the same time and in his anxious commitment to a certain exclusive historical model, fighting the decomposition of the past, the impermanence and indeterminacy of history. And thus, in the end, Ton Duc Thang's official biography can be read as a textual embalmment. An all-enveloping narrative has silenced him with a cacophony of praise. We cannot reach a more intricate notion of Ton; rather, his biography places us in front of his sarcophagus. Through the crystal lid we can only see him in the presumed historicity in which his biographers want him to be deciphered: a (grand-)fatherly figure with mild features, cast in golden light, in the midst of party soldiers holding the wake, his worker's jacket decorated with orders, his body draped in the Red Flag from the Black Sea. We are only supposed to read his waxen mask, a text(-ure) stiffened by impenetrable, formalized language. This is "Comrade Ton Duc Thang," the legitimizing model, the "exemplary, staunch communist fighter"; herein lies the political function and the totalizing, definite meaning of this Telling Life. In his biography-mausoleum Ton Duc Thang is preserved, contained, and exhibited right within the transitional zone of half death, between physical existence and indefinite possibilities of memory.

As chapter 7 will show, however, the attempt by the northern core of the VNCP in the posthumous moment to construct and control a definitive version of Ton Duc Thang's life and national achievements could not succeed for long. Beginning in 1986, in the post-socialist moment, southern commemorations of Ton posited subtly critical counter-versions to the central state's official biography. Opposite the socialist biography-mausoleum appeared a traditional peasant home. And in contrast to the celebration of an exemplary communist success story in a textual mausoleum, a museum-shrine nostalgically (re-)called the Revolution's bygone spirit.

CHAPTER 7

Museum-Shrine: The Revolution's Guardian Spirit in the Post-Socialist Moment

IN 1887, Ton Duc Thang's parents Ton Van De (d. 1938) and Nguyen Thi Di (d. 1947) built a house in the hamlet of My An and part of the village of My Hoa Hung.[1] The village is situated on Ong Ho Island in the lower Mekong River, just four kilometers from Long Xuyen, the commercial and administrative center of An Giang province. Ton Duc Thang, born in 1888, was the couple's first child. Because he was a boy, he was tutored, probably from 1897 at the latest to about 1901, by a private teacher in Long Xuyen, receiving instruction in the Chinese script and Chinese history and philosophy. Additionally, Ton's commemorators in An Giang stress the great influence of his teacher, a fervent anticolonialist,[2] on the boy's early politicization. Afterward, in the early 1900s, Ton Duc Thang also learned French in an unidentified "elementary school" in Long Xuyen.[3] He lived in his parents' house until 1906, when, at eighteen, he moved to Sai Gon.

We do not know how frequently Ton Duc Thang returned to his childhood home between 1906 and 1929. After his arrest in 1929, however, Ton Duc Thang would revisit his birthplace only twice. In the wake of the August Revolution of 1945 and his liberation from sixteen years of incarceration on Con Lon prison island, Ton Duc Thang made his way to My Hoa Hung in November 1945 to see his old mother. But since he was in danger of being captured by the French, who had largely retaken control of the south by then, he stayed only one night, as the story goes, before making his way to Ha Noi to join the DRVN government. The next trip back home would not take place until after the end of the American war, in October 1975, after de facto unification of the north and south, when Ton Duc Thang, who had risen in prominence in the meantime and become president, was able to visit his native place one last time.

In 1984, four years after the president's death, the Ministry of Culture, upon the suggestion of local cadres, declared Ton Duc Thang's childhood home a cultural-historic monument. After Ton's brother Ton Duc Nhung (b. 1896) and sister-in-law (b. 1897) both died in 1986, their son's family moved to an adjacent building, and renovations of the original house and the creation of a "commemorative area" *(khu luu niem)* began. Their completion was to coincide with the centennial of Ton Duc Thang's birth in August 1988. The initiative for these undertakings originated with the provincial branch of the VNCP, which planned to use Ton Duc Thang's centennial "to educate the cadres, party members, and the people of the province about [Ton's] great example in struggle, sacrifice, and revolutionary morality."[4] Under the direction of the VNCP's provincial propaganda board and local cadres, the An Giang departments of construction and culture/information, members of the Club of Former Resistance Fighters (CFRF), and the University of Architecture of Ho Chi Minh City, several projects were started. They included the renovation of Ton Duc Thang's home, the construction of an exhibition building in the vicinity, the landscaping of the area, the first-ever electrification of My Hoa Hung, and the building or upgrading of bridges and paved roads to connect Ong Ho Island to the provincial infrastructure in preparation for the expected visitors. In addition, Professor Lam Binh Tuong, a museum curator, and the An Giang provincial museum in Long Xuyen started gathering materials and objects for future displays on Ton Duc Thang's life.[5]

In August 1988, in celebration of Ton Duc Thang's hundredth birthday, the commemorative area in My Hoa Hung was solemnly inaugurated. At around the same time, several other historical displays on Ton's life opened in the south of Viet Nam, most notably the Ton Duc Thang Museum in downtown Ho Chi Minh City, housed in a riverfront villa near Ba Son shipyard.[6] They, too, were conceived and realized by southern VNCP cadres and CFRF members as integral parts of one overarching commemorative project on the deceased president. The exhibits largely contain the same scripts and often share copies of materials, however, and my focus in this chapter therefore will be on My Hoa Hung. It is at Ton Duc Thang's birthplace that the commemoration is most elaborate, both in a museum and in the Ton family home, which has been transformed into a shrine.

AT FIRST SIGHT, IT IS INCONSISTENCY in message and form that appears in the object of this chapter's investigation, for the commemoration of Ton Duc Thang in his native place contains an ostensible paradox. It can be found in the remembrance by the party of one of its heroes having taken on openly religious forms since the mid- to late 1980s. Put differently, a paradox suggests itself when, under a self-proclaimed secular, even areligious, political regime, Ton's childhood home in My Hoa Hung has been turned into a shrine where, as I will argue, rituals of hero spirit worship are performed. Yet, religious or quasi-religious forms of popular or state-led veneration of revolutionary heroes are by no means a new phenomenon—one might only mention the widespread talismanic use of renderings of Mao Zedong's image among Chinese—and have been observed in East and Southeast Asia, including Viet Nam.[7] But especially in the last case, too little attention has been paid thus far to explaining the societal conditions in which these worship practices appear, or the ideological-cultural concepts undergirding them and lending these rituals their meanings (and which would steer us away from superficially seeing them as paradox). How have local Vietnamese contexts shaped the specific forms in which these exhibits have appeared?

Often, analyses of the constructions of historical memory, the Hobsbawmian "invention of tradition," public ceremonies, symbols, and the refashioning of historic sites—in Viet Nam and elsewhere—have emphasized disjunctures, shifts, contestations, and tensions, discursive and otherwise. While these foci certainly can yield important insights and help undermine long-held assumptions, they have, on the other hand, been remarkably weak in constructing counterarguments of an explanatory inclusiveness. In the case of the Commemorative Area for Ton Duc Thang in An Giang, an analysis of the shrine and the adjacent museum can easily, and legitimately, demonstrate the stark contrast between the two structures, their inherent contradictions vis-à-vis the revolutionary master script of Marxian provenance, or the multiplicity of contending voices and signs. I want to move beyond the uncovering of tensions, however, and instead propose a view—one view—of the Ton Duc Thang worship in which its various elements, far from being paradoxical, might merge into a culturally coherent and intelligible message, with the shrine providing the form and the museum exhibit its contents.

In the end, I will propose that such an integrated commemorative statement, veiled as it might manifest itself at the Ton Duc Thang shrine, needs to be read within its proper regional and historical context. State-organized commemoration in Viet Nam is not a unified or uniform project; even the official interpretations of the commemorated past are subject to important spatial and generational differences. In the wake of the sweeping policy changes known as Doi Moi ("renovation," or perestroika), which began in late 1986 and not only brought dramatic economic reforms but also opened new spaces for public expression, the southern museum-shrine—itself an instrument of official memory construction—seeks to modify and even subtly critique the predominant representations of revolution and war emanating from the north. In this sense, Ton's museum-shrine functions as an intervention in a debate where, despite its muted nature, nothing less is at stake than the self-identity of the revolutionary camp.

TON DUC THANG'S CHILDHOOD HOME is a rather large structure on pillars, with at least four separate rooms, the main living room, and a spacious porch. Some of the walls show elaborate wood carvings, and valuable furniture and several pieces of lacquer art decorate the interior. The main item on display, in the center of the house and its living room, is an altar with Ton Duc Thang's portrait, electric candles, decorative plants, and incense burners. Behind Ton's altar and standing along a wall is a second altar that can more easily be identified as a traditional place for ancestral veneration. This function is underscored by the display around it of photos of Ton Duc Thang's parents, brother, and sister-in-law. The gravesites of these four relatives are situated behind the building, neatly kept—equally important in Vietnamese practices of ancestral worship—and consciously drawn into the overall exhibit by way of a well-maintained, well-marked path.

The nearby exhibition building (erected about fifty meters from the Ton family home) is a large, rectangular concrete structure on pillars standing in water. Inside is a large open exhibition hall with freely movable partitions on which most of the exhibits (photos, paintings, plates, and panels with quotes) are hung. Facing the entryway, a large bust of Ton Duc Thang stands on a slightly elevated platform and underneath a ceiling-high red panel with a gold star, the insignia of the state. The bust is framed by vases depicting a scene from 1958, when Ho Chi Minh conferred on Ton Duc Thang the DRVN's highest order. Adjacent to the exhibition hall are smaller rooms for guest receptions and a few staff offices.

The exhibit itself consists mainly of pictures tracing Ton Duc Thang's life in chronological manner: from his native place and family, his vocation as a mechanic in Sai Gon and France, his alleged role in the Black Sea Mutiny (symbolized by a painting of a warship with a hoisted red flag), his early revolutionary activities in Viet Nam leading to his arrest, trial, and imprisonment on Con Lon, to his rise to prominence at the side of Ho Chi Minh in the newly independent state, and finally to his own presidency. In addition, glass cases present everyday items once belonging to Ton Duc Thang.

Overall, the commemorative area in My Hoa Hung serves as a destination point for secular pilgrimages. Since 1988, schools and factories have frequently organized tours to My Hoa Hung, and in the short time span until the Eastern European revolutions of 1989, delegations of "fraternal" East bloc countries have paid their respects. The museum displays photos of these organized visits, and a visitors' album further attests to this function of the site. According to museum personnel, especially around nationally symbolic dates—Ho Chi Minh's and Ton Duc Thang's birthdays, Independence Day—the commemorative area hosts youth camps. During my sojourn in My Hoa Hung, however, the education cadre accompanying me from Ha Noi and I remained the only visitors, and my companion's worshiping with incense in front of Ton Duc Thang's altar was the only ritual act I witnessed. In particular, none of the local people came to the compound. Several staff members were at hand but seemed to have few duties.

As indicated before, the commemorative area is filled with contrasting images and messages. For example, Ton Duc Thang's veneration results in the partial superseding of the standard biographical script. In My Hoa Hung, the official claim that Ton came from a family of poor peasants is rejected, and no attempt is made to hide the family's being, in the words of Ton Duc Thang's nephew, "rather rich" (and could, after all, afford a private education for the firstborn son). Further, the Ton family home, nicely decorated and built mainly of wood in the traditional style of a peasant home, stands in stark contrast to the adjacent modern museum cast of concrete. While the former is centered on popular ritual and ancestral veneration and, thus, looks backward in time, the latter tells a story of heroic struggles and secular successes along Marxist-Leninist interpretative lines and has its eyes set on the future into which time is moving in a linear and predictably progressive fashion. But even this narrative with its emphasis on Ton Duc Thang's proletarian circumstances and class consciousness is hardly without ambiguity. Its model of a universalist historical materialism is effectively undermined by a strong nativist, essentialist message about a spirit of resistance to foreign aggression with which Ton Duc Thang's home region supposedly imbued the young boy.

WHAT, THEN, CAN ONE MAKE of the commemorative area that is apparently so filled with contrasts and contradictions and that in its quasi-religious worship of a communist leader creates tensions with the state's secular orientation? Is it possible to distill from the site a unified theme, with a form and contents that fit?

In order to identify a mold for the site, I propose that it is not only ancestral worship rituals with which Ton Duc Thang is venerated. Rather, his childhood home resonates even more with the Vietnamese traditional religious belief in the spiritual properties of the country's landscape and history. Although the building is always only referred to as "President Ton Duc Thang's childhood home," in fact it is meant to be a shrine or temple *(den)* for Ton's hero spirit, a tutelary deity for the locale as well as the nation that has entered the pantheon of Vietnamese heroic guardian spirits. By this I do not mean that Ton Duc Thang was made the village patron spirit *(thanh hoang)* of My Hoa Hung. In prerevolutionary Viet Nam, the cult of a village patron spirit was always performed in the village's communal hall *(dinh)* and was based on the respective community's own choice of its guardian deity, which clearly is not the case here.[8] The local population, which traditionally would enjoy the benevolent acts of its patron spirit, is not really meant to be the recipient of the kind deeds by Ton Duc Thang's spirit; it is thus not the primary audience for the shrine's message. And since veneration takes place at Ton Duc Thang's birthplace—and not at the local communal hall—"origins" of some sort appear as a primary concern of the commemorative project.

Rather, Ton Duc Thang's temple consciously models itself on the religious belief (or state ideology, as Stephen O'Harrow calls it)[9] that bestows superhuman spiritual powers not only on Viet Nam's geography—

its mountains, earth, and waters[10]—but also upon its past: historical hero figures as guardian deities continue to watch over the nation's affairs and, thus, transcend and tie together past and present. For long stretches of time, inclusion into (and exclusion from) the national pantheon was a process entailing a formalized court procedure and one that, especially with regard to the question of who among the more prominent cases of historical personae should be "in" and who "out," was of an eminently political and self-serving nature. Among the uncontested hero spirits are, for example, leaders who rebelled against Chinese domination or who defended Vietnamese independence against Chinese attacks, like Trung Trac and Trung Nhi (both died in A.D. 43), Ngo Quyen (897–944), Ly Thuong Kiet (1030–1105), Tran Hung Dao (1220s–1300), Le Loi (1384–1433), and Nguyen Trai (1380–1442), who to this day continue to be worshiped in respective shrines all over Viet Nam.[11]

Vietnamese hero spirit tales form a genre with a set of conventional features from which Ton Duc Thang's shrine liberally quotes. To describe their generic makeup, I will briefly turn to the most prominent collection of such stories of tutelary deities, Ly Te Xuyen's fourteenth-century compilation *Spiritual Powers of the Viet Realm* (Viet Dien U Linh Tap). Keith Taylor and Oliver Wolters have written detailed studies on the *Spiritual Powers of the Viet Realm* in which they argue the compilation of heroic spirit tales was used for the interests of the court elites.[12] What was the spirits' utility to these elites? Taylor traces the tales back to two main concerns: first, to what he terms "Ly dynasty religion" in which royal authority is sanctioned by spiritual powers. Second, at the time of compilation, when dynastic succession was contested and irregular, these spirits functioned as examples of loyalty to rulers. But also highlighting the psychological comfort the belief in protective deities continued to give later ruling classes in dangerous times, he concludes that the "spirit world . . . was a protective screen . . . seen by the Vietnamese as a shelter from alien threats and domestic disorder." Further, "by ritually acknowledging these spiritual powers, Vietnamese kings opened legitimizing space for their claims upon the obedience of the people."[13]

Wolters places his emphasis differently: in the spirit tales he sees reflections of elite anxieties about village value systems of a potentially rebellious nature as well as concerns over "wild" (animist) village ritual practices that do not conform with the court's agenda. The hero spirit tales are used to control and assimilate village customs and are thus primarily didactic tools to disseminate court concepts of "good government" and "loyal behavior" among the population. Such domesticated spirits become the ruler's loyal servants and "local surrogates." The potentially rebellious energies of the spirits as well as those of "villagers of prowess" are harnessed by royal recognition and employment in the ruler's aid.[14] Wolters has characterized the tales' often uniform plots in two ways. First, in instances of outward threats, there is

> the invariably successful relationship between Vietnamese rulers . . . and the local spirits, but only if the ruler alertly apprehends a spirit's presence, if necessary testing it, appoints it to a post of military responsibility, and rewards it for its contribution to victory. The spirit, who always salutes the ruler, now joins the entourage. When this procedure is followed, victory is "certain."[15]

Second, concerning domestic order, the genre would present "a spirit's marvellous 'manifestations' of spiritual power, its dramatic disclosure to a ruler . . . , the ruler's wonder and grateful provision of a 'shrine,' the villagers' 'incessant' worship at the shrine, the spirit's 'response' to the villagers' needs, and the 'favours' enjoyed by rulers and villagers alike."[16]

In sum, guardian spirits protect the country from external threats and the ruler against internal, village-level challenges. Their role often is to facilitate a harmonious relationship between elite and village cultures, between rulers and the people. Although both sides benefit from the deity's tutelary services, the spirit's mediation is not one of equidistance but one ultimately done in the ruler's interest. Spirit tales and local temples are didactic tools, then, to focus popular allegiance toward the ruler. Finally, spirits and rulers come together either through the ruler's proper apprehension and recognition—called *goi hon,* "calling up"[17] a worthy spirit—or by way of the spirit announcing itself to a worthy ruler.

IF TON DUC THANG'S CHILDHOOD HOME is indeed a guardian spirit shrine—creating the site's form—and if it were to establish him as a hero spirit belonging to a greater Vietnamese pantheon, does that not make the commemorative project even more of an oddity because of the exhibition hall's unfitting message of communist revolution? I believe not. Rather, instead of doing the obvious—emphasizing contradictions and incongruities with communist orthodoxy—an alternative reading of the exhibit on Ton Duc Thang's life will fit the form of a guardian spirit shrine and afford us a way to see the site in its entirety as communicating a uniform theme. To this end, we need to change our interpretive grid from one focusing on Marxist-Leninist historiographical attitudes and socialist iconography to a more fruitful one attentive to Vietnamese cultural-political concepts and the conventions in which they came to be expressed. In order to identify a message suitable to the form, the exhibit hall's display needs to be approached as a didactic text modeling itself, if only loosely, on historical texts and political thought of the Vietnamese past.

Again, the works of Oliver Wolters and Keith Taylor are of relevance here. Wolters and Taylor have both undertaken structuralist readings of Vietnamese annals and discerned dominant themes—what they call "sentences"[18] or "statements"[19]—to shed new light on the histories the annals are concerned with as well as on their authors and their intentions. Wolters in particular sees such "sentences" as signifying systems representing the totality of "recurrent 'units,'" or words that are syntactically related but do not necessarily always appear with one another. For those portions of the *Complete Historical Records of Dai Viet* (Dai Viet Su Ky Toan Thu), annals compiled in the mid-fifteenth century, he identifies one such "sentence" as signifying "good government."[20]

Coming back to the exhibit on Ton Duc Thang's life, we will disengage ourselves from a primary concern with the ideological (and museological) master script that makes the commemorative site appear paradoxical. Rather, such a master idiom is perhaps only a required stylistic convention in contemporary Viet Nam, where one has to draw from the reservoir of party-sanctioned political-ideological terminology. Once we focus instead on other recurrent expressions, the exhibit reveals a dominant theme that actually makes sense in conjunction with Ton Duc Thang's hero spirit shrine. This is the museum's repeated and prominent emphasis on "simplicity," "sacrifice," "selflessness," "loyalty," and "service"—all, of course, exemplified by and combined in Ton Duc Thang's life. And following further in Wolters's fashion, these five terms (or their equivalences "thriftiness," "unpretentiousness," "faithfulness," etc.) likewise form the exhibit's "statement." Namely, these words equally fuse into an essential portrayal of "good government." Differently phrased, they are a fundamental commentary on the proper attitudes of the Revolution vis-à-vis the people, especially after its successful rise to power.

Similar to the Ton Duc Thang Museum in Ho Chi Minh City, both the exhibits on Ton Duc Thang's life in Long Xuyen and My Hoa Hung indeed pay particular attention to the characteristic frugality, devotion, and unpretentiousness of this revolutionary and national leader. Ho Chi Minh's words of praise of Ton Duc Thang to that effect are prominently displayed right in the entranceways of both exhibits. And we are reminded of the concern Ton Duc Thang showed for others throughout his life: for example, for his own family members, whom he supplied in his youth with sandals he made for them (shown in the exhibits), or for his Vietnamese coworkers, one of them gravely sick, at the Toulon arsenal. We also meet him loyally caring for his fellow prisoners, even for those who initially tried to harm him, during the hellish years on Con Lon Island. We see him caring for the nation as a whole when, in 1945, he visits his mother, whom he had not seen since 1929, for only one night because of "urgent business" awaiting him in the capital. At My Hoa Hung, a painting of this last scene and a related quote ascribed to Ton Duc Thang underscore the importance placed on his unselfishness.

The theme of simplicity and selflessness is successfully reproduced beyond the exhibits. For example, after the symposium on Ton Duc Thang was held in Long Xuyen in 1988, the publication in 1989 of the symposium's proceedings significantly carried the programmatic title "A Great Ordinary Person", a phrase coined by the former Sai Gon party chief during the U.S. war, Tran Bach Dang.[21]

The parts of the exhibits dealing with Ton Duc Thang's life after he became an accomplished national leader focus even more on his thriftiness, self-reliance, similarity with the common people, and modesty. Among the material artifacts presented are Ton Duc Thang's simple presidential clothes and worn shoes, his bicycle, alarm clock (a gift in 1957 from Vietnamese embassy personnel in Moscow), table fan, and camera—all of basic make—and little gifts from ordinary people he used in everyday life, like an ashtray made from the metal of a downed U.S. bomber. The only piece of extravagance shown is a Swiss watch with a portrait of Ho Chi Minh on its face, which Ton Duc Thang is said to have cherished and worn to the end. It was, like most of the other artifacts, given to the museum by Ton Duc Thang's son-in-law Duong Van Phuc. The story goes that Prime Minister Pham Van Dong had seven of these watches made for the DRVN leadership while he attended the 1954 Geneva Conference.

Large black-and-white photos depict Ton Duc Thang's plain attire and rustic furniture in the presidential residence, or his bicycle-repair tools he is said to have used until old age. The explanations given are that, even as president, Ton remained a mechanic at heart who loved to tinker, and that he did not want to impose upon his presidential guard for repairs to his bicycle. Other pictures show him involved in practical, down-to-earth, hands-on, even mundane activities, like chatting with factory workers, reading to children, and tending his garden. It is here that the core of the exhibits' didacticism is found. What is emphasized is clearly not his revolutionary struggles, successes, and fame—a focus much more pronounced, as discussed in chapter six, in the official biography emanating from the center of party power—but that power, once achieved, was for Ton Duc Thang, not an end in itself but the means to best serve the people. In other words, power left him humble, committed, and uncorrupted. Thus, a plausible reading of the exhibits' statement is one about the correct demeanor of those who govern in the name of the Revolution.

How could this kind of ideal revolutionary leadership, of which Ton Duc Thang is portrayed to possess all the essential characteristics, and of which the Communist Party is the legitimate agent, be conceptualized? Central attributes like "simplicity," "sacrifice," "selflessness," "loyalty," and "service" point to an activist government of officials operating under a set of ethics taking as their reference the common good. Its sense of self would be one of idealistic (and at the same time paternalistic) confidence in the righteousness of its initiatives, its unfailing knowledge of "what is best" for the people, and its predictable success. Its continued power and authority would remain an unchallenged given so long as it remained tightly connected to the people, their experiences and circumstances, and in congruence with their "true wishes."

Ideally, officials would share the conditions of life of the people and remain immune to the corrupting temptations of power, since, in their altruism, their ultimate reward would be the creation of a just and harmonious society free of exploitation.

SUCH A CONCEPT OF PROPER RULE extolled in the exhibits' statement is certainly not without historical precedent. Thus, my contention that Ton Duc Thang's museum-shrine produces both in form (hero spirit temple) and contents (exhibits) a consistent statement must lead us on a detour into premodern Vietnamese intellectual life. For a similar notion of proper rule was once articulated by the great scholar-official Nguyen Trai (1380–1442). Nguyen Trai lived through the tumultuous decades leading to the fall of the Tran dynasty in 1400, the brief reign of Ho Quy Ly (1400–1407), the harsh occupation of the country by an army of China's Ming dynasty (1407–27), and the subsequent restoration of independence under a new dynasty, the Le. Nguyen Trai himself had an important share in the defeat of the Ming; he joined Le Loi in organizing an anti-Ming resistance, begun in 1418, and the two men became the movement's key exponents. As emperor (1428–33), Le Loi would retain Nguyen Trai as his chief official; thereafter, their relationship was made a Vietnamese archetype of the fortunate link between a powerful ruler and his able and loyal minister.[22]

Much has been written on Nguyen Trai in scholarly works. Without doubt, the ascent of Confucian axioms for the first time to a commanding position within Vietnamese elite culture is intimately connected to Nguyen Trai and the early Le dynasty. Tran Quoc Vuong actually called it an "irony of history" that the "Confucian bureaucratic-monarchic regime . . . , an exogenous element originating from north China . . . , received a particular boost from the time Dai Viet shook off the Ming yoke."[23] Nevertheless, Nguyen Trai "took . . . seriously the Confucian dictum of serving the state," as John Whitmore has observed, and "strongly believed in an active role [for scholar-officials]"; in his work "service was his dominant theme."[24] Oliver Wolters accentuates Nguyen Trai's major contributions differently; according to him, it was in

> the selfless way peasants rallied against the Ming invaders [that Nguyen Trai] witnessed the people's response when a heroic style of leadership revived. [Therefore, his writings] stressed the ruler's

> responsibility to the people. . . . The people's well-being now became the test of good government, and the ruler's obligation to use educated officials is confidently formulated.[25]

Finally, Esta Ungar writes that Nguyen Trai's thought "expressed an attachment to traditional Vietnamese values of the ruler as the heroic protector of the people, . . . [onto which] he grafted newer political constructs that . . . enlarged . . . the scope of activity of previous dynastic governments. . . . In his system the people's welfare was the basic concern of the state."[26]

Far from following the inward-looking neo-Confucian interpretation of such central concepts as "humaneness and justice" *(ren yi,* Vietnamese *nhan nghia*), Nguyen Trai instead believed that *nhan nghia* obliged a ruler to "secure the livelihood of the people," an outward-looking, activist stance informed by an "ethic of public service." Significantly, Ungar maintains that Nguyen Trai adapted in such notions the idealistic postulates of the eleventh-century "government school" of Confucianism, an activist reform movement with strong roots in Mencian thought during the times of China's Northern Song dynasty. She sees a particular affinity to the work of Fan Zhongyan (989–1052),[27] who spearheaded the short-lived early Song reforms. Fan Zhongyan's famous precept that officials should "be the first to become concerned with the world's troubles and the last to rejoice in its happiness" became, in Ungar's words, "an article of faith among fifteenth-century Vietnamese public servants and scholars and was greatly encouraged by Nguyen Trai in his writings and his example."[28] James Liu conceptualized the ultimate vision of officialdom in the policies of Fan Zhongyan and his reform movement as an "ethocracy" based on moral principles and a strict sense of responsibility toward the people. This Confucian idealism with its "practical utilitarian spirit and . . . active political interest"[29] nicely complemented the emphases on practicality and dynamic leadership in Vietnamese political thought. However, Nguyen Trai adapted, but did not wholly adopt, the positions of early Song reformist Confucianism. Rather, as Ungar argues, he "merged" them with "the traditional Vietnamese leadership ethic" that envisioned a heroic and just ruler in tune with, and aided by, the spiritual powers of the country.[30]

Nguyen Trai fascinated DRVN intellectuals during the earlier years of the regime's consolidation and resumption of armed struggle. Tran Huy Lieu, the most prominent and influential historian in those days, regularly wrote on Nguyen Trai,[31] and Nguyen Trai's collected works were published in Ha Noi in 1969. Two reasons, one external and one internal, best account for Nguyen Trai's appeal to the DRVN. He, too, had put his service to the ultimately successful task of expelling foreign occupants. And by championing a Vietnamese version of Fan Zhongyan's "government school" of Confucianism with its "ethocracy," Nguyen Trai spoke directly to the revolutionaries' concern, now that they were in power, about building an efficient bureaucracy. In prescribing, as it were, how cadres could avoid the corrupting internal dynamics of government and stay selfless and "close to the people," Nguyen Trai reaffirmed the Revolution's positive self-image.

Did the Vietnamese Revolution consciously utilize Northern Song and early Le thought on good government? Tran Huy Lieu writes that Ho Chi Minh

> often used Pham Trong Yem's [Fan Zhongyan's] precept to educate the cadres. Communists fight for the happiness of humanity and therefore must "be the first to become concerned with the world's troubles and the last to rejoice in its happiness," and only the communists' "being the first to become concerned with the world's troubles and the last to rejoice in its happiness" is really consequential and complete.[32]

If I were to argue for an affinity between Confucianism and Vietnamese communism, I would have no better grounds than those provided by the intellectual links from Fan Zhongyan via Nguyen Trai to Ho Chi Minh. All stress the more practical questions of public service and (outward) moral conduct. The neo-Confucian emphasis on political orthodoxy and self-cultivation, however, neither seemed "to relate to Vietnamese considerations" in Nguyen Trai's times[33] nor was of much concern to Vietnamese communism with its marked absence of grander ideological designs or contributions. While Nguyen Khac Vien has pointed out that Vietnamese communism needed to stress its divergence from those "backward" aspects of Confucianism that emphasized, for example, social harmony and hierarchic obligations,[34] he nonetheless also admitted to affinities between revolutionary and Confucian ethical positions. In fact, Nguyen Khac Vien quotes from a VNCP handbook that explained "the five revolutionary virtues" to its cadres; these virtues were humanity, a sense of duty, knowledge, courage, and integrity. Fan Zhongyan is, again, very much present (yet unacknowledged) in the handbook's statement that "the cadre who displays [humanity] . . . will not hesitate to be the first to endure hardship and the last to enjoy happiness."[35]

Much more needs to be done to understand the connections between Confucian idealism/humanism and Vietnamese communism. For the latter, I suggest that it is helpful to distinguish between the party *in struggle* and the party *in power,* as these different positions conditioned the Revolution's varying judgments of Confucianism either as obstacle and opponent or as (partial) paragon and precursor. Alexander Woodside has hinted at this split perception with regard to the "mandarin" revolutionaries' concern over how to bridge the divide between their elite social backgrounds and the "masses" they were supposed to lead:

> In East Asia, the Confucian gentleman was the universalist concerned with other people's troubles and with the troubles of the universe, the free spirit least bound by the particular concerns of the "petty man." If memories of the self-serving "feudal" bureaucrat were anathema to the "proletarianized" intellectuals of the 1930s and 1940s, recollections of the classical "gentleman" whose universal humanitarianism recognized no social class boundaries, in its reactions to human misery, were probably far less repellent.[36]

To the party in struggle, "self-serving 'feudal' bureaucrats" did not only figure in its memory, I might add, but were, as French- or Emperor Bao Dai-serving "Confucian" bureaucrats, real-life adversaries. Further, the influence of specific and to varying degrees "Confucian" thinkers like Fan Zhongyan or Nguyen Trai on the twentieth-century revolutionary leadership needs to be studied much more thoroughly. When Ho Chi Minh freely inserted Fan Zhongyan's famous eleventh-century dictum into a "rectification" speech in April 1961, he was not just using "old symbols . . . creatively" and in a calculated and conscious way, as David Marr suggests.[37] Rather, he revealed a mind-set very much familiar with, and receptive to, Confucian humanism (and not just "less repelled" by it, as Woodside would have it).

WE CAN NOW END OUR DETOUR through Viet Nam's intellectual past and return to present-day My Hoa Hung by observing that

Nguyen Trai's thought and his precedent as enshrined national hero spirit resonate clearly in the presentation of Ton Duc Thang's own museum-shrine. Although no specific mention is made of Nguyen Trai at Ton's commemorative area, the exhibits' statement about the proper ways of a revolutionary government bears such resemblance to the particular activist-idealist strand of Confucian ethics espoused by Nguyen Trai (and, as we have just seen, consciously utilized as a guideline for DRVN cadres), that it is safe to presume a powerful allusion of the former to the latter.

Ton Duc Thang's commemorators implied the correlation with Nguyen Trai's thought and hero spirit status hardly in an arbitrary or random manner. Rather, the timing of important events likely suggested and reinforced it.[38] The year in which Ton Duc Thang died, 1980, marked also the 600th anniversary of Nguyen Trai's birth. Nguyen Trai's anniversary was widely and prominently observed in Viet Nam—not the least because Nguyen Trai's role as heroic defender of the nation against Ming aggression fit neatly with the pervasive anti-Chinese atmosphere just one year after the brief but costly Chinese invasion of northern Viet Nam in 1979. A number of conferences on Nguyen Trai were organized and related publications appeared in subsequent years. Therefore, during the early to mid-1980s, the public celebration of Nguyen Trai as a model advocate of good government and as a protective spirit in the "heroic tradition of resistance" overlapped with, and likely had considerable influence on, the formative stage of the commemoration of Ton Duc Thang.

I have offered ways of reading Ton Duc Thang's museum-shrine against a background of historical allusions and a multitude of cultural quotations and memories. On the one hand, his birthplace shrine establishes Ton Duc Thang as a guardian spirit who has joined the Vietnamese pantheon of historical hero deities. On the other, the museum exhibit propagates an ethos of the simple and selflessly devoted cadre, which similarly reaches back in time and connects with certain Confucian concepts espoused by a famous Vietnamese scholar-official. But are we not dealing here with two quite different, even incompatible, cultural statements, the markedly non- and pre-Confucian tutelary spirits of the *Spiritual Powers of the Viet Realm* and Nguyen Trai's version of Confucian idealist humanism? I would not agree. According to Esta Ungar, in Nguyen Trai's thought, Song reformist Confucianism was "merged with" or "grafted onto" long-established Vietnamese notions of heroic leadership and the interplay between worldly and spiritual powers. And dynamic relations between these concepts, not incompatibility, existed, as described by Alexander Woodside when he writes of Vietnamese intellectuals:

> [Their] inclination to [study popular traditions] *accompanied* the Confucianization of Vietnamese intellectual life, was provoked by it, and sometimes collided with its this-worldly sensibilities. . . . The mixture of acceptance and rejections varied with each thinker. . . . But it was the *interplay* between Confucian moral theories and the great ancient reservoir of Vietnamese religious and mythical formulations which most decisively shaped Vietnamese views of change before 1860.[39]

Even more so, there is an area of commonality in the two concepts. Nguyen Trai was concerned with an "ethocracy" of officials who would aid the ruler for the welfare of the people, for social order and harmony. Hero spirits likewise take a mediating position between ruler and ruled: as similar guarantors of a stable social order, they ensure protection from the top down and loyalty, ideological adherence, and support from the bottom up. Both concepts are thus concerned with the harmonious relationship between ruler and the people and emphasize the crucial role of the ruler's agents in bringing it about in a proper way.

It is in this fundamental concern that Ton Duc Thang's spirit temple and museum exhibit finally coalesce in a meaningful way. In its personification by Ton Duc Thang, the statement about an idealistic, selfless, and uncorrupted governing officialdom—an ethos of revolutionary cadres—itself is the enshrined spirit of My Hoa Hung. Simple and selfless communist cadres are the agents of an abstract ruler, the Vietnamese Revolution. Properly called upon and utilized, these officials ensure the Revolution's success against outward threats and domestic disorder. Their primary concern with the people's livelihood constitutes the protection the people expect from their government. In exchange, the people recognize the party's legitimacy and are loyal. Instead of tensions, paradox, and subversion, this is the unifying theme that can make sense of the commemorative area. At Ton Duc Thang's birthplace, the uncorrupted cadre, who tirelessly and selflessly works for the benefit of both the Revolution and the people, is enshrined as a guardian spirit of the Revolution, and the museum functions as a modern temple inscription announcing the spirit's merit, achievements, and outstanding character.

I HAVE PROPOSED AN INTERPRETATION that makes sense of what appeared to be a highly contradictory commemoration of a communist leader at his birthplace. While this search has taken me all the way back to the eleventh century, the site's contemporary context, the late 1980s, requires some attention as well. The waning of the Cold War and the decline and ultimate demise of the socialist camp in the 1980s increasingly weakened the external moral authority and political legitimacy that Marxism-Leninism had long afforded the ruling Vietnamese Communist Party. This process opened up space for a popular re-embracing of the "traditional"[40] at the same time the Revolution itself was compelled to seek an alternative model of authority, one that would have to come from within the prerevolutionary Vietnamese range of experiences. Popular reclaiming of ritual practices and the party's need to reaffirm its legitimacy by self-consciously anchoring ("localizing") itself in much more traditional concepts and language occurred side by side. It is no coincidence that the mid-1970s saw the erection of a monumental mausoleum to Ho Chi Minh in Ha Noi, with a structure and a cultic-ritual form outside Vietnamese practices, while spirit shrines/museums resonating with traditional political-cultural concepts appeared in the late 1980s in the countryside.

Commemorative confidence is one aspect that needs to be considered in this context. The Ho Chi Minh mausoleum is one such expression of confidence; here the Vietnamese Revolution felt a "belonging." It was certainly Vietnamese, but belonged—on equal terms, as symbolized by the chosen architectural-ritual form—to the larger moral order and authoritative structure of the socialist camp. Intoxicated by its military triumph of the mid-1970s, it felt firmly embedded in a grander historical design, the validity of which had just been proven by the Revolution's singular feat of successfully achieving, against great odds, its outward goals of uniting the country and ending foreign domination.[41]

In contrast, at the core of the commemoration in My Hoa Hung lies a deep crisis of confidence. Gone were the days of triumphalism and the shelter of a greater outside moral authority that would have provided a familiar choice of commemorative form. The Revolution had lost its sense of purpose, and the split between the trajectory it had prescribed for the country and the material-cultural tendencies of the people widened. There were the dramatic economic downturn of the mid-1980s, rising social ills, widespread popular dissatisfaction with, or, worse yet, disinterest in, the revolutionary government, rampant corruption and loss of morale among its cadres, and the ominous decline of the global socialist camp. Amid these crises, the organizers of Ton Duc Thang's museum-shrine "turned nativist" and (re-)discovered in the traditional a new/old source of legitimacy and guidance. In exchange for one historical model of predictability, the increasingly discredited Marxism-Leninism, they tapped into a model within the Vietnamese cultural repertoire that equally promised historical certainty, a predictable course of events, the invincible alliance between Vietnamese worldly and spiritual powers. Instead of the mausoleum, the spirit temple was (re-)created.

But this should not be confused with a change of allegiance or a turning away from the Revolution. Despite the confidence crisis, Ton Duc Thang's commemorators remained committed and fiercely loyal to the Revolution. Their fundamental concern lay with its survival, and they were anxious to improve the quality of the revolutionary ranks. And so, triggered by the disconcerting changes in the fortunes of the socialist camp, yet another imagined ancestry of Vietnamese communism was established through Ton Duc Thang. This ancestry was found in traditional concepts of authority and order of the country's spiritual and worldly realms and in the unbroken sequence of national heroes, who, with the aid of the spirit world to which they themselves would belong after death, had risen to defend the country and reaffirm these concepts. Placing the communist Revolution and Ton Duc Thang (and, of course, Ho Chi Minh) within this continuum reasserted a sense of pride in times of bedeviling self-doubts. But the veneration of guardian spirits also provided Ton Duc Thang's commemorators with the safe and prudent form, and Confucian idealism afforded them with a consistent language, to express their warnings about revolutionary decline in the present. In that sense, the site entails more of an act of "talking back" at the state than of lecturing down to the people. Through Ton Duc Thang's museum-shrine, the selfless, activist, and uncorrupted cadre who would ensure harmony between the Revolution and the people was idealized. The nostalgia and criticism in this message only become explicit because of the statement's incompatibility with present times, times that to the commemorators likely appeared out of joint.

Amid the loud signals of distress is a faint message of hope. To explain this, let us briefly revisit Ton Duc Thang's commemorators and again consider the aspect of regionalism. The museum-shrine in My Hoa Hung and the symposium on Ton Duc Thang's life that coincided with the site's inauguration in 1988 were organized jointly by local cadres in Long Xuyen and former southern party leaders and important CFRF members who were equally instrumental in establishing the Ton Duc Thang Museum in Ho Chi Minh City: Tran Van Giau, Tran Van Tra, Tran Bach Dang, Luu Phuong Thanh, and others. All were critical of the present and tried to highlight the south's contributions to the successes of the Vietnamese Revolution and national reunion. Therefore, what characterized their outlook was, on the one hand, their deep loyalty to the Revolution they had helped to succeed and, on the other, their intense feelings of having been overlooked in the process, pushed aside and marginalized both as idealistic cadres (by careerists) and as southerners (by northerners).

And thus, in the end, the enshrined revolutionary ethos of loyal service at My Hoa Hung can be seen as the commemorators' *self-image,* and they themselves, along with Ton Duc Thang, embody the Revolution's guardian spirits. Just like the tutelary deities, they "announce" their willingness to serve the ruler. We will remember that Oliver Wolters described the attraction between ruler and guardian spirit as "the automatic response of local tutelary spirits to a ruler's presence, provided that the ruler had already shown signs of achievement and leadership," but also that spirits can admonish a ruler to "seek and follow virtue" *(duc).*[42] Both dynamics, response and admonition, are at work here and undertaken by people who are, on the one hand, loyal to the Revolution and, on the other—amplified by their memories of past glories—pained by its present state.

Their hopeful message is that the Revolution can be saved if it is able to refocus on its fundamental purpose, go back to its origins (symbolized by the temple at a prominent revolutionary's birthplace), "clean up its act," and rediscover, accept, and use all the talents available, including those in the south. In a remarkable parallelism to traditional notions of authority and legitimacy, this message implies that the people, when recognizing such a rejuvenated and reinvigorated rule, would certainly abandon their errant ways and once again follow the Revolution. In their idealization of the earlier days of the Communist Party-led society, when, supposedly, a revolutionary ethos of service guided officialdom and the people and their leaders were in harmony, Ton Duc Thang's commemorators reveal their distress over, and protectiveness of, the Revolution in its present endangered state. Idealization and protectiveness are thus both at work in this act of *goi hon,* of "calling the spirits": enshrined and re-called in the little village of My Hoa Hung are, at once, heady memories of the Revolution's spirit and—waiting so very anxiously to be called to its aid—the Revolution's tutelary spirit.

Conclusion

MY STORY HAS FOLLOWED TON DUC THANG and the imagined ancestries of Vietnamese communism, covering a period of about seventy years. It led me from the early 1920s, when Ton began telling his impressive tale of the Black Sea Mutiny, to the early 1990s, when Ton was invoked as a guardian of the revolutionary spirit—now (re-)conceptualized in traditionalist terms—by those who lamented the shortcomings of the party's leadership and the people's loss of revolutionary fervor. This biographical and historiographical case study thus spans the entire period of the communist-led Vietnamese Revolution, which shared with countless other social-political movements in history the familiar life cycle of rise and decline: timely appeals and visions, parallel struggles for both political power and legitimizing symbolic language, followed by initial idealism and confidence once in command, then increasing doctrinairism and stagnation, and finally inner contradictions and decay.

Ton Duc Thang's life and public images mirrored this cycle. He initially came to symbolize the radical novelty of the Revolution, its rejection of what was old and established, its liberating message, and its adherence to a larger, internationalist order. However, the Red Flag marked the transition from confidence to dogmatism. In the end, he became the personification of rediscovered national traditions and of traits of a nostalgically recalled revolutionary past.

To briefly revisit the various moments of this story: In the late colonial moment, before the August Revolution of 1945, Ton Duc Thang built his authority among the young workers of Sai Gon, and later among his fellow prisoners, on the story of his participation in the Black Sea Mutiny at Sevastopol. His account, however, was in fact sustained by his experiences of organized mass protests in Toulon. Toulon/Sevastopol was *the* life-changing event for Ton. It was a preview of what he hoped would happen in Viet Nam—mass action leading to revolution, liberation, and a new, just community—and henceforth he devoted his life to the struggle to make this vision become reality.

In Cochinchina of 1920, such a goal must have appeared further away than ever. There were no kindred organizations around to turn to, and Ton needed to become a leading activist himself in order to work for radical change. But he was also a quiet, simple, and modest man. In his efforts to organize the workers of Sai Gon, the Black Sea story became his sign of personal distinction that attracted loyal followers. It was employed in a measured way to give him a necessary authoritative edge, yet without making him a celebrity. In his leadership style, Ton did not aspire to greatness, to reaching the top, to standing out. He thrived on *being a part of,* on shared experiences, and on the close and trusting personal associations he then used to give support, counsel, and guidance.

These characteristics might explain why Ton survived sixteen years on Con Lon, the longest prison record among the party leaders. Others cracked and perished, perhaps like the brilliant and driven Nguyen An Ninh, because they experienced confinement as unbearable isolation that stifled their great ambitions, drained their energies, and suffocated their will. But Ton found community in confinement; the island penal colony was an environment almost conducive to his personality. It might explain why fellow inmates would later recall Ton's unfailing optimism, and why he himself remembered those many years on the island as a period when "we were happy all the time."[1]

After 1945, Ton Duc Thang had the rare and good fortune that the Revolution recognized these traits of his and made him what I have termed the leader of followers. His representational functions in the DRVN state apparatus corresponded well with his unique leadership style, and his seniority and southernness served the political and propagandistic needs of the regime.

But with regard to the account of the Black Sea Mutiny, Ton's control over the story slipped away in the revolutionary moment of the second half of the 1940s. The DRVN adopted his account as one of its tales of origin. Any regime in power needs to assert its legitimacy through the imagination and printed and publicly reenacted displays of its presumed origins and the establishment of genealogies that can carry those identified ancestries from the past to the present. The central items of origin from which legitimacy is derived become, in what is inherent in the process of imagination, extremely essentialized: "the ancient culture of X," or "the tradition of resistance," or "the epic struggle of Y," or "zero hour," or "the revolution of Z," et cetera, turn into rhetorical figures exalting wanted traits and excluding those that are undesirable. For the DRVN and the ICP, Ton's Black Sea story thus established the crucial link between Vietnamese communism and the Russian October Revolution. And in the dark days of diplomatic isolation and military pressure around 1947/48, the Revolution found in Ton's participation in the Sevastopol mutinies its ancestry of revolutionary internationalism, which it so desperately needed at that moment.

In the politically much more orthodox post-recognition moment, when the DRVN firmly became a member of the communist bloc, the party's addition of the Red Flag to the story of the Black Sea signified *proletarian* internationalism as another essential trait of Vietnamese communism. It is necessary to emphasize that Ton Duc Thang was irreplaceable for the party in that regard: no one else could establish such an ancestry for such an early date and with such a direct connection to the October Revolution. With the image of the Red Flag at Sevastopol, Ton became a truly national symbol, which the entire revolutionary movement could embrace.

At the same time, the Red Flag had destructive effects on both Ton Duc Thang and the ability of the party leadership to control the story. First, the boastful Red Flag indicated that the party misunderstood the rather quiet utility the original tale had for Ton; he could no longer recognize himself in the exaggerated story. But the Red Flag also brought the serious danger that the lie of Toulon/Sevastopol would be exposed. Ton managed to avoid such a troubling scenario, but in the process lost the ability to imagine himself part of a revolutionary internationalist movement. Second, with the Red Flag in the Black Sea, Ton Duc Thang became such an unassailable icon of the Revolution that the central party now, too, lost control over the imagery of origins associated with him. From now on, competing interests within the Revolution could use Ton for their particular purposes.

The story of the strike at Ba Son must be considered in the context of the post-partition moment. Ton Duc Thang and Tran Van Giau exaggerated the events at the Sai Gon arsenal in 1925 for overlapping, but not necessarily identical, reasons. An ancestry of proletarian internationalism *in Viet Nam* could be imagined through the strike, and after the calamity of the Red Flag, Ton found in the story a new venue for his preferred intimate association with the masses. The story of Ba Son, after all, would not have him hoist a Red Flag. Recounting the tale of the organized political walkout at the navy shipyard was the last time Ton Duc Thang involved himself personally in the imaginations connected with his status as a revolutionary icon. On the other hand, with his version of the strike at Ba Son, Tran Van Giau started a process in which southern revolutionary identities could find expression around the veneration of Ton's life and work. In the forced northern exile in which many southern communists found themselves after 1954, regional tensions emerged with northerners, who seemed condescending toward the southerners, more austere perhaps, and—with the DRVN now consolidated on "their" territory—more accomplished as revolutionaries. Against this background, the strike at the arsenal in Sai Gon not only provided southern revolutionary credentials but also placed the origins of the politicization of Vietnamese labor squarely in the south. Not surprisingly, such an image met with northern resistance, finding expression in the ideological-historiographical dispute between Tran Van Giau and Tran Huy Lieu.

The passion with which regional differences surfaced in the historical debates over the so-called "secret labor union" was only possible in the post-socialist moment of the later 1980s, when the intellectual climate had warmed considerably. However, as an imagined ancestry of revolutionary Vietnamese unionism, which supposedly had its roots in the south, the story of the secret labor union belongs in the post-unification moment. The feeling that, after the long and costly resistance war, southerners did not receive their fair share of revolutionary credit and were, indeed, pushed aside and somehow colonized by the northern-dominated party apparatus became widespread after the end of the war in 1975 and the return home of the exiled southern revolutionaries. As early as around 1979/80 attempts were made to demand broader recognition for the historical contributions of Ton's "union."

After Ton's death in 1980, there was common ground for the whole party to commemorate the deceased president. Various factions together still could see in Ton idealized reflections of their political origins and political dreams. Ton had been the nice old man with a big heart, thrifty and unassuming, a little bumbling and harmless. Through Ton, people could momentarily indulge in the essential desire for harmonious and simple human relations in a conflict-free and easily comprehensible world. Through Ton, they could take comfort in knowing he had risen and fought to set things straight, when imperialism, capitalism, outsiders, and others had encroached on this peaceful arrangement. Next to Ho Chi Minh, only Ton Duc Thang was able to give the Vietnamese Revolution—like the other institutionalized socialist revolutions of the twentieth century, at its cultural/social core a petty bourgeois project—its sense of home, of *Heimat.* The Vietnamese word *nho* means "to remember" but also "to miss" a person, indicative of the extraordinary role that idealized pasts play in the construction of Vietnamese presents. After Ton's death, therefore, and in the accelerating decline of the revolution in the 1980s, remembering Ton was to miss the things he had come to symbolize.

Differences in commemorative emphasis, however, also became apparent. Ton's northern party biography in 1982 attempted, perhaps for the last time, to draw the image of Ton Duc Thang into the national domain. It emphasized the Red Flag in the Black Sea, the long imprisonment, and his shining career in the DRVN after 1945. Likewise, the strike at Ba Son and the secret labor union, episodes open to regionalist imaginations, were downplayed. Ton Duc Thang thus came to legitimize the entire party again. In the immediate posthumous moment, when party confidence and resilience were still relatively high but economic conditions worsened rapidly, the biographical emphases on the Red Flag, Ton's imprisonment, and his post-1945 career also produced a message that revolutionary heroism and sacrifice would ultimately be prominently recognized and handsomely rewarded.

Southern commemorators, on the other hand, emphasized Ton Duc Thang's lifelong simplicity and modesty in connection with all his fine revolutionary contributions, including, of course, the strike at the arsenal and his early labor activism. The southern message was that one could achieve great victories and still stay true to one's ideals. In the post-socialist moment, Ton Duc Thang was thus used for a veiled critique of what was by then perceived as a corrupted Revolution.

The liberalization of the political climate after the Sixth Party Congress in late 1986 finally created space for the southern revolutionary discourse to become more assertive. It demanded that its ancestral line, now also informed by traditional concepts of leadership and notions of good government, be included in an improved power structure. Yet, in an odd twist, the Doi Moi liberalization inadvertently also moved Vietnamese society away from the wartime revolutionary paradigm that had emphasized heroism, solidarity, and endurance, and irrevocably directed it toward a market paradigm focused on individualism, competition, and gratification. In this new environment, the ways of an idealized Revolution no longer fit and, increasingly, no longer mattered.

Paradoxically, the southern revolutionaries, historians, and Ton Duc Thang commemorators lost the possibility for their version of the Revolution to become reality in the very process that finally gave them a certain amount of opportunity to voice their demands. With their vision for the future obstructed, perhaps permanently, what was left for them to do was to project the imagined ancestries, which they had worked so hard to establish through Ton Duc Thang, back in time. At long last they had claimed a coveted place on the stage, but their audience was leaving for the alluring new show next door, and their voices echoed back at them with the sounds of nostalgia.

AT THE TURN OF THE MILLENNIUM, while the veneration and commemoration of Ho Chi Minh continue to saturate Vietnamese public life, Ton Duc Thang has been largely forgotten. To be sure, major boulevards in Ha Noi and Ho Chi Minh City bear his name, as does a wide coastal highway on Con Lon Island,[2] and several commemorative sites in the south, while certainly underutilized, remain open. But a majority of the Vietnamese are in their thirties or younger, too young to know much about, or to show much interest in, their country's second revolutionary president. Moreover, most of those who knew and closely worked with Ton in the Revolution and, as argued in this book, found through his images idealized versions of the Revolution's origin and meaning have passed away or are too old to keep his public memory alive.

What about the generation, then, that came of age during the thirty-odd years of the pre-Doi Moi socialist system, those now in their forties, fifties, and sixties? Like citizens of other "real existing" socialist countries,[3] they were extraordinarily adept at reading the subtle signs of power currents within their country's ruling communist hierarchy. Some leaders projected great power, and the policies, party factions, and ideological lines they represented therefore demanded reckoning in the everyday lives of the population. Regardless of whether one admired or feared them, exponents of the system like Truong Chinh and Pham Hung, the admired Vo Nguyen Giap and Pham Van Dong, or the hard-liners Le Duan and Le Duc Tho—sarcastically referred to as the "later Le dynasty" in reference to their control of the party since the mid-1960s—therefore remain vivid in the memories of this generation. But Ton Duc Thang, despite his prominence and likable public persona, obviously enjoyed little actual political influence and, as mere figurehead, did not require much monitoring by the citizenry's political-atmospheric weathervanes. Thus, twenty-some years after his death, he has long faded from the consciousness of the now middle-aged, notwithstanding the occasional quips about his rhetorical slipups, modest intellectual range, and earthy demeanor.

THIS CASE STUDY has not just examined one historiographical construction of the political biography of Viet Nam's second president, nor the glorification of the communist-led Revolution. Rather, it shows that the process in which Vietnamese communism defined itself, imagined where it had come from, and envisioned where it was going, was a complex one. Ancestries were imagined through the life of Ton Duc Thang in the changing contexts of various historical moments, which determined how these ancestries were perceived, what purposes they served, and who embraced and who contested them. Certainly the widespread (and still lingering) Cold War perceptions in the West of communist regimes as being monolithic and immutable fall far short of reality. Despite strong tendencies in the Communist Party leadership to rigidly prescribe but a single past, there is and never has been just one history of the Vietnamese Revolution. Among others, one purpose of this book is to sharpen our understanding of the diversity and pluralism of the people and ideas that sustained this remarkable historic movement and to invite additional fresh inquiries.

More generally, the extraordinary richness of Viet Nam's most recent century awaits further study. Within and beside the Vietnamese Revolution—and, indeed, sometimes dissociated from the teleological reach of its orbit—much remains to be discovered or reevaluated: social transformations and economic-ecological changes, the great variety of Vietnamese intellectual life, literary and artistic expressions, the country's array of regional and local identities, religious and ethnic communities, political visions and historical memories—myriad experiences, many voices, and multiple pasts.

Notes

INTRODUCTION

1. By the 1880s, the rest of the country had been conquered by the French. It was divided into the artificial units Annam (to the Vietnamese, Trung Ky/the Center) and Tonkin (Bac Ky/the North), which became French protectorates under the nominal authority of what was by then a Vietnamese puppet monarchy. Together with the neighboring kingdoms of Cambodia and Laos, which the French also conquered, the three Vietnamese regions Tonkin, Annam, and the colony of Cochinchina would form French Indochina.

2. From: Centre des archives d'Outre-Mer (CAOM), Aix-en-Provence: Archives d'Outre-Mer (AOM), Fonds de l'Indochine/Archives centrales: Fonds du gouvernement général ([GG), série F: affaires politiques, sous-série 7F: Sûreté générale (7F), carton (c.) 55: Crime de la rue Barbier/Affaire Tran Truong et consorts; Section Outre-Mer (SOM), Direction des affaires politiques; Service de liaison avec les originaires des territoires français d'Outre-Mer (SLOTFOM), série III: Sûreté intérieure de la France et des ses colonies, c. 129: Affaire de la rue Barbier. The material includes several files with interrogations, the bill of indictment, and articles from various periodicals. Also from Hue-Tam Ho Tai, *Radicalism and the Origins of the Vietnamese Revolution* (Cambridge, Mass.: Harvard University Press, 1992), 214ff., and from several interviews of mine with historians in Viet Nam.

3. Alias Bao Luong. She and her cousin Tran Truong lived with Ton's family.

4. The revolutionary events of 1945, in their narrower sense, are referred to as the "August Revolution."

5. Peter Zinoman, *The Colonial Bastille: A History of Imprisonment in Vietnam, 1862-1940* (Berkeley: University of California Press, 2001).

6. Keith Taylor, "Surface Orientations in Vietnam: Beyond Histories of Nation and Region," *Journal of Asian Studies* 57, no. 4 (November 1998): 949-78.

7. Glenn Anthony May, *Inventing a Hero: The Posthumous Re-creation of Andres Bonifacio* (Quezon City: New Day, and Madison: University of Wisconsin-Madison Center for Southeast Asian Studies, 1997).

1. THE BLACK SEA MUTINY IN THE LATE COLONIAL MOMENT

1. Thai Nguyen province is composed of the two former provinces of Thai Nguyen and Bac Can.

2. Interview with Duong Van Phuc and Ton Thi Hanh, Ha Noi, 14 May 1992. For information on the marriage, see Thep Moi, "Bac Ton: nguoi dai bieu Quoc hoi mien Nam tieu bieu" (Uncle Ton: A typical southern member of the National Assembly), transcript of speech given at the Ton Duc Thang symposium in Long Xuyen in 1988, in: *Mot con nguoi binh thuong: vi dai. Ky yeu Hoi thao khoa hoc ve Chu tich Ton Duc Thang nhan dip ky niem 100 nam ngay sinh 20–8–1888–20–8–1988* (A great ordinary person: Proceedings of the symposium on President Ton Duc Thang commemorating the centennial of his birth), Ban tuyen giao Tinh uy An Giang (An Giang provincial propaganda commission), ed., To Thanh Tam (An Giang, 1989), 241.

3. Specifically, two other alleged participants, Pham Van Dong and Le Van Luong, made no mention of the event in Vo Nhai in earlier communications with me. Interview with Le Van Luong (also known as Pham Van Khuong, Nguyen Cong Mieu), Ho Chi Minh City, 9 May 1992; communications received from Pham Van Dong, through his secretary Nguyen Tien Nang, Ha Noi, 12 May 1992. I had, of course, not yet heard about Vo Nhai then; my follow-up letters to Le Van Luong and Pham Van Dong, in which I asked for information on the meeting, were not answered.

4. According to the Gregorian calendar, but 23/24 October according to the Julian calendar in use in Russia, hence "October Revolution."

5. Later renamed Leningrad and in recent years renamed Saint Petersburg, its name before being called Petrograd.

6. The following general discussion is mainly informed by Philippe Masson, *La Marine française et la Mer Noire (1918–1919)* (Paris: Sorbonne, 1982). See also Jacques Raphaël-Leygues and Jean-Luc Barré, *Les Mutins de la Mer Noire: Avril 1919: Des Marins français se revoltent* ([Paris]: Plon, 1981).

7. Warships involved to various degrees in these incidents were the *Diderot,* the *Ernest Renan,* the *Guichen,* the *Patrie,* the *Provence,* the *Voltaire,* and even a few units in the Baltic Sea and the Russian Far East.

8. Masson, *La Marine française,* 345–46.

9. See, for example, ibid., 448–49.

10. See for example, André Marty, *La Révolte de la Mer Noire* (Paris: Éditions Sociales, 1949 [4th ed.]); André Marty, *The Epic of the Black Sea* (London: Modern Books, n.d.); and Jean Le Ramey and Pierre Vottero, *Les Mutins de la Mer Noire* (Paris: Éditions Sociales, 1973).

11. See Yves Le Braz, *Les Rejetés: L'Affaire Marty-Tillon: Pour une histoire différente du PCF* (Paris: Table Ronde, 1974), for the vicissitudes of Marty's life and FCP career.

12. See the detailed lists of court-martials in both Marty, *La Révolte,* 643–53, and Masson, *La Marine française,* 617–19.

13. The alias only appears in police files beginning in 1929; see Centre des archives d'Outre-Mer (CAOM), Aix-en-Provence: Archives d'Outre-Mer (AOM), Fonds de l'Indochine/Archives centrales: Fonds du gouvernement général (GG), série F: affaires politiques, sous-série 7F: Sûreté générale (7F), carton (c.) 55: Crime de la rue Barbier/Affaire Tran Truong et consorts; Section Outre-

Mer (SOM), Direction des affaires politiques; Service de liaison avec les originaires des territoires français d'Outre-Mer (SLOTFOM), série III: Sûreté intérieure de la France et des ses colonies, c. 129: Affaire de la rue Barbier. No other source ever mentioned an alias for Ton Duc Thang.

14. Services historiques de la marine, France (hereafter SHM): Archives de la IIe région maritime (hereafter IIe région), Brest, série 4E (rôles d'équipages), nos. 2782 *(Algol)*, 2807, 2808 *(Bruix)*, 2866, 2867 *(Chamois)*, 2920 *(Du Chayla)*, 2943, 2944 *(France)*, 2952, 2953 *(Hussard)*, 2958, 2959, 2960, [2961] *(Jean-Bart)*, 2977 *(Scarpe)*, 2995, 2996, 2997 *(Mirabeau)*, 3009 *(Protet)*, 3042, 3043, 3044 *(Waldeck-Rousseau)*. Archives de la IIIe région maritime (hereafter IIIe région), Toulon, série 2E7 (rôles d'équipages), nos. 1670, 1671, 1672 *(Justice)*, 1731 *(Touareg)*, 1735, 1736, 1737, 1738 *(Vergniaud)*, 1916, 1917 (*Waldeck-Rousseau* in 1920). I also checked the *Jules Michelet* (Brest, nos. 4E-2964, 2965, 2966) and the *Paris* (Toulon, nos. 2E7–1420 [1918 crew], 1697, 1698), which were in or near the Black Sea during that period, but saw no or little unrest on board.

Archivists in Brest and Toulon examined the crew lists of the *Dehorter, Ernest Renan, Escaut, Fauconneau,* and *Mameluck*. Further searches and cross-checks of the *rôles* of French warships in the Black Sea produced the same, negative result. Official letter, IIe région, 20 September 1996. About a year after my work in Toulon and Brest, the Ton Duc Thang Museum in Ho Chi Minh City commissioned similar inquiries with the archives. Letter from archivist Patrick Petit, Brest, 19 September 1996.

15. Marty, *La Révolte,* 31. Marty never mentions Ton Duc Thang.

16. Hoang Quoc Viet, "A Glorious Son of the Vietnamese Working Class and Nation," *Viet-Nam Advances: A Social and Cultural Review* (Ha Noi) 3, no. 10 (October 1958): 3.

17. Bao tang Cach Mang (Museum of the Revolution), Ho Chi Minh City: "École des mécaniciens asiatiques, registre, brevets d'études techniques 1906–1966, promotion de 1915–1917." The register was rediscovered in 1980 and handed over to the museum. See also document nos. 114 and 117 at the Bao tang Ton Duc Thang (Ton Duc Thang Museum), Ho Chi Minh City.

18. Bao tang Cach Mang, Ho Chi Minh City: "École des mécaniciens, registre matricule, commence le 1er Décembre 1907, terminé le . . . 1918. Thang Ton duc." See also document no. 115 at the Bao tang Ton Duc Thang, Ho Chi Minh City.

19. During a police interrogation on 30 July 1929, a week after his arrest, Ton himself claimed that he "incurred a voluntary enlistment as a skilled worker for the duration of the war" when he attended the École des mécaniciens asiatiques from 1913 to September 1915. After graduating with a *diplôme d'ouvrier mécanicien,* he had left for France at the end of 1915 to work at the Toulon arsenal. But the value of the statement about his voluntary war service—wrong dates and all—is of a somewhat limited nature. After all, the claim was made during the stress of a (violent?) police interrogation and under grave accusations, when a pro-French image would have been of greatest

benefit. See CAOM, AOM, GG, 7F, c. 55: Crime de la rue Barbier /Affaire Tran Truong et consorts; here: protocol of interrogation on 30 July 1929.

20. For example, Dinh Xuan Lam and Pham Xanh, "Bac Ton voi phong trao cach mang o Sai Gon cuoi nhung nam 20" (Uncle Ton and the revolutionary movement in Sai Gon in the late 1920s), *Tap chi cong san* (Communism) (June 1988): 13; Ha Huy Giap, "Tuong nho Bac Ton" (Remembering Uncle Ton) *Tap chi cong san* (July 1988): 18.

21. See, for example, Hoang Quoc Viet, "A Glorious Son," 3; "Tieu su tom tat cua Chu tich nuoc Viet-Nam Dan Chu Cong Hoa Ton-Duc-Thang" (Summarized biography of Ton Duc Thang, President of the DRVN), *Tap chi Hoc tap* (Study) (October 1969): 23–24.

22. "Vi ly tuong ma phan dau" (For the ideal we fight), *Quan doi nhan dan* 6754 (2 April 1980): 3. The article is a reprint of a conversation Ton had in early 1957 with Ha Noi youths aspiring to become party members. My emphases.

23. "Nhung gio Hac-hai doi voi toi" (How I experienced the times in the Black Sea), *Tien phong* 232 (26–29 October 1957): 1. My emphases. This is Ton's article "Ya uchastvoval v vosstanii-na chernom morie," describing his part in the mutinies, trans. A. Shiltovoi, in *Sovietskii Moriak,* 24 (1957): 6–7, *re*translated into Vietnamese. Kurihara Hirohide kindly made the Russian original available to me.

24. SHM-IIIe région, Toulon, 395C, Division navale de l'Indochine/ Cochinchine, majorité, nos. 152 (Cahier d'ordres de l'arsenal no. 9, 6 April 1911–6 June 1912) and 153 (Cahier d'ordres de l'arsenal no. 10, 7 June 1912–19 November 1913) have no entry referring to strikes or protests at the arsenal. See also nos. 149–151 (5 October 1908–6 April 1911).

25. Ban nghien cuu lich su Dang trung uong (Central Commission for the Research of Party History, hereafter BNCLSDTU), *Dong chi Ton Duc Thang, nguoi chien si cong san kien cuong mau muc* (Comrade Ton Duc Thang, an exemplary, staunch communist fighter) (Ha Noi: NXB Su that, 1982), 8–9.

26. Luu Phuong Thanh: "Dong chi Ton Duc Thang, lanh tu dau tien cua giai cap cong nhan Viet Nam" (Comrade Ton Duc Thang, the first leader of the Vietnamese working class), in *Nhung nguoi con trung dung cua thanh pho* (The City's Loyal and Courageous Children), ed. Luu Phong Thanh (Ho Chi Minh City: NXB Thanh pho Ho Chi Minh, 1987): 10–11. Also in part personal interview with Luu Phuong Thanh, 11 May 1992, Ho Chi Minh City.

27. See Bao tang Cach Mang, Ho Chi Minh City: "École des mécaniciens asiatiques, registre, brevets d'études techniques 1906–1966, promotion de 1915–1917."

28. "Nhung mau chuyen ve Chu tich Ton Duc Thang" (Stories about President Ton Duc Thang), handwritten transcript of a conversation between Nguyen Tang Tan of the Ton Duc Thang Museum and Ton's daughter and sons-in-law, Ton Thi Hanh, Duong Van Phuc, and Tuong Bich Truc, at Ha Noi, 6 December 1989; document no. 185, Ton Duc Thang Museum, Ho Chi Minh City, 7.

29. AOM, GG, 7F, c. 55: protocol of interrogation on 30 July 1929. See also article on court proceedings in *Duoc Nha Nam,* Sai Gon, 16/17 July 1930.

30. Ha Huy Giap, "Tuong nho," 18.

31. André Dumarest, *La Formation de classes sociales en pays annamite* [Lyon, 1935?]: 64.

32. CAOM, SOM, Séries géographiques, Asie, Indochine, Nouveau Fonds, from 1920 (hereafter ICh NF), c. 21, dossier (hereafter d.) 227: Rapport du contrôle postal indochinois, Mai 1919, 4. Original emphasis.

33. During roughly the same period, one should remember, Nguyen Ai Quoc in Paris, after reading Lenin's treatise on the national and colonial questions (1920), privately burst out into the famous exclamation to his compatriots that now he had finally found the road to national liberation. BNCLSDTU, *Nhung su kien lich su Dang* (Events in Party history), vol. 1: 1920–1945 (Ha Noi: NXB Su that, 1976): 26.

34. Personnel records of the Toulon port and arsenal for 1916–20 are inconclusive. Those files that are accessible list mostly Frenchmen (and a few French women). See, for example, SHM-IIIe région, Toulon, *série* 2E4 (bureau des revues et services de la solde), nos. 888, 903, *série* 2G1 (bureaux matricules et statistiques, matricules du personnel ouvrier des constructions navales et artillerie navale), nos. 107, 130, 131, 132, 133, 199, 200, 207, 231, 234, 253, 256, 257, 258, 260. Other files are not systematically accessible unless one knows specific matriculation numbers to look for; see, for example, nos. 201–202, and especially *séries* 2G2 (bureaux matricules et statistiques, dossiers d'ouvriers) and 1M1 (matricules du personnel non officier).

35. BNCLSDTU, *Dong chi Ton,* 13.

36. In the absence of more concrete information, neither Patrick Fridenson's *Histoire des usines Renault: I. Naissance de la grande entreprise, 1898–1939* (Paris: Seuil, 1972) could contribute to clarifying the matter, nor did the central Renault archives. Correspondence with Regie nationale des usines Renault, Boulogne Billancourt, France, October 1994.

37. The passage from "École des mécaniciens, registre matricule" (Bao tang Cach Mang, Ho Chi Minh City) reads as follows:

"Sujet de peu de confiance: S'en présenté à l'École au retour de France, demandant sa préparation gratuité au Brevet, pension comprise, avec la promesse de servir comme chauffeur à l'École; sur le point d'être nommé, a quitté brusquement l'École." (illegible signature)

The word *nommé* is ambiguous here. On 9 May 1992, museum cadres told me they understood this passage to mean that Ton abruptly left when he was "about to have the degree conferred" *(den khi gan tot nghiep),* that is after he must have been enrolled and taken courses for a certain amount of time.

The matriculation page ends with an additional single line; in a different handwriting someone entered the words "Condamné politique au Poulo-Condore."

38. BNCLSDTU, *Dong chi Ton,* 13.

39. Trung tam luu tru quoc gia II, Ho Chi Minh City, files IA.3/172 and

177 (i.e., former files 1302 and 1310 GouCoch [gouvernement Cochinchine]): Chambre de commerce, *Bulletin quotidien des mouvements du port de Saigon, et renseignements commerciaux,* 36e année (January-September 1919) and 37e année (January-July 1920), especially nos. 143 (30 June, 1 July), 151 (9/10 July), 153 (12/13 July). See file IA.3/171(3) (i.e., 1301 GouCoch) for the *Bulletin* of September-December 1919.

40. In Thanh Nien, the challenge that Le Van Phat posed to Ton's customary role as the elder might well have contributed to the disastrous rivalries that led to the murder at the rue Barbier and the destruction of the southern revolutionary movement in 1929.

41. Tran Tu Binh, narr., Ha An, rec., *The Red Earth: A Vietnamese Memoir of Life on a Colonial Rubber Plantation,* trans. John Spragens, ed. David Marr (Athens, Ohio: Ohio University Press, 1985): 84: On Con Lon, Tran Tu Binh "met Ton Duc Thang, a mature communist, a sailor who had been in the *impressive* struggle on the Black Sea. . . . He regarded younger prisoners like me as *younger brothers*. He felt very sorry for us and shouldered all the heavy, difficult work." In this account, Ton is a "teacher" in the prison's "party school," and criticizes, directs, and encourages his "youngsters." Note how the Black Sea story impressed Tran Tu Binh. My emphasis. See also the reformative work Ton undertakes on a prison labor assignment with young, dangerous criminals in Nguyen Cong Hoan's semi-fictional, semi-biographical *Nguoi cap rang ham xay lua* (The *capelan* of the rice mill) (Ha Noi: NXB Kim Dong, 1978).

42. Marty, *La Révolte,* 459–76, and Masson, *La Marine française,* 453–78.

43. My interview with Luu Phuong Thanh, 11 May 1992, Ho Chi Minh City. See Luu Phuong Thanh, *Nhung nguoi con trung,* 10–11. Vo Van The stayed in contact with Ton throughout the 1920s but steered clear of any political activity. Before Ton was sent off to Con Lon in 1930, Vo Van The visited his friend in the Sai Gon central prison. They would meet again only in 1975, when then-president Ton Duc Thang received a letter from Vo Van The, remembered his old friend, and paid a private visit during his presidential trip to postwar Sai Gon/Ho Chi Minh City.

44. See Luu Phuong Thanh, "Bac Ton nguoi cong nhan uu tu, lanh tu cong doan dau tien o Viet Nam va o thanh pho Sai Gon" (Uncle Ton, the outstanding worker, the first labor union leader in Viet Nam and in Sai Gong), in *Mot con nguoi binh thuong—vi dai,* 186–91.

45. Interview with Duong Quang Dong, Ho Chi Minh City, 9 May 1992.

46. See unnumbered document of the Bao tang Ton Duc Thang, Ho Chi Minh City: handwritten, twenty-five-page transcript of one of Duong Quang Dong's interviews at the Museum of the Revolution, Ho Chi Minh City, June 1984, to which the interviewer (name illegible) attached an urgent note ("DO NOT TYPE THIS UP") with a list of inaccuracies, contradictions, and illogical claims made by the interviewee. See also document no. 107, Bao tang Ton Duc Thang, Ho Chi Minh City: speech given by Duong Quang Dong on the 101st anniversary of Ton's birthday in 1989.

47. See his memoirs, "Dom lua dau tien cua Nam Ky luc tinh trong thang

nam chua co Dang" (The first sparks of the Six Provinces South [i.e., Cochinchina] during the years before there was the party), recited at the symposium on Ton Duc Thang in 1988; published in *Mot con nguoi binh thuong—vi dai,* 110–16, with an editor's note that these were only extracts of the original memoirs of forty-six pages. One can imagine the poor symposium participants suffering through the inevitable ordeal . . .

48. My conversations with Luu Phuong Thanh, Ho Chi Minh City, and Dang Hoa and Pham Xanh, who expressed similar views and frustrations, Ha Noi, May 1992.

49. Communications received from Ha Huy Giap, through Pham Xanh, Ho Chi Minh City, 4 May 1992.

50. Phan Trong Binh's recollections, "Bac Ton Duc Thang" (Uncle Ton Duc Thang), written in May 1984, published in *Mot con nguoi binh thuong—vi dai,* 231–32. In this version, Ton is already hoisting a red flag on the French warship, but I interpret this and other such details not as concrete recollections but as additions by Phan Trong Binh to give his essay more historical depth.

51. Communications received from Pham Van Dong, through his secretary Nguyen Tien Nang, Ha Noi, 12 May 1992.

52. Tran Tu Binh, *The Red Earth,* 84.

53. Interview with Le Van Luong, Ho Chi Minh City, 9 May 1992.

54. Nguyen Thanh, "Bac Ton trong cuoc noi day o Bien Den" (Uncle Ton in the revolt of the Black Sea), in *Mot con nguoi binh thuong—vi dai,* 224. He specifically cites memoirs of Phan Trong Quang, which were not available to me. Again, Ton is said to have talked about hoisting a red flag on the *France.* As with the case of Phan Trong Binh's recollections, I have strong reservations about these details. The red flag, after all, does not appear in the public story until the mid-1950s, years after the initial propagation of the tale. Regardless of specifics, Ton's mention of his role in the mutinies is important here.

55. Interview with Duong Van Phuc and Ton Thi Hanh, Ha Noi, 14 May 1992.

56. Tran Tu Binh, *The Red Earth,* 84.

2. THE BLACK SEA MUTINY IN THE REVOLUTIONARY MOMENT

1. Harold R. Isaacs, *No Peace for Asia* (Cambridge, Mass.: MIT Press, 1967), 150–51. See Phuong Hanh, "Ve su kien Bac Ton tro ve dat lien sau Cach mang Thang 8" (About Uncle Ton's return to the mainland after the August Revolution), in *Mot con nguoi binh thuong—vi dai,* 234–37: The fleet consisted of twenty-eight vessels, which transported some twenty-three hundred inmates back to the mainland. Most of them landed in the vicinity of the provincial center of Soc Trang. Among those liberated with Ton were Le Duan, Pham Hung, Le Van Luong, Nguyen Van Linh, Nguyen Duy Trinh, Mai Chi Tho, and others. See also Bao tang Cach Mang (Museum of the Revolution),

Ha Noi, document no. 33–TTTD/17, "Toa dam 'Don chinh tri pham o dao Con Lon ve dat lien'" (Conference about 'Taking Political Prisoners from Con Lon Island Back to the Mainland'), 24 September 1965.

2. Just like the returning Dutch, who during the same period unleashed a similar war against "their" former colony, newly independent Indonesia, the French appeared undisturbed by the irony that their own country had experienced military occupation and subjugation at the hands of German fascism. What called for a just *résistance* there was termed "continuing the civilizing mission" here.

3. Huynh Van Tieng, "Hoat dong cua Bac Ton o Nam bo va o Phap trong nam 1945–1946" (Uncle Ton's activities in Cochinchina and France during 1945–1946), in *Mot con nguoi binh thuong—vi dai,* 244–48.

4. Interviews in Ha Noi with the author Le Minh and with Duong Van Phuc and Ton Thi Hanh, April/May 1992. The husband of Le Minh was a fellow prisoner of Ton's, was liberated with him, and served as his escort before and after the operation.

5. Philippe Devillers, a French officer in Cochinchina in 1945, told me in Copenhagen on 21 August 1993 that Ton had become the most wanted revolutionary in the south by late 1945. The French believed him to be behind the most ruthless anti-French attacks and called him "the butcher of the South." Here, however, I suspect that Devillers confused persons in his memory. For he further claims that, according to French intelligence sources, Ton Duc Thang clandestinely appeared in Ha Noi as early as in November, before the dissolution of the ICP, was criticized for "discrediting the southern Viet Minh," and fell from grace until about 1949. But in the recollections of Huynh Van Tieng, a coleader of the Southern Resistance Committee, Ton was in the south throughout this period. Devillers's descriptions better fit instead Tran Van Giau, who is placed by Huynh Van Tieng in the south in late September or early October, but whom Harold Isaacs talked to in Ha Noi in November. Huynh Van Tieng, in *Mot con nguoi binh thuong—vi dai,* 245; Isaacs, *No Peace,* 172–73 and, perhaps, 176. Philippe Devillers, *Histoire du Viêt-Nam de 1940 à 1952* (Paris: Seuil, 1952): 166, when describing the period in question, is himself preoccupied with the "fanaticism and violence" of Tran Van Giau. He also mentions Tran Van Giau's trip to a conference in Ha Noi, coming at the "opportune" moment when the Binh Xuyen, organized bandits who controlled the environs of Sai Gon, sought to liquidate Tran Van Giau. Tran Van Giau was sent to Bangkok to head the Viet Minh mission there in early 1946, an indication that he was removed from leading positions in the resistance; Motoo Furuta, "The Indochina Communist Party's Division into Three Parties: Vietnamese Communist Policy toward Cambodia and Laos, 1948–1951," in *Indochina in the 1940s and 1950s,* ed. Takashi Shiraishi and Motoo Furuta (Ithaca, N.Y.: Cornell University SouthEast Asia Program Publications, 1992): 146. Some glimpses of Tran Van Giau's activities during the early southern resistance can be found in Subrata Banerjee, *Viet Nam Fights for Freedom*

(Bombay: People's Publishing House, 1947): 22, 26ff. The information was likely provided by Tran Van Giau himself when he headed a DRVN delegation to the Asian Relations Conference in New Delhi in the spring of 1947.

6. Huynh Van Tieng, in *Mot con nguoi binh thuong—vi dai,* 244, mentions an election date of 23 December 1945, only for Cochinchina.

7. Bernard Fall, *The Viet-Minh Regime: Government and Administration in the Democratic Republic of Viet-Nam* (New York: Institute of Pacific Relations, jointly with Cornell University SouthEast Asia Program Publications, 1954, 1956 [2d ed.]): 16.

8. Friedrich Sembdner, *Das kommunistische Regierungssystem in Vietnam* (The communist government system in Viet Nam) (Cologne: von Nottbeck, 1978): 75ff.

9. Thep Moi and Huynh Van Tieng, in *Mot con nguoi binh thuong—vi dai,* 238–39, 244–45, report anti-DRVN violence and perhaps dozens of dead election activists. Clearly, the question of elections in the south warrants further inquiry.

10. Based on Thep Moi and especially Huynh Van Tieng, who played a major role in the events described, in *Mot con nguoi binh thuong—vi dai,* 238–39, 244ff.

11. Thep Moi and Huynh Van Tieng differ on this point. Possibly, the fighters retreated from Rach Gia further south to Ca Mau, for the French captured Rach Gia on 26 January, but Ca Mau not until 5 February. Devillers, *Histoire du Viêt-Nam,* 165.

12. Ton Thi Hanh (b. 1926) and Ton Thi Nghiem (1928–91) were very young when their father was taken away to prison. In 1946, in their late teens, they accompanied their father north to receive better schooling. Their mother, Ton's wife Doan Kim Oanh (1897–1974), remained in the south during the resistance war, and the family was reunited in the north only in 1954. Doan Kim Oanh was pregnant at the time of Ton's arrest in 1929; Ton saw his son only once while in prison in Sai Gon. The little boy died at age three or four. Interview with Ton Thi Hanh, Ha Noi, 14 May 1992. Cf. Thep Moi in *Mot con nguoi binh thuong—vi dai,* 240.

13. Thep Moi, in *Mot con nguoi binh thuong—vi dai,* 239.

14. Premier de Gaulle's resignation in France on 20 January 1946 and unfulfilled prospects of a successor government of the Left might have been an additional reason. Cf. Edward Rice-Maximin, *Accommodation and Resistance: The French Left, Indochina and the Cold War, 1944–1954* (New York: Greenwood, 1986): 27.

15. The Viet Minh would destroy their rival nationalist parties during the second half of 1946, when Chinese troops left the north of Viet Nam. The returning French certainly had no objections to the demise of the violently anti-French VNQDD and DMH. For an excellent discussion of the complex and often murky scene of Vietnamese nationalist efforts in southern China from 1938 to 1945, on their internal relations, rivalries, alliances, and violent conflicts, and on their varying Chinese and foreign backers, see King C.

Chen, *Vietnam and China, 1938–1954* (Princeton, N.J.: Princeton University Press, 1969).

16. Thep Moi, in *Mot con nguoi binh thuong—vi dai,* 239. See also a description of the scene by Vo Nguyen Giap, *Unforgettable Days* (Ha Noi: Foreign Languages Publishing House, 1975): 159–67, especially 164.

17. After the official reconstitution of the Communist Party (as the Labor Party) in 1951, the Viet Minh Front rapidly lost its utility. It merged with the Lien Viet in March 1951, only weeks after the founding of the Vietnamese Labor Party.

18. This post has been erased from biographical sketches of Ton, possibly because of the Stockholm Appeal's association with Stalinism. See the weekly *Viet-Nam Information,* Rangoon: Viet-Nam News Service, 1950, passim. See Rice-Maximin, *Accommodation,* 81, for a brief description of the Stockholm Appeal movement.

19. BNCLSDTU, *Dong chi Ton,* 30; Fall, *Viet-Minh Regime* (1956): 44. Probably Ho Tung Mau held the post from 1949 until his death in July 1951; cf. Nguyen Q. Thang, Nguyen Ba The, *Tu dien nhan vat lich su Viet Nam* (Dictionary of Vietnamese historic personalities) (Ha Noi: NXB Khoa hoc xa hoi, 1992): 289–90.

20. Devillers, *Histoire du Viêt-Nam,* 401. For a different assessment of these two government posts held by Ton, see Pierre Célerier, *Menaces sur le Viet-Nam* (Sai Gon: Imprimerie d'Extrême-Orient, 1950): 194.

21. Thep Moi, in *Mot con nguoi binh thuong—vi dai,* 240, writes that Ton was already informally admitted to the party's Central Committee in early 1948, possibly at the ICP's third, extended cadre conference, 15–17 January 1948, at "Mount Stalin" (Pac Bo) in the northern guerrilla base. See Furuta, in *Indochina in the 1940s,* 155.

22. Thep Moi, in *Mot con nguoi binh thuong—vi dai,* 241.

23. *Le Monde,* Paris, 1946: 27 April, 4, 2 May, 2, 14 May, 2.

24. Jean Sainteny, *Histoire d'une paix manquée: Indochine 1945–1947* (Paris: Fayard, 1953, 1967 [2d ed.]): 217–20, especially 220. Sainteny might have interpreted as colonial subjects' gratitude what was actually meant as a political hint: Henri Azeau, *Ho Chi Minh, dernière chance: La Conférence franco-vietnamienne de Fontainebleau, juillet 1946* (Paris: Flammarion, 1968): 137, 141, argues that the delegates' singing the *Marseillaise* was in reference to French revolutionary ideals.

25. Huynh Van Tieng, in *Mot con nguoi binh thuong—vi dai,* 247. He incorrectly dates the delegation's trip in October 1946. His point about the delegation's early return is unconvincing. There is no indication the trip was cut short or that its purpose was in any way to prepare the Fontainebleau conference.

26. Huynh Van Tieng, in *Mot con nguoi binh thuong—vi dai,* 247. "Marti" in the original. My emphasis in the quote.

27. Rice-Maximin, *Accommodation,* 119.

28. This is what Ha Huy Giap, "Tuong nho," 18, suggests. There is no evi-

dence to support the assertion, though; in particular, Marty's whereabouts during the period in question could not be ascertained.

29. Isaacs, *No Peace,* 174.

30. Rice-Maximin, *Accommodation,* 53, 56–57.

31. Isaacs, *No Peace,* 173.

32. Ibid., 172–73.

33. Ibid., 173–74. As reported by Edgar Snow, the FCP members in Sai Gon were disappointed that the ICP did not share their own confidence in the "New France," in which the FCP was to play a prominent role; *Saturday Evening Post,* 2 February 1946, quoted in Virginia Thompson and Richard Adloff, *The Left Wing in Southeast Asia* (New York: William Sloane/Institute of Pacific Relations, 1950): 40.

34. Mark Bradley, "An Improbable Opportunity: America and the Democratic Republic of Vietnam's 1947 Initiative," in *The Vietnam War: Vietnamese and American Perspectives,* ed. Jayne S. Werner and Luu Doan Huynh (Armonk, N.Y.: M. E. Sharpe, 1993): 5, 19 n. 9. Wu Xiuquan, *Eight Years in the Ministry of Foreign Affairs (1/50–10/58): Memoirs of a Diplomat* (Beijing: New World, n.d.): 19. On Stalin's negative attitudes toward the Vietnamese Revolution and on the role of FCP leader Maurice Thorez as intermediary between Stalin and Ho Chi Minh from about 1945 to 1950, see János Radványi, *Delusion and Reality: Gambits, Hoaxes, & Diplomatic One-Upmanship in Vietnam* (South Bend, Ind.: Gateway, 1978): 4–5.

35. See Bradley, in *Vietnam War.*

36. Chen, *Vietnam and China,* 188–96.

37. Ibid., 176–79.

38. Ibid., 175–76, 189–90. Bradley, in *Vietnam War,* 8: One of the DRVN-GMD contacts occurred at the New Delhi conference. For a good example of the solidarity publications after the Asian Relations Conference, see Banerjee, *Viet Nam.* The other conference delegates were Tran Van Luan and Mai The Chau. For American and more Asian voices of support, see Viet Nam American Friendship Association, *Transcript of the Proceedings at the Meeting in Celebration of the Second Anniversary of the Independence of the Republic of Viet-Nam, 1947* (New York: 1947). David K. Wyatt, *Thailand: A Short History* (New Haven: Yale University Press, 1984): 264. Furuta, in *Indochina in the 1940s,* 147. Fall, *Viet-Minh Regime* (1956): 58–59.

39. Thep Moi, in *Mot con nguoi binh thuong—vi dai,* 240.

40. Chen, *Vietnam and China,* 193ff; Furuta, in *Indochina in the 1940s,* 147.

41. Paul Mus, *Viêt-Nam: Sociologie d'une guerre* (Paris: Seuil, 1952): 312–16. Philippe Devillers, *Vietnam and France* (Paris: Comité d'études des problèmes du Pacifique, and New York: Institute of Pacific Relations, 1950): 10. Neil L. Jamieson, *Understanding Vietnam* (Berkeley: University of California Press, 1993): 211. Nguyen Khac Vien, *The Long Resistance (1858–1975)* (Ha Noi: Foreign Languages Publishing House, 1975): 127.

42. Jamieson, *Understanding,* 211ff., 221; Chen, *Vietnam and China,* 179–86; Devillers, *Vietnam and France,* 11–17.

43. Chen, *Vietnam and China,* 191–92; Furuta, in *Indochina in the 1940s,* 155; Rice-Maximin, *Accommodation,* 57; J. H. Brimmell, *Communism in South East Asia* (London: Oxford University Press, 1959): 167, 251–55.

44. Brimmell, *Communism,* 167.

45. Rice-Maximin, *Accommodation,* 57.

46. Furuta, in *Indochina in the 1940s,* 155.

47. Ruth McVey, *The Calcutta Conference & the Southeast Asian Uprisings* (Ithaca, N.Y.: Cornell, 1958): 15, quoted in Chen, *Vietnam and China,* 191–92. Cf. Brimmell, *Communism,* 258–59.

48. Furuta, in *Indochina in the 1940s,* 155–56, 157.

49. At several instances in 1949 and 1950, the FCP actually invoked the example of the Black Sea Mutiny in its increasingly radical opposition to the French war in Indochina. Rice-Maximin, *Accommodation,* 78, 96, and compare 124.

3. THE BLACK SEA MUTINY IN THE POST-RECOGNITION MOMENT

1. Furuta, in *Indochina in the 1940s,* 145 n.4, 158 n.68.

2. Thep Moi, in *Mot con nguoi binh thuong—vi dai,* 241. At that time, Zhou Enlai, Liu Shaoqi, and Chen Yun were the second-, third-, and fifth-ranked men in the CCP leadership. Chen, *Vietnam and China,* 251–52, reports that Ton traveled to China in September and October 1951 for the PRC's National Day celebrations. Thep Moi might actually make reference, albeit incorrectly dated, to that trip.

For more on Thep Moi, see Thep Moi (Ha Van Loc): *Cay tre Viet Nam* (Vietnamese bamboo) (Ha Noi: NXB Chinh Tri Quoc Gia, 2001).

3. Devillers, *Histoire,* 460; see also 8. The correct dates of Ton's imprisonment are 1929–45. I was unfortunately unable to ascertain on which source Devillers had based his account in 1952; personal correspondence, 25 August 1995.

4. *Regards sur le monde du travail* (Paris, 1953) 357: 21. Clare Crowston kindly provided me with this source.

5. Fall, *Viet-Minh Regime* (1954): 34, 67; (1956): 39, 75. Bernard Fall, *The Two Viet-Nams: A Political and Military Analysis* (New York: Praeger, 1963): 91. Jean Chesneaux, *Geschichte Vietnams* (History of Viet Nam), a revised and enlarged edition of his *Contribution à l'histoire de la nation vietnamienne* (Paris, 1955), trans. Ernst-Ulrich Kloock (Berlin: Rütten & Loening, 1963): 305.

6. There were five other recipients: the Mexican Lazaro Cardenas, the Syrian Sheikh Mohammed al-Ashmar, the German Josef Wirth, the Japanese Akiko Seki, and the Norwegian Ragnar Forbek. *The New York Times,* 21 December 1955.

7. Tran Huu Nghiep, "Nhung ngay toi lam thay thuoc rieng cho Bac Ton" (When I was Uncle Ton's personal doctor), in *Mot con nguoi binh thuong—vi dai,* 133.

8. *The New York Times,* 10 June 1956, 1 and 27, and 8 September 1956, 3.

9. See Brimmell, *Communism,* 297–98.

10. Thep Moi, in *Mot con nguoi binh thuong—vi dai,* 241, makes a similar point.

11. For example, *Neues Deutschland* (New Germany), East Berlin, 6 January 1956, 3.

12. What would the 1905 mutiny of the *Potemkin* at Odessa be without a red flag? I have seen one version of Sergei Eisenstein's famous black-and-white film *Bronenosez Potjemkin* (1925), in which the red flag fluttering above the armored cruiser was colored red at a later date. This was the only scene to be recolored, apparently to make sure the correct hue was not lost on the audience.

And during the last days of the final Soviet assault on Berlin, why did the Red Army focus more on storming the Reichstag rather than Hitler's headquarters in the Reichs Chancellery? Stalin had ordered a red flag to fly on the Reichstag before Labor Day, 1 May. At terrible human cost, the militarily meaningless, but more symbolic, Reichstag was taken late on 30 April 1945.

13. Marty, *La Révolte,* 460, especially 467.

In the English version of Marty's account, *The Epic,* 10, a red flag is said to have flown above the *Waldeck-Rousseau.* This short propaganda pamphlet is unreliable, though, and the original Marty, *La Révolte,* does not support the claim. Masson, *La Marine française,* 351–52, only hints at an unsuccessful attempt to hoist a red flag on the *Waldeck-Rousseau.* In any case, Ton Duc Thang was not a crew member of that cruiser either.

14. Chen, *Vietnam and China,* 216, also 221.

15. Ibid., 222–23, 242–45, especially 244–45. See also Brimmell, *Communism,* 278.

16. Chen, *Vietnam and China,* 238.

17. My interview with Ton Thi Hanh, Duong Van Phuc, and Tuong Bich Truc, 14 May 1992. Document no. 185, Ton Duc Thang Museum, Ho Chi Minh City, "Nhung mau chuyen ve Chu tich Ton Duc Thang," transcript of a conversation between Nguyen Tang Tan and Ton's daughter and sons-in-law, Ha Noi, 6 December 1989, 2, 4.

18. Document no. 185, Ton Duc Thang Museum, Ho Chi Minh City, 4.

19. Bao tang Cach Mang, Ha Noi, document no. 70–NVat/18, "Bac Ton: Ban goi y ve yeu cau tu thuat cua dong chi Ton Duc Thang" (Uncle Ton: List of suggestions for requested autobiography of Comrade Ton Duc Thang), 14 January 1966.

20. Le Minh, *Nguoi tho may Ton Duc Thang* (The mechanic Ton Duc Thang) (Ha Noi: Thanh Nien, 1981, 1987 [2d ed.]): 5–6. Also my interview with Le Minh, Ha Noi, April 1992.

21. Thep Moi, in *Mot con nguoi binh thuong—vi dai,* 242.

22. As previously discussed, mutinies on the *Waldeck-Rousseau, Bruix, Condorcet, Touareg,* and possibly the *Fauconneau* and *Mameluck* took place on sea off Odessa or at a nearby isolated island navy base; the *Dehorter* saw unrest off the Crimea.

23. Communications received from Ha Huy Giap, through Pham Xanh, Ho Chi Minh City, 4 May 1992.

24. Huynh Van Tieng, in *Mot con nguoi binh thuong—vi dai,* 248.

25. In Russian: "Ya uchastvoval v vosstanii-na Chernom Morie," trans. A. Shiltovoi, in *Sovietskii Moriak* 24 (1957): 6–7. In Vietnamese: "Nhung gio Hac-hai doi voi toi" (How I experienced the times in the Black Sea), in *Tien phong* 232 (26–29 October 1957): 1, 4; and also distributed by the Vietnamese News Agency (Thong tan xa Viet Nam) in November 1957.

26. Editor's introduction to Ton's article, in *Tien phong* 232 (1957): 1.

27. Ibid. The quotes in the remainder of this section are all taken from this article.

28. Ibid. My emphasis of the past-perfect tense.

29. Ibid. During the Allied intervention in the Black Sea in the spring and summer of 1919, no "Red Navy" was in existence.

30. Ibid. My emphasis.

31. Ibid. My emphasis.

32. For information on the *Paris,* see Masson, *La Marine française,* 420, 480, 493.

33. Marty, *La Révolte,* 530, and Masson, *La Marine française,* 390, 414. The court eventually cut Marty off by ordering a psychiatric examination. His second trial took place on 4 July 1919, at Constantinople on board the *Condorcet.*

34. SHM-IIIe région, Toulon, nos. 2E7–1420 (1918), 1697, and 1698 (1919), *rôle d'équipage* of the *Paris.*

35. I am reminded of Wilhelm Busch's immortal line, "daß nicht sein kann was nicht sein darf" (that cannot be what may not be).

36. Nguyen Van Hoan, "Bac Ton song o nha tu Con Lon nhung nam 1930" (Uncle Ton's life on Con Lon during the 1930s), in *Mot con nguoi binh thuong—vi dai,* 92–93. Plagiarized parts are from Marty, *La Révolte,* especially 283, 286, 293, 297–98. The symposium participants, among them a number of historians, most likely did not realize what this dubious historical "witness" was doing.

37. Nguyen Thanh, in *Mot con nguoi binh thuong—vi dai,* 219, 224.

38. His definitive answer was, of course, Sevastopol/*France*/20–4/8 A.M./Red Flag.

39. In addition to those I have already cited, these were, for example: BNCLSDTU, *Nhung su kien lich su Dang* (Events in party history), vol. 1 (1920–1945) (Ha Noi: NXB Su that, 1976): 18ff.; Nguyen Cong Hoan, *Nguoi cap rang ham xay lua* (The *capelan* of the rice mill) (Ha Noi: NXB Kim dong, 1978); a series of four articles all titled "Co do tren Bien Den" (The Red Flag in the Black Sea), ed. Le Kim, in *Quan doi nhan dan* (People's Army) (Ha Noi, 22, 23, 26, 27 October 1987); Tran Thanh Phuong, ed., *Bac Ton cua chung ta* (Our Uncle Ton), (NXB Tong hop An Giang, 1988); Ban khoa hoc xa hoi Thanh uy (Social Science Commission of the Municipal Party Committee), ed., *Bac Ton va chung ta* (Uncle Ton and we) (Ho Chi Minh City: NXB Ban khoa hoc xa hoi Thanh uy, 1988); Dang Hoa and Viet Chinh, *Nguoi thuy thu phan chien*

o Bien Den (The antiwar sailor in the Black Sea) (Ha Noi: NXB Thong tin ly luan, 1988), with a picture of the Red Flag in the Black Sea on its cover; So Van hoa va thong tin An Giang (An Giang culture and information department), ed., *Chu tich Ton Duc Thang (1888–1980)* (President Ton Duc Thang) (An Giang, 1988); To Thanh Tam, ed., *Chuyen ke ve Bac Ton* (Stories about Uncle Ton) (NXB Tong hop An Giang, 1988); Ban chap hanh Tinh Dang bo An Giang (Party Executive Central Committee of An Giang province), ed., *Bac Ton (1888–1980), cuoc doi va su nghiep* (Uncle Ton, life and work) (Ha Noi: NXB Su that, 1988).

40. *Saigon Times,* 10 June 1996; Nora Taylor kindly made me aware of the article. Unfortunately, I could not utilize this film for my analysis. After a rather lengthy search, Nguyen Van Kim of the National University Ha Noi in 2001 kindly found a copy for me. But the Ministry of Culture denied him the export permit required to send the cassette to me. Personal communications, September 2001.

41. *Thong Nhat* (Ha Noi), 10 November 1967, quoted in Tran Thanh Phuong, ed., *Bac Ton cua chung ta,* 88.

42. See Tran Thanh Phuong, ed., *Bac Ton cua chung ta,* 244–60, 268–71. A VNA report in *Quan doi nhan dan* 6757 (5 April 1980): 1, states that during the street-naming ceremony in Odessa on 3 April 1980, the recently deceased Ton was remembered for hoisting the Red Flag on the *Waldeck-Rousseau.* See also document nos. 36 and 46, Bao tang Ton Duc Thang, Ho Chi Minh City, for Soviet images of the Red Flag hoisted by Ton.

4. STRIKING IMAGES: BA SON IN THE POST-PARTITION MOMENT

1. Ho Chi Minh City has been the official name for Sai Gon since 1975.

2. This chapter is an abbreviated and reworked version of my "Ba Son 1925: The Strike at the Arsenal in Sai Gon: A Closer Look at Events and Their Interpretations" (M.A. thesis, Cornell University, Ithaca, N.Y., 1989).

3. Vietnamese *u tau* (*u,* bulge, swelling; *tau,* boat), meaning a little bay for use as a natural harbor. The Sai Gon River indeed forms a *bassin* roughly at the location of Ba Son, running along one side of the zoological garden. This basin is integrated into the shipyard now. I am indebted to Ho Ton Trinh, Ha Noi, for explaining the term to me.

4. Le Minh, *Nguoi tho may,* 29.

5. Huynh Ngoc Trang, Truong Ngoc Tuong et al., eds., *Sai Gon-Gia Dinh xua: Tu lieu & hinh anh* (Old Sai Gon-Gia Dinh: Documents and pictures) (Ho Chi Minh City: NXB Thanh Pho Ho Chi Minh, 1996): 33. Tran Van Giau et al., *Dia chi van hoa,* 258. Nguyen: the last Vietnamese dynasty (1802–1945), with Hue as its capital. By the 1880s, it had become a mere puppet monarchy of French colonialism.

6. The arsenal was bounded to the northwest by the rue de la Ste. Enfance, which by 1867 had been renamed the rue Isabelle II; sometime before 1905

it became the rue d'Espagne. Since about 1956, the street has been named after emperor Le Thanh Ton. Along the arsenal's southwestern side with its main gate ran the boulevard de la Citadelle, which became the boulevard Luro sometime after 1905. During the period of the Sai Gon government, the street was called after the anticolonial Nguyen prince Cuong De; since 1975, it has had the name of Ton Duc Thang.

Also in 1864, Vietnamese and ethnic Chinese workers transformed the entire riverfront between the mouths of the Thi Nghe canal, called Arroyo de l'avalanche by the French, and the Ben Nghe canal, called Arroyo chinois in French, into an eighteen-hundred-meter-long jetty. The pier, initially called the quai Napoleon in the 1860s, soon became the quai Francis Garnier-quai Primauguet, and after World War I, the quai le Myre de Vilier-Quai de l'Argonne. Since 1975, the whole riverfront, too, has been known as Ton Duc Thang Avenue. Huynh, Truong et al., eds., *Sai Gon-Gia Dinh xua,* 24, 49–51, 71, 78. Tran Van Giau et al., *Dia chi van hoa,* 258, and Tran Van Giau, *Giai cap cong nhan Viet Nam* (1961): 45. *Lich su Xi nghiep lien hop Ba Son (1863–1998)* (History of the united enterprise Ba Son) (Ha Noi: NXB Quan Doi Nhan Dan, 1998): 54.

7. Tran Van Giau, *Giai cap cong nhan Viet Nam* (1961): 45; Tran Van Giau et al., *Dia chi van hoa,* 258, 261.

8. See CAOM, SOM, ICh AF, c. 316: Cochinchine: École professionnelle de mécaniciens indigènes, projet d'organisation, etc.

9. Tran Van Giau et al., *Dia chi van hoa,* 261. Dumarest, *La Formation,* 82, is skeptical about its success. Since instruction was in French, graduates rather used their new language skills for higher salaried administrative jobs.

10. Some five hundred Vietnamese were posted at the Toulon arsenal alone in 1918, about half of whom were specialized. SOM, ICh NF, d. 226; SOM, Aff. polit. 1920–57, c. 1462.

11. See official communications in SOM, ICh NF, ds. 225, 233. The need for highly trained personnel is evident when considering that, according to Dumarest, Ba Son's shipyard ranked among those colonial "establishments whose technical activity is very complex and in every respect comparable with European industries"; *La Formation,* 70.

12. Tran Van Giau, *Giai cap cong nhan Viet Nam* (1961): 413. Nguyen An Ninh (1900–43), from a southern literati family, graduated from law school and was active in anticolonial groups in France. Back in Sai Gon in 1923, he began publishing *La Cloche fêlée* and rose to intellectual leadership and fame with his courage and unconventionality. In the face of colonial realities, he shifted from advocating collaboration and reform to radical opposition and revolution. He was first arrested in 1926. Political activity and persecution would alternate until his death in prison on Con Lon.

13. Tran Van Giau, alias Ho Nam (b. 1912), was a student in France around 1930–31, became an active revolutionary there, and for a short while even attended Moscow's Stalin School. Back in Cochinchina in the early 1930s, he was instrumental in rebuilding the Indochinese Communist Party in the

south, whose structure had been destroyed in 1931. A leading cadre in the southern resistance from the mid-1930s to the mid-1940s, he lost his influential party posts in 1951 for "excesses" during the August Revolution. He became (and, now more than ninety years old, still is) one of the foremost historians of the DRVN/SRVN. The late Huynh Kim Khanh kindly shared with me his insights into Tran Van Giau's life.

14. Tran Van Giau, *Giai cap cong nhan Viet Nam* (1957): 249–57; (1961): 353–63, 371ff. See his (et al.) *Lich su can dai*, vol. 4, 138–42, and his (et al.), *Dia chi van hoa*, 281–84.

15. From C. R. Pennell, *A Country with a Government and a Flag: The Rif War in Morocco, 1921–1926* (Wisbech, Cambridgeshire: Menas, 1986), and David S. Woolman, *Rebels in the Rif: Abd el Krim and the Rif Rebellion* (Stanford, Calif.: University of Stanford Press, 1968).

16. Woolman, *Rebels*, 196; in all of 1925, there were approximately twelve thousand French dead, including Algerian and Senegalese soldiers.

17. Heavy reinforcements and joint French-Spanish operations on three fronts soon rendered the rebels' situation hopeless. Abd el Krim surrendered in May 1926.

18. Quoted in Woolman, *Rebels*, 194.

19. From Safiuddin Joarder, *Syria under the French Mandate: The Early Phase: 1920–27* (Dacca: Asiatic Society of Bangladesh, 1977), and from Stephen Hemsley Longrigg, *Syria and Lebanon under French Mandate* (London: Oxford University Press, 1958).

20. In Syria, a provisional government established itself, again. But after heavy French bombing, the all-out, open insurrection came to an end by November 1925.

21. Ku Hung-ting, *Urban Mass Movement*, 21; AOM, GG, d. 38,788: Grève à Shanghai (1925), télégrammes officiels, 1–13 June 1925.

22. Kuo Heng-yü, *Die Komintern und die chinesische Revolution*, 93–94. Thanh Nien, for example, reported this internationalist help in its nos. 4 and 8 (12 July, 15 August).

23. See AOM, GG, d. 27,180 (X3). Beginning in the early 1900s, these Hoa Kieu supported the nationalist cause in China and developed many ties with the GMD.

24. Henry Chavigny (self-styled de Lachevrotière) is a telling example of this species of *colons:* He abandoned his Vietnamese wife and children, refusing to support them, while he lived in luxury. He started out as a small-time journalist, was convicted of fraud at one point, became a police informer at another, and was a draft evader during World War I. After the war, he quickly rose to power as one of Cognacq's cronies. In his semiofficial newspaper, he assumed the role of an aggressive defender of French values and "interests." See Walter Langlois, *André Malraux: The Indochina Adventure*, 86ff.

25. Nguyen An Ninh went to France and remained until June 1925. A much more radical *La Cloche fêlée* resumed publication in November 1925.

26. Malraux (1901–76) became a towering literary and political figure in

France. In Sai Gon in 1925, he was an angry young man who honed his unchallenged literary abilities in journalistic battles with reactionaries. See the excellent, if only lacking the Vietnamese perspective, Langlois, *André Malraux*.

27. Langlois, *André Malraux,* 90ff., 102ff. Another scandal involved attempts to manipulate Cochinchina's Chamber of Agriculture through a Cognacq "marionette."

28. For a concise presentation of the effects of Varenne's nomination on Sai Gon society, see Cedric Allen Sampson, "Nationalism and Communism" (Ph.D. diss., University of California, Los Angeles, 1975): 69–70, and William Frederick, "Alexandre Varenne," in *Aspects of Vietnamese History,* ed. Walter Vella, 104–11.

29. Langlois, *André Malraux,* 143, 153–58: By 14 August, the Sûreté had coerced *L'Indochine*'s printer to cancel the contract with Malraux and Monin. No other printer dared to accept them, and Monin and Malraux had to set up their own printing press. However, Malraux had to travel to China to buy the type. Facing some government obstruction in Sai Gon, Malraux finally succeeded in importing the type in October. Malraux and Monin began publishing *L'Indochine enchaînée* on 4 November 1925.

30. According to Langlois, *André Malraux,* 79–80, Le Quang Trinh served as a French-designated "spokesman for the Annamite community" who "faithfully supported every oppressive policy of the government," which naturally had him on its payroll. Sampson, "Nationalism and Communism in Viet Nam," 106, calls him a "government favorite."

31. Sampson, "Nationalism and Communism in Viet Nam," 93. See also Shawn McHale, "Printing, Power, and the Transformation of Vietnamese Culture, 1920–1945" (Ph.D. diss., Cornell University, Ithaca, N.Y., 1995).

32. The procedure was described in *L'Écho annamite* (abbr. *L'Écho*) (Sai Gon) 21 July 1925, "Une manifestation à l'Arsenal de Saigon," in *L'Impartial* (abbr. *Impa*) (Sai Gon), "Une grève à l'Arsenal," and in *L'Indochine* (abbr. *Indo*) (Sai Gon), "Une grève importante à Saigon," both 5 August. Unless otherwise noted, dates refer to 1925.

33. *L'Écho,* 21 July; *Impa* and *Indo,* 5 August, also date the incident on 18 July.

34. *L'Écho,* 21 July. See *Indo,* 5 August, and *Le Progrès annamite* (abbr. *ProA*) (Sai Gon), 14 August, "La Grève de l'Arsenal": the power failure at the arsenal happened on 16 July. Workers might only have found out about the wage cut when getting paid on 18 July.

35. *Indo,* 5 August.

36. *North-China Herald,* 1925, vol. 383 (19 September). The article specifies: "*Michelet,* however, has been delayed by a strike of workmen in the dock at Saigon where she is being overhauled. Work is being rapidly pushed ahead at the moment and it is expected that [she] will arrive in Hong Kong before the end of this month."

37. *Indo,* 4 August, *Impa,* 4/5 August, *L'Écho, La Voix annamite* (Sai Gon), 5 August, *L'Avenir du Tonkin* (abbr. *AvTo*), *Bao Dong Phap* (abbr. *BDP*) (Ha Noi),

6–8 August, *Cong Luan Bao* (abbr. *CLB*) (Sai Gon), *Trung Bac Tan Van* (abbr. *TBTV*) (Ha Noi), 7 August, *Temps d'Asie* (abbr. *TemA*) (Sai Gon), 9 August, *Dong Phap Thoi Bao* (abbr. *DPTB*) (Sai Gon), 10 August.

38. *Impa,* 5 August.

39. *Indo, Impa,* 5 August, *L'Écho,* 6 August, *DPTB,* 7 August, *TBTV,* 7/9 August, *ProA,* 14 August.

40. *Indo,* 6 August, *Impa,* 6–8 August, *L'Écho,* 7 August, *AvTo,* 9 August.

41. *Indo,* 5 August. It was impossible to verify the authenticity of this letter (and another of 6 August) through a second source.

42. Note that the letter mentioned only rationales, not demands. Newspapers reported no demands until 11 August, when the situation changed significantly with the lockout.

43. *Impa,* 5 August.

44. *Impa,* 6 August. *L'Impartial* was not the only newspaper to connect the strike with the arrival of the *Jules Michelet.* Others at least mentioned the workers' rationale—the change in working hours—but also saw the strike in connection with delays on the *Jules Michelet's* repairs. Others still, like *Temps d'Asie,* interpreted the walkout at Ba Son only as a manifestation of discontent about the changes in working hours. *CLB,* 8 August, *TBTV,* 9 August, *TemA,* 9 August.

45. *Indo,* 6 August.

46. *ProA,* 14 August.

47. *Impa,* 8 August. Reports also in *AvTo, TBTV, BDP,* 11 August.

48. *Impa,* 10 August. See *CLB,* 10 August, *L'Écho,* 11 August, *AvTo, TBTV,* 12 August, *ProA,* 14 August.

49. On the document of 11 August, the ultimatum, and the return of the workers, see *L'Écho,* 12/13 August, *Impa,* 12–14 August, *ProA, DPTB,* 14 August, *AvTo,* 15/18 August, *TemA,* 16/23 August, *LTTV,* 17 August, *BDP,* 18 August, *TBTV,* 19 August.

50. *AvTo,* 15 August.

51. Cited in *BDP,* 18 August, *TBTV,* 19 August, *AvTo,* 18/23 August.

52. *L'Écho,* 12 September, *CLB,* 15 September, *AvTo,* 9, 12, 13, 16, 23, 24 September, *BDP,* 12, 15 September, *TBTV,* 12, 13, 23 September. *BDP* and *TBTV,* however, confuse the two sister ships *Jules Ferry* and *Jules Michelet.*

53. A few days later, however, it was reported that the ship had suffered renewed engine damages and lay crippled off the southern central coast of Indochina. *AvTo,* 26, 27 November, 1, 3, 4 December, *TBTV,* 4 December, *BDP,* 5 December.

54. (C)AOM, GG, d. 45,823: Arsenal de Saigon, Correspondances diverses, 1921–33.

55. All quotes in preceding section, ibid.

56. SOM, SLOTFOM XI, c. 1: Renforcement des forces navales; letter of the minister of the navy to the minister of foreign affairs, 7 November 1925, 3 pages.

57. Some concessions lay deep in China, for example in Chongqing on the Yangzi. Thus, French naval forces in China with ten patrol and gunboats,

but only one cruiser, were "particularly adapted for the protection of our interests" in China.

58. AOM, GG, d. 45,833: L'Affaire dite "Grève de l'arsenal de Saigon," 1925 (copy).

59. All quotes in preceding section, ibid.

60. *Indo,* 5 August. Tran Van Giau also wrote that the workers were "waiting for the director's answer." *Giai cap cong nhan Viet Nam* (1961): 356.

61. This is the only logical explanation for the confusion in August over where the ship would be repaired. Its "mission report" for August 1925 is missing in the archives.

62. It was precisely the workers' unity that *Thanh Nien,* organ of the Vietnamese Revolutionary Youth League (VRYL), which Nguyen Ai Quoc had recently founded in Canton, highlighted in a brief note on the troubles at Ba Son on 23 August, just one week after the event: "In Sai Gon, 800 workers who are employed at a navy arsenal went on strike, but none of them got arrested by the French because they all marched hand in hand." From the start of its publication on 21 June 1925, the weekly *Thanh Nien*—only partially preserved in French language extracts the Sûreté prepared ("La Jeunesse")—had stressed the need for the people in Indochina to unite, exhorting the Vietnamese in numerous articles to organize to be able to rid themselves of French occupation and exploitation of their homeland. On several occasions, the paper juxtaposed anti-imperialist activities in other countries with what it saw as lamentable passivity and social fragmentation in Indochina. The Riffian rebellion served as a good example: why, an article on 9 August asked anxiously, should 20 million Vietnamese be unable to do what barely 3 million Moroccans had achieved against France and Spain? *Thanh Nien's* report of the strike must be seen in this context: Ba Son's walkout was proof of the merits of concerted action, for "marching hand in hand."

It is surprising, however, that the strike was seen as significant only for its internal unity that protected against persecution, but not for its possibly internationalist solidarity. After all, *Thanh Nien* had drawn a connection between imperialist reinforcements and strike threats of English workers in solidarity with China. It enjoyed good communication channels with Indochina, usually reported promptly on events, obviously had access to colonial newspapers (see, for example, a reprint on 11 October [no. 15] of an article that *L'Eclaireur* published on 29 September in Ha Noi), and therefore likely knew about the *Jules Michelet.* But the paper, the most radical organ of Vietnamese anticolonialism at that time, never used the strike for internationalist propaganda. Along with the silence of Sai Gon's progressive *L'Indochine* after its initial coverage of the strike, *Thanh Nien's* one rather subdued article remains a perplexing aspect of the otherwise lively media coverage of Ba Son.

63. See details in my M.A. thesis, Cornell University, 1989. In Paris, Vietnamese anticolonialism was thriving in the Union Intercoloniale, an association of radical African and Asian colonial subjects living in France. Since the outbreak of the May Thirtieth Movement, the Union Intercoloniale had col-

laborated with Chinese expatriates to support the protests in China. The "Indochinese-Chinese cooperation against imperialism" was an issue that both sides frequently stressed. It topped the agenda of an 9 October 1925 public meeting organized by the Union Intercoloniale, and as a result, the roughly two hundred participants sent a telegram to Canton to inform the GMD, among other things, of the strike at Ba Son. The telegram stated that "a united front of the peoples of Indochina and China against imperialism is necessary and possible to form." About Ba Son's labor action, allegedly called "the beginning of the liberating revolution" in Indochina, it read: "800 Vietnamese workers of the Arsenal in Sai Gon struck at the very moment that they should have repaired a French cruiser ordered to sail to China and bomb its territory." Thus, for the first time, the Left, too, interpreted the strike as an internationalist act. Obviously ignorant of details about the walkout, this interpretation served its purpose when Chinese-Indochinese cooperation was given special prominence. (SOM, ICh NF, d. 1036: Note sur la propagande, 31 October 1925, 8–11, 15.)

64. Tran Van Giau, *Giai cap cong nhan Viet Nam* (1961): 516, 520 for lists of newspapers used in his study.

65. So far, Vietnamese historical writing rarely provides references for source material and research data. Tran Van Giau's accounts are practically never cited, even though whole passages of his are sometimes copied word for word. See, for example, Ban nghien cuu lich sụ cong doan Viet-Nam, *(So thao lan thu nhat) Lich su phong trao cong nhan,* 74; BNCLSDTU, *Dong chi Ton,* 14–15; Uy ban khoa hoc xa hoi Viet Nam, *Lich su Viet Nam, tap II,* 220–21; Dinh Xuan Lam and Pham Xanh, in *Tap chi Cong san* (June 1988): 13–16, 32; Ha Huy Giap, in *Tap chi Cong san* (July 1988): 14; Ngo Van Hoa and Duong Kinh Quoc, *Giai cap cong nhan,* 327–28, among others. For Western accounts that are based on Tran Van Giau, see, most important, Phan Thanh Son, "Le Mouvement ouvrier Vietnamien des origines à 1945" (Ph.D. diss., Sorbonne, 1968): 142–51, and "Le Mouvement ouvrier vietnamien de 1920 à 1930," in *Tradition et révolution au Vietnam,* ed. Jean Chesneaux et al. (Paris: Anthropos, 1971): 164–88. Others, such as Thomas Hodgkin's *Vietnam: The Revolutionary Path* (New York: St. Martin's, 1981): 220, in turn rely on Phan Thanh Son.

66. Tran Van Giau, *Giai cap cong nhan Viet Nam* (1961): 355. Another historical witness was Le Van Luõng. Le Van Luõng (with "Luong" having the tilde tone marker) should not be confused with the Le Van Luong ("Luong" without a tone marker), who introduced Ton Duc Thang's story of the mutiny at Sevastopol to the communist leadership meeting in 1947 at Vo Nhai. The Le Van Luong of Vo Nhai had been a radical anticolonial activist in early 1930s Sai Gon, had been convicted of criminal offenses by the French, and served time with Ton Duc Thang in Con Lon island penitentiary, rose to the inner circle of the ICP after 1945, and later, in the mid-1950s, was among those blamed for the violent excesses of the land reform in northern Viet Nam. On the other hand, Le Van Luõng had been a worker at Ba Son in 1925 and subsequently became a labor activist in Cambodia and Cochinchina and a mid-

level cadre during the anti-French resistance war. Exiled in northern Viet Nam after the Geneva ceasefire accords of 1954, he worked in the DRVN state bureaucracy in the fields of agricultural mechanization and light industry when Tran Van Giau interviewed him and Ton Duc Thang about the events of 1925. But Tran Van Giau never revealed which of the two historical witnesses provided particular pieces of information, and henceforth only Ton Duc Thang was celebrated as the clandestine leader of the strike at Ba Son. It is for these reasons that I will focus only on Ton Duc Thang and Tran Van Giau in the following analysis.

See a copy of Le Van Luõng's personnel file, Ha Noi, 17 March 1962 (unnumbered document, Ton Duc Thang Museum, Ho Chi Minh City); handwritten extracts made by Pham Thi Mong Trinh in 1989 of Le Van Luõng's memoirs, Ha Noi, 1 March 1960 (Ton Duc Thang Museum, document 23); speech delivered at a Ba Son cadre conference, Ho Chi Minh City, 26 May 1977 (copy of handwritten notes displayed at Ba Son, typed copy at the Ton Duc Thang Museum, document 24).

67. Tran Van Giau, *Giai cap cong nhan Viet Nam* (1961): 353. At the time of the labor conflict at Ba Son, the French-kidnapped Phan Boi Chau had not yet been returned from China to Indochina, and Nguyen An Ninh spent a good part of 1924/25 in France. The significance of Nguyen Ai Quoc's congress appearance in 1924 for Tran Van Giau's description of the strike also remains unexplained. The same applies to Khai Dinh, the second-to-last Nguyen king, who died in November 1925: his influence in Cochinchina (which was under direct French rule) was minimal.

68. Ibid., 354. The ahistorical term "Annamites" was used by the French and other Westerners to refer to the Vietnamese. The term was used by many Vietnamese themselves before 1945, when reference to Viet Nam and Vietnamese in itself became a politically charged act. Especially after 1945, the continued application of "Annamites" was deemed insulting. Tran Van Giau also notes that when asked about his intentions to implement "socialist policies" in Indochina, an embarrassed and supposedly exposed Varenne fell silent.

69. Ibid., 355. My emphases. "Krupp" here is not the German militarist and industrialist, but a colonial enterprise called Kropff & Cie. Tran Van Giau contradicts himself seventeen pages later, where Ton is a mechanic at Cho Quan power station in 1925. Mai Van Ngoc is identified in the 1957 edition of Tran Van Giau's book (252) as "the grandson-in-law of Do Chieu." Do Chieu was the pen name of Nguyen Dinh Chieu (1822–88), a blind southern "scholar-poet" (Marr, *Vietnamese Tradition,* 265).

70. The original article identifies him as Zinovieff (in Riga). Grigori Zinoviev (1883–1936) was a close associate of Lenin's. During the mid-1920s, at the height of his political career, he was chairman of the Executive Committee of Comintern. In 1925, he opposed Stalin and (in stages) fell from power. He was executed after a show trial during the Stalinist purges. (Lazitch, Branko

et al., *Biographical Dictionary of the Comintern* [Stanford, Calif.: Hoover Institution, 1973]: 454–57.)

71. The exaggerated number of Ba Son workers appears in Tran Van Giau, *Giai cap cong nhan Viet Nam* (1961): 355; the 1957 version, 252, even speaks of two thousand workers. In fact, Ba Son had only about 720 workers in 1925.

72. Tran Van Giau, *Giai cap cong nhan Viet Nam* (1957): 253, and (1961): 356.

73. Tran Van Giau, *Giai cap cong nhan Viet Nam* (1957): 254, and (1961): 356–57.

74. It should be noted that Ton Duc Thang and Tran Van Giau do not inform their readers about what happened to the workers' initial grievances regarding fired colleagues and extended work hours on paydays.

75. Tran Van Giau, *Giai cap cong nhan Viet Nam* (1961): 356, 357. Tran Van Giau et al., *Dia chi van hoa,* 284, gives a figure of ten thousand supporting workers.

76. Tran Van Giau, *Giai cap cong nhan Viet Nam* (1961): 357. The delegate's alias was An. According to William Duiker, *The Comintern and Vietnamese Communism,* 12, "An" really was Nguyen Van Tao. Nguyen Van Tao (1908–72) likely had been a witness of the Ba Son strike in 1925. In 1926, expelled from school in Sai Gon for political activities (which, again, involved the arsenal), he fled to France, where he became an active revolutionary. Deported back to Indochina in 1931, he was an exponent of "Stalinists" within the Indochina Communist Party during the 1930s. He became a minister in DRVN governments later (Huynh Kim Khanh, *Vietnamese Communism,* 198 n. 10). "An" mentioned the strike at Ba Son in the section of his speech where he disputed allegations made by unspecified "people" that Indochina had no proletariat. To the contrary, "An" argued, the proletariat was a "concentrated" one and had "clearly shown its revolutionary abilities," for example through the walkout at Ba Son ("Tham luan cua dai bieu Dong-Duong," in *Tap chi hoc tap* 2 [1961]: 38). It is noteworthy that Tran Van Giau, who used the same reprint of the speech, did not quote An's figure of eight hundred strikers, which came much closer to facts.

77. Huynh Kim Khanh, *Vietnamese Communism,* 106, 107.

78. Masson, *La Marine française,* 355–56.

79. Tran Van Giau et al., *Dia chi van hoa,* 284.

80. Tran Van Giau, *Giai cap cong nhan Viet Nam* (1961): 354 and 359–63. See also Tran Van Giau, *Lich su can dai,* (1963): 140–42.

81. Tran Van Giau, *Giai cap cong nhan Viet Nam* (1961): 354.

82. Ibid., 360–61.

83. Ibid., 363. Tran Van Giau's count of "several thousand" striking Ba Son workers reflects his tendency to exaggerate the strike unnecessarily to prove his arguments about the importance of the workers' movement around 1925. See Huynh Kim Khanh, *Vietnamese Communism,* 46 n.22, for the Jeune Annam arrests and subsequent protests.

84. Tran Huy Lieu (1901–69), pen names Nam Kieu and Dau Nam, from a patriotic literati family in Tonkin, came to Sai Gon in late 1924, where he soon became one of the most active journalists of the national-democratic opposition. A cofounder of the Jeune Annam party in early 1926, he later joined the Viet Nam Quoc Dan Dang. Arrested in the roundup following the rue Barbier killing in 1929 (discussed in the introduction), he served five years on Con Lon, where he converted to communism. After 1934, he published various leftist papers in Ha Noi. Imprisoned during most of World War II, he became a minister of the provisional government in the August Revolution of 1945 and personally received the abdication of the last puppet monarch Bao Dai of the Nguyen dynasty. See AOM, GG, 7F, c. 22, Sûreté cochinchine, Rapport annuel 1924–26; *Nghien cuu lich su,* no. 125 (8/1969): 1, 2, 21ff., with full bibliography.

85. This and the preceding quotation are from Tran Huy Lieu, *Lich su 80 nam,* quyen II-thuong (1958): 6–7. My emphases.

86. *DPTB,* 7 August.

87. For the decade of the 1920s, Tran Huy Lieu, in *Lich su 80 nam,* q. II-thuong, 5–8, and ibid., q. I, 223ff., spends just six pages on the Vietnamese working class. See also Tran Huy Lieu et al., *Tai lieu tham khao, tap VI* (1956): 40–44.

88. Radványi, *Delusion,* 24, 25.

89. I thank Hjorleifur Jonsson and Nora Taylor for personally delivering the documents.

90. Among those present were Dang Hoa, Dao Phieu, Nguyen Thanh, Nguyen Van Kim (whom I thank for translating the finer points), and Pham Xanh.

91. See, for example, Nguyen Quang Ngoc, Vu Minh Giang, Pham Xanh et al., eds., *Tien trinh Lich su Viet Nam* (Advanced history of Viet Nam) (Ha Noi: NXB Giao Duc, 2000): 261–62; the relevant passage in this book was written by Pham Xanh.

Lich su Xi nghiep lien hop Ba Son (1863–1998) (History of the united enterprise Ba Son) (commissioned by the Party Committee and the Board of Directors of Ba Son) (Ha Noi: NXB Quan Doi Nhan Dan, 1998): 6, 98–106, 463–68: In a foreword, Tran Van Giau declares Ton Duc Thang the "spirit" of this book, and says that "reading it is like sitting around Uncle Ton and listening to his stories of olden times." In perhaps a reaction to the documents I provided, the strike itself is presented in a convoluted story where the *Michelet* was already docked inside Ba Son in late July 1925, thus giving Ton and his comrades a good week to plan for the ship's paralyzation. Page 106 n. 1, mentions that the Ministry of Defense in October 1997 allowed Ba Son to designate 4 August 1925 as the shipyard's "Day of Tradition."

See also Nguyen Khac Vien and Huu Ngoc, eds., *From Saigon to Ho Chi Minh City: A Path of 300 Years* (Ha Noi: The Gioi, 1998): 54–55 (on Ba Son), 138–41 (on the Black Sea). There is indication that the Ton Duc Thang Museum in Sai Gon already knew by the mid-1990s from its own inquiries with the French navy archives in Brest and Toulon that Ton Duc Thang did not appear on any of the mutinous ships' *rôles d'équipages*.

5. THE SECRET LABOR UNION IN THE POST-UNIFICATION MOMENT

1. Directive no. 222–CT-TU of 25 June 1983. Quoted from *Ngay thanh lap cong doan Viet Nam, 28 thang 7 nam 1929* (7/28/29: The founding day of the Viet Nam Labor Union), Ban tuyen giao Tong cong doan (VFTU Propaganda Commission) (Ha Noi: NXB Lao dong, 1984), by Vu Lan, "Hay tra lai su that lich su cho lich su ra doi cua cong doan Viet Nam" (The historical truth should be given back to the history of the creation of the Vietnamese Labor Union), in *Mot con nguoi binh thuong—vi dai,* 197.

2. Cf. Ban tuyen giao Tong cong doan Viet Nam, *Cong doan Viet Nam tu dai hoi I den dai hoi V* (Vietnamese Labor Union from the first to fifth congress) (Ha Noi: NXB Lao dong, 1984): 169. Since 1961, the "General Labor Confederation of Viet Nam" (of 1946) has been called the "Viet Nam Federation of Trade Unions." I use the English term from the Vietnam Federation of Trade Unions, *The Trade Union Movement in Vietnam* (Ha Noi: Foreign Languages Publishing House, 1988): 50.

3. Tran Van Giau, *Giai cap cong Viet Nam* (1958): 393–94; see also 3d ed. (1961): 371–73.

4. Tran Van Giau et al., *Dia chi van hoa,* 282. It is often stated in this context in Vietnamese literature; see also, for example, Dinh Xuan Lam and Pham Xanh, "Bac Ton voi phong trao cach mang o Sai Gon cuoi nhung nam 20,"13.

5. Tran Van Giau, *Giai cap cong nhan Viet Nam* (1961): 373.

6. See Langlois, *André Malraux,* 63, and AOM, GG, 7F, c. 22, Sûreté cochinchine, Rapport annuel 1926/27 (1 July 1927), vol. 1, 102–10. Tran Van Giau himself, in *Giai cap cong Viet Nam* (1961): 372, explicitly acknowledges the existence of Hoa Kieu unionism, but remains ambiguous about the number of unions.

7. The issues of Chinese organizations in colonial Viet Nam, their influences on Vietnamese anticolonial movements, and their "disappearance" from Vietnamese historiography cry out for detailed examinations. Recently, Sophie Quinn-Judge, in her unpublished manuscript "Rethinking the History of the Vietnamese Communist Party" (2003): 7, writes of "the failure to mention the influence of Chinese organizations within Vietnam on the early revolutionary movement. (The whole idea of Chinese influence on Vietnam's revolution became a taboo topic in the late 1970s.)" See also relevant passages in her *Ho Chi Minh: The Missing Years, 1919–1941* (Berkeley: University of California Press, 2003).

8. Tran Van Giau, *Giai cap cong nhan Viet Nam* (1961): 372.

9. Ibid., 372–73.

10. Ibid. Dinh Xuan Lam and Pham Xanh, "Bac Ton voi phong trao cach mang o Sai Gon cuoi nhung nam 20," 14–15, have Ton work as a mechanic

at KROFF Co. and call the others Nguyen Van *Cam,* N. Manh, and Dang Van Sam. Tran Van Giau et al., *Dia chi van hoa,* 282, spells the deputy Nguyen Van *Con.*

11. AOM, GG, 7–8, c. 55: Crime de la rue Barbier/Affaire Tran Truong et consorts, Index alphabetique, 11, 16. Ban nghien cuu lich su Dang trung uong (here Phuong Dinh, Duc Vuong), *Dong chi Ton Duc Thang, nguoi chien si cong san kien cuong mau muc* (Ha Noi: NXB Su that, 1982): 13. No evidence is cited.

12. Tran Van Giau, *Giai cap cong nhan Viet Nam* (1961): 373. As mentioned before, the VRYL (Viet Nam Thanh Nien Cach Mang Dong Chi Hoi), or just Thanh Nien, was the first in the twentieth century to root the previously fragmented and regionalized anticolonial resistance in the entire country, and the first to apply a conclusive ideology (Marxism-Leninism) to its cause. As the forerunner organization to the Communist Party, the VRYL trained a first nucleus of revolutionary cadres. In Cochinchina, for example, Ton's secret union was used as a basis to establish and develop a regional VRYL committee, which then in turn recruited parts of the union (Dinh Xuan Lam and Pham Xanh, "Bac Ton voi phong trao cach mang o Sai Gon cuoi nhung nam 20," 16). In 1929, during the "proletarianization movement," Thanh Nien disintegrated when factions broke away to form rival communist groups. They were united again by Nguyen Ai Quoc in February 1930, when the ICP was founded. On the VRYL see, for example, Tap the tac gia, *Viet Nam Thanh Nien,* and Duiker in *The China Quarterly* 51: 475–99.

13. Ban nghien cuu lich su cong doan Viet Nam (Commission for the Research of Vietnamese Labor Union History) *(So thao lan thu nhat) Lich su phong trao cong nhan va cong doan Viet Nam (1860–1945)* ([A first sketch of] the history of Viet Nam's workers' and labor union movement) (Ha Noi: NXB Lao dong, 1974): 69, 74.

14. The arguments are detailed in ibid., 83–88, 92.

15. Note that Ton Duc Thang met Ho Chi Minh for the first time only in 1946.

16. Regional tensions within the Revolution are detailed in, for example, Bui Tin, *Following Ho Chi Minh* (Honolulu: University of Hawai'i Press, 1995), and Truong Nhu Tang, *A Viet Cong Memoir* (New York: Vintage Books, 1986).

17. Ban nghien cuu lich su Dang Thanh pho Ho Chi Minh (Ho Chi Minh City Commission for the Research of Party History), *Su truyen ba chu nghia Mac-Lenin va cac to chuc cong san dau tien o Thanh pho Ho Chi Minh* (Propagation of Marxism-Leninism and the first communist organizations in Ho Chi Minh City) (Ho Chi Minh City: NXB Thanh pho Cho Chi Minh, 1980), passim.

18. Ban nghien cuu lich su Dang trung uong, *Dong chi Ton Duc Thang* (1982): 13.

19. Quoted from *Ngay thanh lap,* op. cit. (1984): 8, by Vu Lan, in *Mot con nguoi binh thuong—vi dai,* 202–3. The original booklet was unfortunately not available to me.

20. A later VFTU pamphlet, published coincidentally with the Long Xuyen symposium on Ton Duc Thang, *The Trade Union Movement in Vietnam* (Ha

Noi: Foreign Languages Publishing House, 1988), confirmed 28 July 1929 as the beginning of Vietnamese unionism.

21. Tran Van Giau et al., *Dia chi van hoa,* 282.

22. Luu Phuong Thanh, *Nhung nguoi con,* 13–16.

23. Cf. Huynh Kim Khanh, *Vietnamese Communism, 1925–1945* (Ithaca, N.Y.: Cornell University Press, 1982): 113–22, especially 120–21.

24. The year 1988/89 saw a flurry of publications on Ton Duc Thang, including, of course, accounts of the secret labor union. I have, however, chosen to focus on the symposium proceedings, because the opinions there were usually more pointedly expressed. Cf. Ban khoa hoc xa hoi thanh uy, *Bac Ton va chung ta;* Dang Hoa, Viet Chinh, *Nguoi thuy thu;* So van hoa va thong tin An Giang, *Chu tich Ton;* To Thanh Tam, *Chuyen ke ve Bac Ton;* Tran Thanh Phuong, *Bac Ton cua chung ta.* A rather independent article by Ngo Quang Lang, a researcher from Long Xuyen, about the union, in Ban chap hanh tinh dang bo An Giang, *Bac Ton (1888–1980),* 59–83, should nevertheless be mentioned here. As the "exception to the rule" of my argument, Ngo does mention the Hoa Kieu unions in Cho Lon and does not see Ton's union as the country's "first"—at a time when even northerners proposed just that.

25. Zachary Abuza, *Renovating Politics in Contemporary Vietnam* (Boulder, Colo.: Lynne Rienner, 2001): 168. Much of the following information comes from Abuza's chapter 5 on the club, 161–82, to date one of the best accounts of the CFRF.

26. My repeated inability to meet with Tran Van Giau during my research in Ho Chi Minh City in 1992 likely was due to his lingering political problems as a prominent exponent of the CFRF.

27. Vu Lan, "Hay tra lai su that," in *Mot con nguoi binh thuong—vidai,* 202–4.

28. Phan Van Nhan, "Cong hoi bi mat ra doi nam 1920 o Sai Gon la to chuc Cong doan dau tien o Viet Nam" (The secret labor union founded in 1920 in Sai Gon was the first labor union organization in Viet Nam), in *Mot con nguoi binh thuong—vi dai,* 195–96.

29. Dang Hoa, "Ve to chuc Cong hoi bi mat do Bac Ton to chuc" (About the secret labor union organized by Uncle Ton), in *Mot con nguoi binh thuong—vi dai,* 206–10, passim. It should be emphasized again that the argument over 1925 or 1929 as the beginning of Vietnamese unionism was a revolutionary one. An anticommunist author, Trinh-Quang-Quy, *Phong trao Lao-dong Viet-Nam: Le Mouvement du travail au Vietnam: The Labor Movement in Viet-Nam* (Sai Gon, 1970), dates the origin of the Vietnamese labor movement in 1947 and dismisses prior communist organizations as, in fact, set to destroy an independent union movement.

30. Luu Phuong Thanh, "Bac Ton, nguoi cong nhan uu tu, lanh tu cong doan dau tien o Viet Nam" (Uncle Ton, outstanding worker and leader of the first labor union in Viet Nam), in *Mot con nguoi binh thuong—vi dai,* 186–91.

31. To Thanh Tam, "Ton Duc Thang va to chuc Cong hoi bi mat" (Ton Duc Thang and the secret labor union), in *Mot con nguoi binh thuong—vi dai,* 211–17, especially 215–16.

32. Tran Bach Dang, "Mot con nguoi binh thuong—vi dai" (A great ordinary person), in *Mot con nguoi binh thuong—vi dai,* 29–32, especially 30.

33. To Thanh Tam, "Ton Duc Thang," in *Mot con nguoi binh thuong—vi dai,* 216, 217.

34. Phan Huy Le, "Vai suy nghi ve su hoc Viet Nam tren duong doi moi" (A few thoughts about the Viet Nam historical sciences on the road of renovation), in *Nhan dan chu nhat* 2, no. 153 (12 January 1992): 12.

6. TELLING LIFE

1. This chapter was originally published as an essay in Keith W. Taylor and John K. Whitmore, eds., *Essays into Vietnamese Pasts* (Ithaca, N.Y.: Cornell University, SouthEast Asia Program Publications, 1995): 246–71, and is, in its shorter, revised form, reprinted with permission. Its title has been adapted from a book by Leon Edel et al. on "the biographer's art."

2. Ban nghien cuu lich su Dang trung uong (BNCLSDTU) (Phuong Dinh, Duc Vuong), *Dong chi Ton Duc Thang, nguoi chien si cong san kien cuong mau muc* (Ha Noi: NXB Su that, 1982).

3. This characterization truly set standards: it is quoted in both *Quan doi nhan dan* (People's Army, hereafter *QDND*) 6752 (31 March 1980): 1, in the biographical sketch, and *QDND* 6755 (3 April 1980): 4, "Xa luan" (Leading article).

4. Cf. *QDND* 6752 (31 March 1980): 1.

5. *QDND* 6756 (4 April 1980): 1.

6. See "Special Communiqué," "Biographical Sketch," "Leading Article," "Memorial Address," in *QDND.*

7. The prominence and attention given those three countries (always in the order USSR-Laos-Kampuchea) in official writing continued throughout the 1980s.

8. BNCLSDTU, *Dong chi Ton,* 7; Ha Huy Giap, "Tuong nho," 18; *QDND* 6752 (31 March 1980): 1.

9. "Tieu su tom tat cua Chu tich nuoc Viet-Nam dan chu cong hoa Ton-Duc-Thang" (Summarized biography of Ton Duc Thang, president of the DRVN), in *Tap chi Hoc tap* (Study, hereafter *TCHT*) (Ha Noi) (October 1969): 23–24. Also in: *Nghien cuu lich su* (Historical research) (Ha Noi), no. 127 (October 1969): 2–3.

10. BNCLSDTU, *Dong chi Ton,* 7. Note that a *nation,* not a social class, has "revolutionary tradition."

11. Ha Huy Giap, "Tuong nho," 18, states (without proof) that Ton came to Sai Gon only in 1914.

12. *QDND* 6752 (31 March 1980): 1.

13. BNCLSDTU, *Dong chi Ton,* 11.

14. Quoted in Cao Van Bien, "Nhung chuyen bien cua giai cap cong nhan Viet Nam duoi anh sang chu nghia Mac-Le-nin" (Transformations of the

Vietnamese working class under the light of Marxism-Leninism), 228, in Nguyen Cong Binh, Vu Huy Phuc et al., *Mot so van de ve lich su giai cap cong nhan Viet Nam* (Some questions concerning the history of the Vietnamese working class) (Ha Noi: NXB Lao Dong, 1974): 223–52. Also in Tran Van Giau, *Giai cap cong nhan Viet Nam* (1961): 372–73.

15. *QDND* 6754 (2 April 1980): 3.

16. For example, Ton's alleged helplessness during "the crisis of September-December 1957" in the anticommunist book by P. J. Honey, *Communism in North Vietnam: Its Role in the Sino-Soviet Dispute* (Cambridge, Mass.: MIT, 1963): 52–54, and his (ed.) *North Vietnam Today: Profile of a Communist Satellite* (New York: Praeger, 1962): 55–57.

17. With raging anticommunism, Gérard Tongas, *(J'ai vécu dans) l'enfer communiste au Nord Viêt-Nam (et j'ai choisi la liberté)* (Paris: Nouvelles Éditions Debresse, 1960): 114, is not able to see anything else in Ton than a "fanatique moscoutaire de vieille obédience."

18. BNCLSDTU, *Dong chi Ton,* 25. Quoted from the 1957 "recollections."

19. Le Minh, *Nguoi tho may,* 108–19.

20. Tran Huy Lieu, *Lich su tam muoi nam chong Phap* (History of eighty years against the French), vol. 1 (1858–1929) (Ha Noi: NXB Ban nghien cuu Van Su Dia, 1957 [2d ed.]): 273. Tran Huy Lieu's italics. Convicted of political activities at the trial in 1930, Tran Huy Lieu served five years on Con Lon.

21. Tap the tac gia (Authors' collective, i.e., Nguyen Thanh, Pham Xanh, Dang Hoa, Dao Phieu), *Viet Nam Thanh Nien Cach Mang Dong Chi Hoi* (The VRYL) (Ha Noi: NXB Thong tin ly luan, 1986): 199 n.2. My accentuations. It is an interesting passage, hidden in a "mumbled" footnote ("etc."). Regarding the somewhat skewed logic of the argument ("but"), I wonder whether the authors really expected a "gentlemen's war" between the French and the resistance. The defensive-deterrent word "internal" seems much more aimed at the 1986 Vietnamese reader than at the 1928 French police. In an adaptation, the account was reprinted by one of the collective's authors, Dao Phieu, in *Chu tich Ton Duc Thang (1888–1980)*: 27n.

22. Ngo Quang Lang, chap. 4 of *Bac Ton (1888–1980)*: 81.

23. Tai, *Radicalism,* 214ff.

24. Chesneaux, *Geschichte Vietnams,* 305; Fall, *Viet-Minh Regime,* 39, 75, and *Two Viet-Nams,* 91.

25. The destruction of the Cochinchinese VRYL also had its positive effects from the point of view of the VNCP: By weakening the entire league, it accelerated a process in which the VRYL came under increasing pressure from breakaway factions demanding the movement's "proletarianization" (in accordance with a recent shift in Comintern policy). This process finally led to the dissolution of the league and to the foundation of a unified Communist Party, the first one on a national level, in February 1930.

26. Tongas, *L'enfer communiste,* 114; Honey, *Communism in North Vietnam,* 131.

27. Werner Holzer, *Bei den Erben Ho Tschi Minhs: Menschen und Gesellschaft in Nordvietnam* (With Ho Chi Minh's heirs: People and society in North Viet Nam) (Munich: Süddeutscher Verlag, 1971): 29.

28. "Loi phat bieu cua Chu tich nuoc Viet-Nam Dan chu Cong hoa Ton-Duc-Thang" (Statement of Ton Duc Thang, president of the DRVN), reprinted in *TCHT* (October 1969): 27.

29. BNCLSDTU, *Dong chi Ton,* 29. We know, of course, that Ton's two teenage daughters accompanied their father north. Only his wife remained south until 1954.

30. Ibid., 12.

31. "Vi ly tuong," in *QDND* 6754 (2 April 1980): 3.

32. Wang Gungwu, in *Self and Biography,* 4, 189, 194.

33. David Marr, "Vietnamese Historical Reassessment, 1900–1944," in *Perceptions of the Past in Southeast Asia,* ed. Anthony Reid and David Marr (Singapore: Heinemann Educational Books, 1979): 313–39.

34. I borrow here from David Marr.

35. Tran Tu Binh, *The Red Earth,* 84: Ton Duc Thang, a "mature communist," "felt very sorry for us [young prisoners] and shouldered all the heavy work." He is also the (unexplained) herald of news about the outcome of revolutionary struggles in which Tran Tu Binh had been involved.

36. Huynh Kim Khanh, *Vietnamese Communism, 1925–1945* (Ithaca, N.Y.: Cornell University Press, 1982): 254–55 n.49.

37. The right of "earth returning to earth" was one of the main contemporary arguments against Lenin's embalmment before it became a taboo subject. Only in the last years of perestroika USSR did the whole concept of mausolea as an ersatz religion of officially atheist regimes become heatedly debated again. And in Bulgaria, the embalmed corpse of Georgii Dimitrov (d. 1949) was cremated shortly after the 1989 revolution. In China and Viet Nam the subject remains sacrosanct. The conflict over Lenin's preserved corpse continues in the USSR's successor polity. Here, the course of the Commonwealth of Independent States toward capitalism is mirrored in one symptomatic episode of the mausoleum debate. News reports from Moscow in the winter of 1991/92 disclosed suggestions to send Lenin's corpse on a "World Exhibition Tour" for hard currency. Under the liquidators of the exclusive historical model, the mausoleum is undergoing a transition: from cult to commodity.

7. MUSEUM-SHRINE

1. This is an adaptation of my article "Museum-Shrine: Revolution and Its Tutelary Spirit in the Village of My Hoa Hung," in *The Country of Memory: Remaking the Past in Late Socialist Vietnam,* ed. Hue-Tam Ho Tai (Berkeley: University of California Press, 2001): 77–105. It is reprinted with permission of the University of California Press.

2. The tutor likely had contacts with the famed anticolonialist Phan Boi Chau when the latter came to An Giang in 1902 to recruit for his Travel East

(Dong Du) movement, and with the anti-French conspiracy of 1916 under emperor Duy Tan.

3. Information provided by Bui Cong Duc and Ngo Quang Lang, cadres of the An Giang province culture and information department and the provincial VNCP propaganda board, Long Xuyen, 4 May 1992.

4. An Giang provincial branch of the VNCP, circular no. 06/TT-TU, Long Xuyen, 13 March 1987 (document no. 39, Ton Duc Thang Museum, Ho Chi Minh City).

5. See Lam Binh Tuong, "Trung tu di tich voi viec phuc hoi noi that ngoi nha cua Chu tich Ton Duc Thang o My Hoa Hung (An Giang)" (Reconstructing historic sites with interior renovations of President Ton Duc Thang's house in My Hoa Hung [An Giang]), and "Bao ve ngoi nha luu niem Chu tich Ton Duc Thang o My Hoa Hung, tinh chat phong canh va canh quan" (Protecting President Ton Duc Thang's home in My Hoa Hung, landscape character and beauty), in Ban tuyen giao Tinh uy An Giang (Propaganda commission of An Giang province), To Thanh Tam, ed., *Mot con nguoi binh thuong—vi dai. Ky yeu Hoi thao khoa hoc ve Chu tich Ton Duc Thang nhan dip ky niem 100 nam ngay sinh 20–8–1888–20–8–1988* (A great ordinary person: Proceedings of the symposium on President Ton Duc Thang commemorating the centennial of his birth) (An Giang, 1989): 59–64. Articles on the constructions in An Giang (27 July, 5, 12 August 1988) and pamphlet of An Giang culture and information department about the commemoration site, 1988 (documents no. 149 and no. 84, Ton Duc Thang Museum, Ho Chi Minh City). Dang Kim Quy, "Ngoi nha luu niem thoi nien thieu Chu tich Ton Duc Thang" (President Ton Duc Thang's childhood home), in *Tap chi Lich su Dang* (Journal of party history) (October 1991): 36. Interview with Ton's nephew Ton Duc Hung, My Hoa Hung, 4 May 1992.

6. Other displays in Ho Chi Minh City are at Cao Thang vocational school, the former École des mécaniciens asiatiques de Saïgon, at the Museum of the Revolution, and in the Hall of Tradition of Ba Son shipyard. In addition to the commemorative area in nearby My Hoa Hung, Long Xuyen's Museum of An Giang Province also boasts a large section devoted to Ton Duc Thang.

7. For a comprehensive treatment of the post-Tiananmen "craze" of Mao Zedong, see Geremie R. Barmé, *Shades of Mao: The Posthumous Cult of the Great Leader* (Armonk, N.Y.: M. E. Sharpe, 1996). See also the very brief but promising treatment of a Mao Zedong temple in Gushui, Shaanxi, by Begonia Lee, "Houses of the Holy," *Far Eastern Economic Review* 6 June 1996, 52.

Shrines of Ho Chi Minh are briefly mentioned by Hue-Tam Ho Tai, "Monumental Ambiguity: The State Commemoration of Ho Chi Minh," in *Essays into Vietnamese Pasts,* ed. K. W. Taylor and John K. Whitmore (Ithaca, N.Y.: Cornell University SouthEast Asia Program Publications, 1995): 273, 278.

For Indonesia and its commemoration of *pahlawan,* see Klaus H. Schreiner, *Politischer Heldenkult in Indonesien: Tradition und Moderne Praxis* (Political hero cult in Indonesia: Tradition and modern practice) (Berlin, Hamburg: Reimer, 1995).

8. Whitfield, *Historical and Cultural Dictionary,* 275–76. See also the helpful, if only awkwardly presented, materials in Nguyen Tien Huu, *Dörfliche Kulte im traditionellen Vietnam* (Village cults in traditional Viet Nam) (Munich: UNI, 1970).

9. Stephen O'Harrow, "Men of Hu, Men of Han, Men of the Hundred Man: The Biography of Si Nhiep and the Conceptualization of Early Vietnamese Society," *Bulletin de l'École française d'Extrême-Orient* LXXV (1986): 251.

10. See, with such an emphasis, Yamamoto Tatsuro, "Myths Explaining the Vicissitudes of Political Power in Ancient Vietnam," *Acta Asiatica: Bulletin of the Institute of Eastern Culture* (Tokyo: The Toho Gakkai) 18 (1970): 70–94.

11. For example, Nguyen Trai's retreat on Con Son Mountain in Hai Hung province was turned into a national hero shrine. Nguyen Trai became canonized and continues to be venerated as among the most important guardian spirits of the Vietnamese realm. Whitfield, *Historical and Cultural Dictionary,* 48.

12. Keith W. Taylor, "Notes on the Viet Dien U Linh Tap," *The Vietnam Forum* 8 (summer/fall 1986): 26–59. See also an earlier brief discussion in his *The Birth of Vietnam* (Berkeley: University of California Press, 1983): 352ff. Oliver W. Wolters, "Preface," in his *Two Essays on Dai-Viet in the Fourteenth Century* (New Haven: Council on Southeast Asia Studies, Yale University, 1988), vii–xl.

13. Taylor, "Notes," 45.

14. Wolters, "Preface," xix, xxviii, xxxv. The author worked mainly with later versions of the *Spiritual Powers of the Viet Realm.*

15. O. W. Wolters, "On Telling a Story of Vietnam in the Thirteenth and Fourteenth Centuries," *Journal of Southeast Asian Studies* 26, no. 1 (March 1995): 67.

16. Wolters, "Preface," xvi.

17. See David G. Marr, *Vietnamese Tradition on Trial, 1920–1945* (Berkeley: University of California Press, 1981): 263.

18. Oliver W. Wolters, "Possibilities for a Reading of the 1293–1357 Period in the Vietnamese Annals," *The Vietnam Forum* 11 (winter/spring 1988): 97 passim.

19. Keith W. Taylor, "Looking behind the Vietnamese Annals: Ly Phat Ma (1028–54) and Ly Nhat Ton (1054–72) in the Viet Su Luoc and the Toan Thu," *The Vietnam Forum* 7 (winter/spring 1986): 51.

20. Wolters, "Possibilities," 116–17.

21. *Mot con nguoi binh thuong—vi dai,* To Thanh Tam, ed.

22. The archetypical image persisted despite the violent end in a court intrigue Nguyen Trai and most of his family met several years after Le Loi's death.

23. Tran Quoc Vuong, "Traditions, Acculturation, Renovation: The Evolutional Pattern of Vietnamese Culture," in *Southeast Asia in the 9th to 14th Centuries,* ed. David G. Marr and A. C. Milner (Singapore: ISEAS et al., 1986): 271.

24. John K. Whitmore, "From Classical Scholarship to Confucian Belief in Vietnam," *The Vietnam Forum* 9 (winter/spring 1987): 58.

25. Oliver W. Wolters, "Assertions of Cultural Well-Being in Fourteenth-Century Vietnam," in his *Two Essays,* 42.

26. Esta S. Ungar, "Vietnamese Leadership and Order: Dai Viet under the Le Dynasty (1428–1459)" (Ph.D. diss., Cornell University, Ithaca, N.Y., 1983): 19, 20. The following exposition is based on subsequent passages in the first chapter.

27. Fan Zhongyan: also transcribed Fan Chung-yen in the Wade-Giles system, or, in Sino-Vietnamese transcription, Pham Trong Yem.

28. James T. C. Liu, "An Early Sung Reformer: Fan Chung-Yen," in: *Chinese Thought and Institutions,* ed. John K. Fairbank (Chicago: University of Chicago Press, 1964 [3d ed.]): 111. Ungar, "Vietnamese Leadership and Order," 41.

29. Liu, "An Early Sung Reformer," 108, 131.

30. Ungar, "Vietnamese Leadership and Order," 10.

31. "Nguyen Trai, mot nha dai chinh tri, dai van hao Viet-nam" (Nguyen Trai, a great Vietnamese politician and writer), *Nghien cuu Van Su Dia* (September 1956), an excerpt of the keynote address Tran Huy Lieu gave at a "commemorative assembly" on Nguyen Trai organized in September 1956 by the Ministry of Culture (Patricia Pelley, "Writing Revolution: The New History in Post-Colonial Vietnam" [Ph.D. diss., Cornell University, Ithaca, N.Y., 1993]: 209); "Nguyen Trai, mot nhan vat vi dai trong lich su dan toc Viet-nam" (Nguyen Trai, a great persona in the history of the Vietnamese nation), *Nghien cuu lich su* 42 (September 1962), but also possibly published in expanded form as a monograph, *Nguyen Trai* (Ha Noi: NXB Khoa hoc xa hoi, 1966, 1969 [2d ed.]). For a more comprehensive bibliography of DRVN writings on Nguyen Trai between 1956 and 1968, see Pelley, "Writing Revolution," 207–12, especially nn. 65, 75, 77, and 78, and Ungar, "Vietnamese Leadership and Order," 268 nn. 4 and 5.

32. Tran Huy Lieu, *Nguyen Trai,* 56.

33. Ungar, "Vietnamese Leadership and Order," 34.

34. Nguyen Khac Vien, *Tradition and Revolution in Vietnam,* ed. David Marr and Jayne Werner (Berkeley: Indochina Resource Center [1974?]), especially his essay "Confucianism and Marxism in Vietnam," 15–52.

35. Nguyen Khac Vien, *Tradition,* 46–51; the quote is from 48. See also Neil L. Jamieson, *Understanding Vietnam* (Berkeley: University of California Press, 1993): 217, and Marr, *Vietnamese Tradition,* 135.

36. Alexander B. Woodside, *Community and Revolution in Modern Vietnam* (Boston: Houghton Mifflin, 1976): 237. Note the echo from Fan Zhongyan in the first sentence.

37. Marr, *Vietnamese Tradition,* 134; Nguyen Khac Vien, *Tradition,* 49–50.

38. I am grateful to Hue-Tam Ho Tai for suggesting this aspect of timing to me.

39. Alexander B. Woodside, "Conceptions of Change and of Human Responsibility for Change in Late Traditional Vietnam," *The Vietnam Forum* 6 (summer/fall 1985): 108. My emphases.

40. See, among others who have observed that phenomenon, Hy Van

Luong, "Economic Reform and the Intensification of Rituals in Two Northern Vietnamese Villages, 1980–1990," in *The Challenge of Reform in Indo-China,* ed. Borje Ljunggren and Peter Timmer (Cambridge, Mass., 1993): 259–91. Here, however, I am less concerned with the effects of economic reforms under the *Doi Moi* policy and more interested in the context of the declining outside models of authority.

41. To draw a parallel to premodern times, equal confidence exudes from the Vietnamese tales of heroic guardian spirits and the underlying concept of the spiritual properties of the land, as Oliver Wolters has pointed out with reference to the *Spiritual Powers of the Viet Realm* (Wolters, "On Telling a Story," 67). Challenges to the ruling powers and threats to the country's security—recurrent themes in the Vietnamese experience—had been warded off, as one could very well see in retrospect, whenever ruler and tutelary deity had established a "winning" rapport in the proper manner described by the tales.

42. Oliver W. Wolters, *History, Culture, and Region in Southeast Asian Perspectives* (Singapore: ISEAS, 1982): 102; and Wolters, "Preface," xix.

CONCLUSION

1. As stated in his "recollections" of 1957, op. cit.
2. Judith Henchy kindly informed me about the road on Con Lon.
3. Rudolf Bahro, an East German dissident, coined this phrase.

Select Bibliography

ARCHIVES AND DOCUMENT COLLECTIONS

Bao Tang Cach Mang (Museum of the Revolution), Ha Noi, Viet Nam
Bao Tang Cach Mang, Ho Chi Minh City, Viet Nam
Bao Tang Ho Chi Minh (Ho Chi Minh Museum), Ha Noi, Viet Nam
Bao Tang Ton Duc Thang, Ho Chi Minh City, Viet Nam
Centre des archives d'Outre-Mer, Aix-en-Provence, France
Nha Truyen Thong Xuong Ba Son (Hall of Tradition of the Ba Son Shipyard), Ho Chi Minh City, Viet Nam
Service historique de l'Armée de terre, Vincennes, France
Services historiques de la marine, France:
Archives centrales, Vincennes
Archives de la IIe région maritime, Brest
Archives de la IIIe région maritime, Toulon
Trung Tam Luu Tru Quoc Gia I (National Archives Center I), Ha Noi, Viet Nam
Trung Tam Luu Tru Quoc Gia II, Ho Chi Minh City, Viet Nam

INTERVIEWS

Bui Cong Duc, So Van Hoa Va Thong Tin An Giang (An Giang department for culture and information), Long Xuyen, Viet Nam, 4 May 1992.
Devillers, Philippe, Copenhagen, Denmark, 21 August 1993.
Duong Quang Dong, Ho Chi Minh City, Viet Nam, 9 May 1992.
Duong Van Phuc, Ha Noi, Viet Nam, 14 May 1992.
Le Minh, Ha Noi, Viet Nam, April 1992.
Le Van Luong (also known as Pham Van Khuong, Nguyen Cong Mieu), Ho Chi Minh City, Viet Nam, 9 May 1992 (now deceased).
Luu Phuong Thanh (also known as Le Van An), Ban Nghien Cuu Lich Su Dang Thanh Pho Ho Chi Minh (Ho Chi Minh City Commission for the Research of Party History), Ho Chi Minh City, Viet Nam, 11 May 1992.
Masson, Philippe, Service historique de la marine, Vincennes, France, 10 June 1992.
Ngo Quang Lang, Ban Tuyen Giao Tinh Uy An Giang (Propaganda and education department, VNCP committee of An Giang province), Long Xuyen, Viet Nam, 4 May 1992.
To Thanh Tam, Ban Tuyen Huan Tinh Uy An Giang (Propaganda and

training department, VNCP committee of An Giang province), Long Xuyen, Viet Nam, 5 May 1992.

Ton Duc Hung, Khu Luu Niem Thoi Nien Thieu Chu Tich Ton Duc Thang (Commemorative area of President Ton Duc Thang's youth), My Hoa Hung, Viet Nam, 4 May 1992.

Ton Thi Hanh, Ha Noi, Viet Nam, 14 May 1992.

Tran Quoc Vuong, Ithaca, N.Y., 30 April 1991, and Ha Noi, Viet Nam, May 1992.

Tuong Bich Truc, Ha Noi, Viet Nam, 14 May 1992.

COMMUNICATIONS RECEIVED

Ha Huy Giap, through Pham Xanh, Ho Chi Minh City, Viet Nam, 4 May 1992 (now deceased).

Nguyen Thanh Son (also known as Nguyen Van Tay), through Pham Xanh, Ho Chi Minh City, Viet Nam, 6 May 1992.

Pham Van Dong, through his secretary Nguyen Tien Nang, Ha Noi, Viet Nam, 12 May 1992 (now deceased).

NEWSPAPERS AND PERIODICALS

An Ha Bao (Organe d'informations agricoles, commerciales et industrielles), Can Tho.

L'Argus Indochinois (Organe de défense des intérêts français et annamites), Ha Noi.

L'Asie française (Bulletin mensuel du comité de l'Asie française [Indochine, Levant, Extrême-Orient]), Paris.

L'Avenir du Tonkin, Ha Noi.

Bao Dong Phap ("France-Indochine"), Ha Noi.

La Cloche fêlée (Organe de propagande démocratique), Sai Gon.

Cong Luan Bao, Sai Gon.

Dong Phap Thoi Bao (Le Courrier indochinois), Sai Gon.

L'Écho annamite, Sai Gon.

L'Extrême Asie, Sai Gon.

L'Impartial (Organe de défense des intérêts français en Indochine), Sai Gon.

L'Indochine (Journal quotidien de rapprochement franco-annamite), 1925 (no. 1, 17 June–no. 49, 14 August), Sai Gon.

L'Indochine enchaînée (beginning 4 November [?] 1925, twenty-three editions), Sai Gon.

La Jeunesse (French Sûreté extracts of *Thanh Nien,* organ of the Viet Nam Thanh Nien Cach Mang Dong Chi Hoi/Vietnamese Revolutionary Youth League), Canton/Guangzhou.

Luc Tinh Tan Van: Nam-Trung Nhut-Bao Reunis, Sai Gon.

Le Monde, Paris.

Nam Phong (Van-hoc khoa-hoc Tap-chi), Ha Noi.
Neues Deutschland, East Berlin.
The New York Times, New York.
Nghien cuu lich su, Ha Noi.
North-China Daily News, Shanghai.
The North-China Herald, Shanghai.
La Presse indochinoise (Périodique illustré: Politique, littéraire, économique), Sai Gon.
Le Progrès annamite, Sai Gon.
Quan doi nhan dan, Ha Noi.
Regards sur le monde du travail, Paris.
Revue du Pacifique, Paris.
La Revue indochinoise, tome XLIV (July-December 1925), Ha Noi.
Saigon Times, Ho Chi Minh City.
The Shanghai Crisis, (no. 1,10 June 1925, published by the students of Tsing Hua College [Qinghua Daxue]), Beijing.
Shanghai Mercury-Emergency Edition (June/July 1925), Shanghai.
Sovietskii Moriak, Moscow (?).
Tap chi Hoc tap, Ha Noi.
Tap chi Lich su Dang, Ha Noi.
Le Temps, Paris.
Temps d'Asie, Sai Gon.
Thanh Nien (see *La Jeunesse*).
Tien phong, Ha Noi.
Trung Bac Tan Van, Ha Noi.
Viet Nam Hon (Tribune libre des etudiants et des travailleurs annamites) (beginning January 1926), Paris.
La Voix annamite, Sai Gon.
La Voix libre (Journal bi-hebdomadaire indépendant, organe de défense de tout français contre l'arbitraire et le favoritisme), Sai Gon.

SECONDARY SOURCES

Abuza, Zachary. *Renovating Politics in Contemporary Vietnam.* Boulder, Colo.: Lynne Rienner, 2001.
Amadiume, Ifi, and Abdullahi An-Na'im, eds. *The Politics of Memory: Truth, Healing, and Social Justice.* New York: St. Martin's, 2000.
Anderson, Benedict. *Imagined Communities. Reflections on the Origin and Spread of Nationalism.* Rev. ed. London: Verso, 1991.
Asselin, Pierre. *A Bitter Peace: Washington, Hanoi, and the Making of the Paris Agreement.* Chapel Hill: University of North Carolina Press, 2002.
Azeau, Henri. *Ho Chi Minh, dernière chance: La Conférence franco-vietnamienne de Fontainebleau, juillet 1946.* Paris: Flammarion, 1968.
Ban Chap Hanh Tinh Dang Bo An Giang (Party Central Executive Com-

mittee of An Giang province), ed. *Bac Ton (1888–1980), cuoc doi va su nghiep* (Uncle Ton, life and work). Ha Noi: NXB Su that, 1988.

Ban Khoa Hoc Xa Hoi Thanh Uy (Social Science Commission of the Municipal Party Committee), ed. *Bac Ton va chung ta* (Uncle Ton and we). Ho Chi Minh City: NXB Ban khoa hoc xa hoi Thanh uy, 1988.

Ban Nghien Cuu Lich Su Cong Doan Viet Nam (Commission for the Research of Vietnamese Labor Union History). *(So thao lan thu nhat) Lich su phong trao cong nhan va cong doan Viet Nam (1860–1945)* ([A first sketch of] the history of Viet Nam's workers' and labor union movement). Ha Noi: NXB Lao dong, 1974, 1977 (3d ed.).

Ban Nghien Cuu Lich Su Dang Thanh Pho Ho Chi Minh (Ho Chi Minh City Commission for the Research of Party History). *Su truyen ba chu nghia Mac-Lenin va cac to chuc cong san dau tien o Thanh pho Ho Chi Minh* (Propagation of Marxism-Leninism and the first communist organizations in Ho Chi Minh City). Ho Chi Minh City: NXB Thanh pho Ho Chi Minh, 1980.

Ban Nghien Cuu Lich Su Dang Truc Thuoc Ban Chap Hanh Trung Uong Dang Lao Dong Viet-Nam (Commission for the Research of Party History at the Central Committee of the Vietnamese Labor Party). *Buoc ngoat vi dai cua lich su cach mang Viet Nam* (A great turning point in the history of the Vietnamese Revolution). Ha Noi: NXB Su that, 1961.

Ban Nghien Cuu Lich Su Dang Trung Uong (Central Commission for the Research of Party History; Phuong Dinh, Duc Vuong). *Dong chi Ton Duc Thang, nguoi chien si cong san kien cuong mau muc* (Comrade Ton Dun Thang, an exemplary, staunch communist fighter). Ha Noi: NXB Su that, 1982.

———. *Nhung su kien lich su Dang* (Events in party history). Vol. 1 (1920–1945). Ha Noi: NXB Su that, 1976.

Ban Tuyen Giao Tong Cong Doan Viet Nam (Propaganda commission of the Viet Nam Federation of Trade Unions). *Cong doan Viet Nam tu dai hoi I den dai hoi V* (Vietnamese Labor Union from the first to fifth congress). Ha Noi: NXB Lao dong, 1984.

Banerjee, Subrata. *Viet Nam Fights for Freedom*. Bombay: People's Publishing House, 1947.

Bao Ninh. *The Sorrow of War. A Novel of North Vietnam*. New York: Riverhead Books, 1996.

Barmé, Geremie R. *Shades of Mao: The Posthumous Cult of the Great Leader*. Armonk, N.Y.: M. E. Sharpe, 1996.

Blatti, Jo, ed. *Past Meets Present: Essays about Historic Interpretation and Public Audiences*. Washington, D.C.: Smithsonian Institution, 1987.

Borofsky, Robert, ed. *Remembrance of Pacific Pasts: An Invitation to Remake History*. Honolulu: University of Hawai'i Press, 2000.

Boudarel, Georges. "Intellectual Dissidence in the 1950s: The Nhan-Van Giai-Pham Affair." *Vietnam Forum* 13, (1990): 154–74.

Boudarel, Georges, and Nguyen Van Ky. *Hanoi: City of the Rising Dragon,* trans. Clare Duiker. Lanham, Md.: Rowman & Littlefield, 2002.

Bousquet, Gisele, and Pierre Brocheux, eds. *Viêt-Nam Exposé: French Scholarship on Twentieth-Century Vietnamese Society.* Ann Arbor: University of Michigan Press, 2002.

Boyarin, Jonathan, ed. *Remapping Memory: The Politics of TimeSpace.* Minneapolis: University of Minnesota Press, 1994.

Bradley, Mark Philip. *Imagining Vietnam and America: The Making of Postcolonial Vietnam, 1919–1950.* Chapel Hill: University of North Carolina Press, 2000.

Brandt, Susanne. "The Memory Makers: Museums and Exhibitions of the First World War." *History & Memory* 6, no. 1 (spring/summer 1994): 95–122.

Brigham, Robert K. *Guerrilla Diplomacy: The NLF's Foreign Relations and the Viet Nam War.* Ithaca, N.Y.: Cornell University Press, 1998.

Brocheux, Pierre. *The Mekong Delta: Ecology, Economy, and Revolution, 1860–1960.* Madison: University of Wisconsin-Madison Center for Southeast Asian Studies, 1995.

Bui Tin. *Following Ho Chi Minh: The Memoirs of a North Vietnamese Colonel,* trans. Judy Stowe and Do Van. Honolulu: University of Hawai'i Press, 1995.

Buttinger, Joseph. *Vietnam: A Political History.* New York: Praeger, 1968.

Célerier, Pierre. *Menaces sur le Viet-Nam.* Sai Gon: Imprimerie d'Extrême-Orient, 1950.

Chen, King C. *Vietnam and China, 1938–1954.* Princeton, N.J.: Princeton University Press, 1969.

Chesneaux, Jean. *The Chinese Labor Movement 1919–1927,* trans. H. M. Wright ("Le mouvement ouvrier chinois de 1919 à 1927," Paris, 1962). Stanford, Calif.: Stanford University Press, 1968.

———. *Geschichte Vietnams* (History of Viet Nam). Rev., enlarged ed. of his *Contribution à l'histoire de la nation vietnamienne,* Paris, 1955, trans. Ernst-Ulrich Kloock. Berlin: Rütten & Loening, 1963.

Chesneaux, Jean et al., eds. *Tradition et Révolution au Vietnam.* Paris: Anthropos, 1971.

Ch'i, Hsi-sheng. *Warlord Politics in China, 1916–1928.* Leland Stanford Junior University, 1976. Reprint, Taibei: Hongqiao, 1983.

Christopher, Renny. *The Viet Nam War/the American War: Images and Representations in Euro-American and Vietnamese Exile Narratives.* Amherst: University of Massachusetts Press, 1995.

Clifford, Nicholas Rowland. *Shanghai, 1925: Urban Nationalism and the Defense of Foreign Privilege.* Ann Arbor: University of Michigan Press, 1979.

Cong Dachang. *When Heroes Pass Away: The Invention of a Chinese Communist Pantheon.* Lanham, Md.: University Press of America, 1997.

Connerton, Paul. *How Societies Remember.* Cambridge: Cambridge University Press, 1989.

Dalloz, Jacques. *The War in Indo-China, 1945–54,* trans. Josephine Bacon. Savage, Md.: Barnes & Noble, 1990.

Dang Hoa. *Nhung mau chuyen ve Bac Ho, Bac Ton* (Stories about Uncle Ho, Uncle Ton). Long Xuyen: NXB Tong hop An Giang, 1990.

Dang Hoa, and Viet Chinh. *Nguoi thuy thu phan chien o Bien Den* (The antiwar sailor in the Black Sea). Ha Noi: NXB Thong tin ly luan, 1988.

Deng Zhongxia. *Anfänge der chinesischen Arbeiterbewegung 1919–1926.* German ed. of *Zhongguo zhigong yundong jianshi* (A short history of the Chinese workers' movement), ed. Werner Meißner and Günther Schulz. Reinbek bei Hamburg: Rowohlt, 1975.

Devillers, Philippe. *Histoire du Viêt-Nam de 1940 à 1952.* Paris: Seuil, 1952.

———. *Vietnam and France.* Paris: Comité d'etudes des problèmes du Pacifique, and New York: Institute of Pacific Relations, 1950.

Dinh Xuan Lam, and Pham Xanh. "Bac Ton voi phong trao cach mang o Sai Gon cuoi nhung nam 20" (Uncle Ton and the revolutionary movement in Sai Gon in the late 1920s). *Tap chi cong san* (Communism) (June 1988): 13–16, 32.

Do Quang Hung. *Cong hoi do Viet Nam* (The Vietnamese red labor union). Ha Noi: NXB Lao dong, 1989.

Duara, Prasenjit. *Rescuing History from the Nation: Questioning Narratives of Modern China.* Chicago: University of Chicago Press, 1995.

Duiker, William J. *The Comintern and Vietnamese Communism.* Athens, Ohio: Ohio University Press, 1975.

———. *Ho Chi Minh.* New York: Hyperion, 2000.

———. "The Revolutionary Youth League: Cradle of Communism in Vietnam." *The China Quarterly* (London), no. 51 (September/December 1972): 475–99.

———. *The Rise of Nationalism in Vietnam, 1900–1941.* Ithaca, N.Y.: Cornell University Press, 1976.

———. *Sacred War: Nationalism and Revolution in a Divided Vietnam.* New York: McGraw-Hill, 1995.

———. *Vietnam Since the Fall of Saigon.* Athens, Ohio: Ohio University CIS, 1989.

Dumarest, André. *La Formation de classes sociales en pays annamite.* Lyon, 1935[?].

Duong Thu Huong. *Novel without A Name.* New York: Morrow, 1995.

Elliott, Duong Van Mai. *The Sacred Willow: Four Generations in the Life of a Vietnamese Family.* New York: Oxford University Press, 1999.

Evans, Grant. *The Politics of Ritual and Remembrance: Laos since 1975.* Honolulu: University of Hawai'i Press, 1998.

Fall, Bernard. *The Two Viet-Nams: A Political and Military Analysis.* New York: Praeger, 1963.

———. *The Viet-Minh Regime: Government and Administration in the Democratic Republic of Viet-Nam.* New York: Institute of Pacific Relations, jointly with the Cornell University SouthEast Asia Program Publications, 1954, 1956 (2d ed.).

Feige, Michael. "Rescuing the Person from the Symbol: 'Peace Now' and the Ironies of Modern Myth." *History & Memory* 11, no. 1 (spring/summer 1999): 141–68.

Franchini, Philippe, ed. *Saigon 1925–1945: De la "Belle Colonie" à l'éclosion révolutionnaire ou la fin des dieux blancs.* Paris: Éditions Autrement, 1993.

Franke, Wolfgang, ed. *China Handbuch* (China handbook). 2d ed. Opladen: Westdeutscher Verlag, 1978.

Franklin, H. Bruce. *M.I.A. or Mythmaking in America: How and Why Belief in Live POWs Has Possessed a Nation.* New Brunswick, N.J.: Rutgers University Press, 1992, 1993.

Fridenson, Patrick. *Histoire des usines Renault: I. Naissance de la grande entreprise, 1898–1939.* Paris: Seuil, 1972.

Fujitani, Takashi, Geoffrey M. White, and Lisa Yoneyama, eds. *Perilous Memories: The Asia-Pacific War(s).* Durham, N.C., London: Duke University Press, 2001.

Gedi, Noa, and Yigal Elam. "Collective Memory: What Is It?" *History & Memory* 8, no. 1 (spring/summer 1996): 30–50.

Giebel, Christoph. "Ba Son 1925: The Strike at the Arsenal in Sai Gon, a Closer Look at Events and Their Interpretations." M.A. thesis, Cornell University, Ithaca, N.Y., 1989.

———. "Museum-Shrine: Revolution and Its Tutelary Spirit in the Village of My Hoa Hung." In *The Country of Memory: Remaking the Past in Late Socialist Vietnam,* ed. Hue-Tam Ho Tai, 77–105. Berkeley: University of California Press, 2001.

———. "Telling Life: An Approach to the Official Biography of Ton Duc Thang." In *Essays into Vietnamese Pasts,* ed. Keith W. Taylor and John K. Whitmore, 246–71. Ithaca, N.Y.: Cornell University SouthEast Asia Program Publications, 1995.

———. "Ton Duc Thang and the Imagined Ancestries of Vietnamese Communism." Ph.D. diss., Cornell University, Ithaca, N.Y., 1996.

Giesenfeld, Günter. *Land der Reisfelder, Vietnam, Laos, Kampuchea: Geschichte und Gegenwart* (Land of the rice fields, Vietnam, Laos, Kampuchea: History and present). Cologne: Pahl-Rugenstein, 1981.

Gillis, John R., ed. *Commemorations: The Politics of National Identity.* Princeton, N.J.: Princeton University Press, 1994.

Goscha, Christopher E. *Thailand and the Southeast Asian Networks of the Vietnamese Revolution, 1885–1954.* Copenhagen: Nordic Institute of Asian Studies and Curzon Press, 1999.

———. *Vietnam or Indochina? Contesting Concepts of Space in Vietnamese Nationalism, 1887–1954.* Copenhagen: Nordic Institute of Asian Studies, 1995.

Ha Huy Giap. "Tuong nho Bac Ton" (Remembering Uncle Ton). *Tap chi cong san* (July 1988): 18–21.

Hayslip, Le Ly. *When Heaven and Earth Changed Places: A Vietnamese Woman's Journey from War to Peace*. New York: Plume, 1990.

Heroes and Heroines of the Liberation Armed Forces of South Vietnam. N.p.: Liberation Editions, 1965.

A Heroic People: Memoirs from the Revolution (Nguyen Luong Bang, Pham Hung, Le Van Luong, Vo Nguyen Giap, Hoang Quoc Viet). Ha Noi: Foreign Languages Publishing House, 1960.

Hilberg, Raul. *The Politics of Memory: The Journey of a Holocaust Historian*. Chicago: Ivan R. Dee, 1996.

Hoang Quoc Viet. "A Glorious Son of the Vietnamese Working Class and Nation." *Viet-Nam Advances: A Social and Cultural Review* (Ha Noi) 3, no. 10 (October 1958): 3ff., 14.

Hobsbawm, Eric. *On History*. London: Weidenfeld & Nicolson, 1997.

Hodgkin, Thomas. *Vietnam: The Revolutionary Path*. New York: St. Martin's, 1981.

Hoi Ky Cach Mang. Tuyen chon (Selected revolutionary memoirs). N.p.: NXB Hoi Nha Van (Writers' association), 1995.

Holzer, Werner. *Bei den Erben Ho Tschi Minhs: Menschen und Gesellschaft in Nordvietnam* (With Ho Chi Minh's heirs: People and society in North Viet Nam). Munich: Süddeutscher Verlag, 1971.

Honey, P. J. *Communism in North Vietnam: Its Role in the Sino-Soviet Dispute*. Cambridge, Mass.: MIT Press, 1963.

———, ed. *North Vietnam Today: Profile of a Communist Satellite*. New York: Praeger, 1962.

Hong Chuong. *Bao chi Viet Nam* (The Vietnamese press). Ha Noi: NXB Su that, 1985.

Hooper-Greenhill, Eilean. *Museums and the Shaping of Knowledge*. London: Routledge, 1992.

Hsü, Immanuel C. Y. *The Rise of Modern China*. 3d ed. New York: Oxford University Press, 1983.

Huynh Kim Khanh. *Vietnamese Communism, 1925–1945*. Ithaca, N.Y.: Cornell University Press, 1982.

Huynh Ngoc Trang, Truong Ngoc Tuong et al., eds. *Sai Gon-Gia Dinh xua: Tu lieu & hinh anh* (Old Sai Gon-Gia Dinh: Documents and pictures). Ho Chi Minh City: NXB TP HCM, 1996.

Huynh Van Tong. *Lich su bao chi Viet Nam tu khoi thuy den nam 1930* (History of Vietnamese journalism from the beginnings to 1930). Sai Gon: Tri Dang XB, 1973.

Isaacs, Harold R. *No Peace for Asia*. Cambridge, Mass.: MIT Press, 1967.

Jacobs, Dan N. *Borodin: Stalin's Man in China*. Cambridge, Mass.: Harvard University Press, 1981.

Jamieson, Neil L. *Understanding Vietnam*. Berkeley: University of California Press, 1993.

Joarder, Safiuddin. *Syria under the French Mandate: The Early Phase: 1920–27.* Dacca: Asiatic Society of Bangladesh, 1977.

Kaes, Anton. "History and Film: Public Memory in the Age of Electronic Dissemination." *History & Memory* 2, no. 1 (fall 1990): 111–29.

Kamala Tiyavanich. *Forest Recollections: Wandering Monks in Twentieth-Century Thailand.* Honolulu: University of Hawai'i Press, 1997.

Kammen, Michael. "Some Patterns and Meanings of Memory Distortion in American History." In *Memory Distortion: How Minds, Brains, and Societies Construct the Past,* ed. Daniel L. Schacter, 329–45. Cambridge, Mass.: Harvard University Press, 1995.

Karnow, Stanley. *Vietnam: A History.* New York: Viking, 1983.

Karp, Ivan et al., eds. *Museums and Communities: The Politics of Public Culture.* Washington, D.C.: Smithsonian Institution, 1992.

Kolko, Gabriel. *Vietnam: Anatomy of a Peace.* London: Routledge, 1997.

Krog, Antjie. *Country of My Skull: Guilt, Sorrow, and the Limits of Forgiveness in the New South Africa.* New York: Times Books/Random House, 1998.

Ku, Hung-ting. *Urban Mass Movement in Action: The May Thirtieth Movement in Shanghai.* Singapore: Nanyang University, 1977.

Kuo Heng-yü. *Die Komintern und die chinesische Revolution: Die Einheitsfront zwischen der KP Chinas und der Kuomintang 1924–1927* (The Comintern and the Chinese Revolution: The United Front between the Communist Party of China and the Kuomintang 1924–1927). Paderborn: Schöningh, 1979.

Langlois, Walter G. *André Malraux: The Indochina Adventure.* London: Pall Mall, 1966.

Lazitch, Branko et al. *Biographical Dictionary of the Comintern.* Stanford, Calif.: Hoover Institution Press, 1973.

Le Braz, Yves. *Les Rejetés: L'Affaire Marty-Tillon: Pour une Histoire différente du PCF.* Paris: Table Ronde, 1974.

Lecalve, Frank. "Liste de la flotte de guerre française; vol. 1: Depuis la naissance de la vapeur à nos jours, vol. 3: Bâtiments réquisitionnés, guerre 1914–1918, guerre 1939–1945." Undated manuscript. Toulon: Service historique de la marine (Archives de la IIIe région maritime).

Lee, Begonia. "Houses of the Holy." *Far Eastern Economic Review,* 6 June 1996, 52.

Le Huu Lap. "Nho Bac Ton" (Remembering Uncle Ton). *Van hoa nghe thuat* (Culture and art) (Ha Noi) 16, no. 242 (August 1988): 2, 9.

Le Minh. *Nguoi tho may Ton Duc Thang* (The mechanic Ton Duc Thang). Ha Noi: NXB Thanh Nien, 1981, 1987 (2d ed.).

Le Ramey, Jean, and Pierre Vottero. *Les Mutins de la Mer Noire.* Paris: Éditions Sociales, 1973.

Lessard, Micheline. "Tradition for Rebellion: Vietnamese Students and Teachers and Anticolonial Resistance, 1888–1931." Ph.D. diss., Cornell University, Ithaca, N.Y., 1995.

Le Van Thu. *Hoi kin Nguyen An Ninh* (The Nguyen An Ninh secret society). 2d ed. Cho Lon: NXB Me Linh, 1961.

Lewin, Moshe. *The Making of the Soviet System: Essays in the Social History of Interwar Russia.* New York: Pantheon, 1985.

Lewis, John Wilson, ed. *Peasant Rebellion and Communist Revolution in Asia.* Stanford, Calif.: Stanford University Press, 1974.

Lich su Xi nghiep lien hop Ba Son (1863–1998) (History of the united enterprise Ba Son). Commissioned by the Party Committee and the Board of Directors of Ba Son. Ha Noi: NXB Quan Doi Nhan Dan, 1998.

Litvak, Meir. "A Palestinian Past: National Construction and Reconstruction." *History & Memory* 6, no. 2 (fall/winter 1994): 24–56.

Liu, James T.C. "An Early Sung Reformer: Fan Chung-Yen." In *Chinese Thought and Institutions,* ed. John K. Fairbank, 105–31. 3d ed. Chicago: University of Chicago Press, 1967.

Lockhart, Bruce M. *The End of the Vietnamese Monarchy.* New Haven: Council on Southeast Asia Studies, Yale Center for International and Area Studies, 1993.

Logan, William S. *Hanoi: Biography of a City.* Seattle: University of Washington Press, 2000.

Longrigg, Stephen Hemsley. *Syria and Lebanon under French Mandate.* London: Oxford University Press, 1958.

Lowenthal, David. "Fabricating Heritage." *History & Memory* 10, no. 1 (spring 1998): 5–24.

———. *Possessed by the Past: The Heritage Crusade and the Spoils of History.* New York: Free Press, 1996.

Lumley, Robert, ed. *The Museum Time-Machine: Putting Cultures on Display.* London: Routledge, 1988.

Luong, Hy Van. "Economic Reform and the Intensification of Rituals in Two Northern Vietnamese Villages, 1980–1990." In *The Challenge of Reform in Indochina,* ed. Borje Ljunggren and Peter Timmer, 259–91. Cambridge, Mass.: Harvard Institute for International Development (dist. Harvard University Press), 1993.

Luu Phuong Thanh. "Dong chi Ton Duc Thang, lanh tu dau tien cua giai cap cong nhan Viet Nam" (Comrade Ton Duc Thang, the first leader of the Vietnamese working class). In *Nhung nguoi con trung dung cua thanh pho* (The city's loyal and courageous children), ed. Luu Phuong Thanh, 9–19. Ho Chi Minh City: NXB Thanh pho Ho Chi Minh, 1987.

Ly Qui Chung, ed. *Between Two Fires: The Unheard Voices of Vietnam.* New York: Praeger, 1970.

Marr, David G. *Vietnam 1945:The Quest for Power.* Berkeley: University of California Press, 1995.

———. *Vietnamese Anticolonialism, 1885–1925.* Berkeley: University of California Press, 1980.

———. *Vietnamese Tradition on Trial, 1920–1945*. Berkeley: University of California Press, 1981.

Marr, David G., and A. C. Milner, eds. *Southeast Asia in the 9th to 14th Centuries*. Singapore: ISEAS et al., 1986.

Martin, Helmut. *Cult & Canon: The Origins and Development of State Maoism*. Armonk, N.Y.: M. E. Sharpe, 1982.

Marty, André. *The Epic of the Black Sea*. London: Modern Books, n.d.

———. *La Révolte de la Mer Noire*. 4th ed. Paris: Éditions Sociales, 1949.

Masson, Philippe. *La Marine française et la Mer Noire (1918–1919)*. Paris: Sorbonne, 1982.

May, Glenn Anthony. *Inventing a Hero: The Posthumous Re-creation of Andres Bonifacio*. Quezon City: New Day, and Madison: University of Wisconsin-Madison Center for Southeast Asian Studies, 1997.

McConnell, Scott. *Leftward Journey: The Education of Vietnamese Students in France, 1919–1939*. New Brunswick, N.J.: Transaction, 1989.

McHale, Shawn F. "Printing, Power, and the Transformation of Vietnamese Culture, 1920–1945." Ph.D. diss., Cornell University, Ithaca, N.Y., 1995.

Mrazek, Rudolf. *Engineers of Happy Land: Technology and Nationalism in a Colony*. Princeton: Princeton University Press, 2002.

Murray, Martin J. *The Development of Capitalism in Colonial Indochina (1870–1940)*. Berkeley: University of California Press, 1980.

Naquin, Susan, and Chün-fang Yü, eds. *Pilgrims and Sacred Sites in China*. Berkeley: University of California Press, 1992.

Ngo Van Hoa, and Duong Kinh Quoc. *Giai cap cong nhan Viet Nam nhung nam truoc khi thanh lap Dang* (The Vietnamese working class in the years before the party was founded). Ha Noi: NXB Khoa hoc xa hoi, 1978.

Nguyen Cao Ky. *Buddha's Child: My Fight to Save Vietnam*. New York: St. Martin's, 2002.

Nguyen Cong Binh, Vu Huy Phuc et al. *Mot so van de ve lich su giai cap cong nhan Viet Nam* (Some questions concerning the history of Viet Nam working class). Ha Noi: NXB Lao Dong, 1974.

Nguyen Cong Hoan. *Nguoi cap rang ham xay lua* (The caporal of the rice mill). Ha Noi: NXB Kim Dong, 1978.

Nguyen Khac Vien. *The Long Resistance (1858–1975)*. Ha Noi: Foreign Languages Publishing House, 1975.

———. *Tradition and Revolution in Vietnam,* ed. David Marr and Jayne Werner. Berkeley: Indochina Resource Center, [1974?].

Nguyen Khac Vien, and Huu Ngoc, eds. *From Saigon to Ho Chi Minh City: A Path of 300 Years*. Ha Noi: The Gioi, 1998.

Nguyen Q. Thang, and Nguyen Ba The. *Tu dien nhan vat lich su Viet Nam* (Dictionary of Vietnamese historic personalities). Ha Noi: NXB Khoa Hoc Xa Hoi, 1992.

Nguyen Quang Ngoc, Vu Minh Giang, Pham Xanh et al., eds. *Tien trinh Lich su Viet Nam* (Advanced history of Viet Nam). Ha Noi: NXB Giao Duc, 2000.

Nguyen Quoc Hung, Vu Duong Ninh et al. *100 nam ngay quoc te lao dong (1–5–1886–1–5–1986)* (The Centennial of international labor day). Ha Noi: NXB Lao Dong, 1986.

Nguyen Thanh. Bao chi cach mang Viet Nam 1925–1945 (Revolutionary Vietnamese journalism). Ha Noi: NXB Khoa Hoc Xa Hoi, 1984.

Nguyen Thanh, Pham Xanh et al. *Viet Nam Thanh Nien Cach Mang Dong Chi Hoi* (Vietnamese Revolutionary Youth League). Ha Noi: NXB Thong Tin Ly Luan, 1985.

Nguyen Thanh Khe. *Die historische Entwicklung und Bedeutung der Volksmacht in Vietnam* (The historic development and meaning of people's power in Viet Nam). Frankfurt/M. : Peter Lang, 1984.

Nguyen Thanh Tam. *Dong chi Le Hong Phong (1902–1942)* (Comrade Le Hong Phong). Ha Noi: NXB Su That, 1989.

Nguyen Thi Dinh. *No Other Road to Take.* Ithaca, N.Y.: Cornell University SouthEast Asia Program Publications, 2000.

Nguyen Tien Huu. *Dörfliche Kulte im traditionellen Vietnam* (Village cults in traditional Viet Nam). Munich: UNI, 1970.

Nguyen Viet Hung. "Doi ngu cong nhan Ba Son tu 1864 den 1945" (Workers' ranks of Ba Son). Historical thesis, Tong Hop (now National) University of Ho Chi Minh City, 1981.

Nhung nguoi cong san (Communists). Ho Chi Minh City: NXB Thanh Nien, 1977.

Ninh, Kim N. B. *A World Transformed: The Politics of Culture in Revolutionary Vietnam, 1945–1965*. Ann Arbor: University of Michigan Press, 2002.

Nong Quoc Chan, Nguyen Thach Giang et al., eds. *Tuyen tap Ha Huy Giap* (Selected works of Ha Huy Giap). Ha Noi: Bo Van Hoa-Thong Tin (Ministry of Culture and Information), 1998.

Norindr, Panivong. *Phantasmatic Indochina: French Colonial Ideology in Architecture, Film, and Literature*. Durham, N.C.: Duke University Press, 1996.

Novick, Peter. *That Noble Dream: The "Objectivity Question" and the American Historical Profession*. Cambridge: Cambridge University Press, 1988.

O'Harrow, Stephen. "Men of Hu, Men of Han, Men of the Hundred Man: The Biography of Si Nhiep and the Conceptualization of Early Vietnamese society." *Bulletin de l'École française d'Extrême-Orient* LXXV (1986): 249–66.

O'Malley, Ilene O. *The Myth of the Revolution: Hero Cults and the Institutionalization of the Mexican State, 1920–1940*. New York: Greenwood, 1986.

Pearce, Susan, ed. *Objects of Knowledge*. London: Athlone, 1990.

Pelley, Patricia M. *Postcolonial Vietnam: New Histories of the National Past.* Durham: Duke University Press, 2002.

———. "Writing Revolution: The New History in Post-Colonial Vietnam." Ph.D. diss., Cornell University, Ithaca, N.Y., 1993.

Pelzer, Kristin: "On Defining 'Vietnamese Religion': Reflections on Bruce Matthews' Article." *Buddhist-Christian Studies* 12 (1992): 75–79.

Pennell, C. R. *A Country with a Government and a Flag: The Rif War in*

Morocco, 1921–1926. Wisbech, Cambridgeshire: Menas (Middle East and North African Studies) Press, 1986.

Pham, Andrew. *Catfish and Mandala: A Two-Wheeled Voyage through the Landscape and Memory of Vietnam*. New York: Farrar, Straus & Giroux, 1999.

Pham Thanh Vinh. *Kinh te mien Nam: Bang so sanh kinh te Dong Duong tu 1913 den 1939* (The economy of the south: Comparative chart of the economy of Indochina from 1913 to 1939). Ha Noi: NXB Su that, 1957.

Pham Thi Hoai. *Crystal Messenger* (Thien su), trans. Ton-That Quynh-Du. Melbourne: Hyland House, 1999.

Phan Huy Le. "Vai suy nghi ve su hoc Viet Nam tren duong doi moi" (A few thoughts about the Vietnamese historical sciences on the road of renovation). *Nhan dan chu nhat* 2, no. 153 (12 January, 1992): 12.

Phan Thanh Son. "Le Mouvement ouvrier vietnamien des origines à 1945." Ph.D. diss., Sorbonne University, Paris, 1968.

Porter, Daniel Gareth. "Imperialism and Social Structure in Twentieth Century Vietnam." Ph.D. diss., Cornell University, Ithaca, N.Y., 1976.

Quinn-Judge, Sophie. *Ho Chi Minh: The Missing Years*. Berkeley: University of California Press, 2002.

———. "Rethinking the History of the Vietnamese Communist Party." Unpublished ms., 2003.

Radványi, János. *Delusion and Reality: Gambits, Hoaxes, & Diplomatic One-Upmanship in Vietnam*. South Bend, Ind.: Gateway, 1978.

Raphaël-Leygues, Jacques, and Jean-Luc Barré. *Les Mutins de la Mer Noire: Avril 1919: Des Marins français se revoltent*. [Paris?]: Plon, 1981.

Reid, Anthony, and David Marr, eds. *Perceptions of the Past in Southeast Asia*. Singapore: Heinemann Educational Books, 1979.

Remnick, David. *Lenin's Tomb: The Last Days of the Soviet Empire*. New York: Vintage Books, 1994.

Rice-Maximin, Edward. *Accommodation and Resistance: The French Left, Indochina and the Cold War, 1944–1954*. New York: Greenwood, 1986.

Rigby, Richard W. *The May 30 Movement: Events and Themes*. Canberra: Australian National University Press, 1980.

Roniger, Luis, and Mario Sznajder. "The Politics of Memory and Oblivion in Redemocratized Argentina and Uruguay." *History & Memory* 10, no. 1 (spring 1998): 133–69.

Said, Edward W. *Culture and Imperialism*. New York: Alfred A. Knopf, 1993.

———. *Orientalism*. New York: Vintage Books, 1979.

Sainteny, Jean. *Histoire d'une paix manquée: Indochine 1945–1947*. Paris: Fayard, 1953, 1967 (2d ed.).

Sampson, Cedric Allen. "Nationalism and Communism in Viet Nam, 1925–1931." Ph.D. diss., University of California, Los Angeles, 1975.

Schreiner, Klaus H. *Politischer Heldenkult in Indonesien: Tradition und moderne Praxis* (Political hero cult in Indonesia: Tradition and modern practice). Berlin: Reimer, 1995.

Sears, Laurie, ed. *Autonomous Histories, Particular Truths: Essays in Honor of John Smail.* Madison: University of Wisconsin-Madison Center for Southeast Asian Studies, 1993.

Sembdner, Friedrich. *Das kommunistische Regierungssystem in Vietnam* (The communist government system in Viet Nam). Cologne: von Nottbeck, 1978.

Shiraishi, Takashi, and Motoo Furuta, eds. *Indochina in the 1940s and 1950s.* Ithaca, N.Y.: Cornell University SouthEast Asia Program Publications, 1992.

Sider, Gerald, and Gavin Smith, eds. *Between History and Histories: The Making of Silences and Commemorations.* Toronto: University of Toronto Press, 1997.

So Van Hoa Va Thong Tin An Giang (An Giang culture and information department), ed. *Chu tich Ton Duc Thang (1888–1980)* (President Ton Duc Thang). An Giang, 1988.

Sommerskill, Michael. *China on the Western Front: Britain's Chinese Work Force in the First World War.* London: Sommerskill, 1982.

Soyinka, Wole. *The Burden of Memory, the Muse of Forgiveness.* New York: Oxford University Press, 1999.

Tai, Hue-Tam Ho. *Radicalism and the Origins of the Vietnamese Revolution.* Cambridge, Mass.: Harvard University Press, 1992.

———, ed. *The Country of Memory: Remaking the Past in Late Socialist Vietnam.* Berkeley: University of California Press, 2001.

Tam Vu. "Chu nghia quoc te vo san, mot trong nhung dong luc tinh than cua cach mang Viet Nam tu sau chien tranh the gioi lan thu nhat den thang 8–1945" (Proletarian internationalism, one among the spiritual driving forces of the Vietnamese Revolution, from after World War I to August 1945). *Nghien cuu lich su* (Historical research) (Ha Noi), no. 185 (March/April 1979): 9–21.

Tap chi lich su Dang (Party history), Vien Mac-Lenin (Marx-Lenin Institute), Ha Noi, May 1991 ("So dac biet ve Chu tich Ton Duc Thang"/Special on President Ton Duc Thang).

Taylor, Keith W. *The Birth of Vietnam.* Berkeley: University of California Press, 1983.

———. "Looking behind the Vietnamese Annals: Ly Phat Ma (1028–54) and Ly Nhat Ton (1054–72) in the *Viet Su Luoc* and the *Toan Thu.*" *The Vietnam Forum* 7 (winter/spring 1986): 47–68.

———."Notes on the *Viet dien u linh tap.*" *The Vietnam Forum* 8 (summer/fall 1986): 26–59.

———. "Surface Orientations in Vietnam: Beyond Histories of Nation and Region." *Journal of Asian Studies* 57, no. 4 (November 1998): 949–78.

Taylor, Keith W., and John K. Whitmore, eds. *Essays into Vietnamese Pasts.* Ithaca, N.Y.: Cornell University SouthEast Asia Program Publications, 1995.

Taylor, Philip. *Fragments of the Present: Searching for Modernity in Vietnam's South*. Honolulu: University of Hawai'i Press, 2001.

Thep Moi (Ha Van Loc). *Cay tre Viet Nam* (Vietnamese bamboo). Ha Noi: NXB Chinh Tri Quoc Gia, 2001.

Thep Moi, Le Quang Vinh, Doan Gioi, and Tran Dinh Van. *Nhung Nguoi Song Mai* (People who will live on forever). Ha Noi: NXB Kim Dong, 2001.

Thompson, Virginia, and Richard Adloff. *The Left Wing in Southeast Asia*. New York: William Sloane, with the Institute of Pacific Relations, 1950.

Thongchai Winichakul. *Siam Mapped: A History of the Geo-Body of a Nation*. Honolulu: University of Hawai'i Press, 1994.

To Thanh Tam, ed. *Chuyen ke ve Bac Ton* (Stories about Uncle Ton). Long Xuyen: NXB Tong Hop An Giang, 1988.

To Thanh Tam, ed. *Mot con nguoi binh thuong—vi dai. Ky yeu Hoi thao khoa hoc ve Chu tich Ton Duc Thang nhan dip ky niem 100 nam ngay sinh 20–8–1888–20–8–1988* (A great ordinary person: Proceedings of the symposium on President Ton Duc Thang commemorating the centennial of his birth). An Giang: Ban Tuyen Giao Tinh Uy An Giang (Propaganda and education department of the VNCP committee of An Giang province), 1989.

Ton Duc Thang. "Nhung gio Hac-hai doi voi toi" (How I experienced the times in the Black Sea). *Tien Phong* 232 (26–29 October 1957): 1, 4.

———. "Ya uchastvoval v vostanii na Chernom More," trans. A. Shiltovoi. *Sovietskii Moriak* [Moscow ?] 24 (1957): 6ff.

Tongas, Gérard. *(J'ai vécu dans) l'enfer communiste au Nord Viêt-Nam (et j'ai choisi la liberté)*. Paris: Nouvelles Éditions Debresse, 1960.

Tong Cong Doan Viet Nam (Viet Nam Federation of Trade Unions). *Phong trao cong nhan va cong doan Viet Nam 55 nam qua (1929–1984)* (Viet Nam workers' and union movement through 55 years). Ha Noi: NXB Lao Dong, 1985.

Tonkin, Elizabeth. *Narrating Our Pasts: The Social Construction of Oral History*. Cambridge: Cambridge University Press, 1992.

Tønnesson, Stein. *The Vietnamese Revolution of 1945: Roosevelt, Ho Chi Minh and De Gaulle in a World at War*. London: Sage Publications, 1991.

The Trade Union Movement in Vietnam. Ha Noi: Foreign Languages Publishing House, with the Viet Nam Federation of Trade Unions, 1988.

Tran Huy Lieu. *(Ban du thao) Su Cach mang can dai Viet-Nam (1858–8–1945)* (Draft of a history of the modern Vietnamese Revolution). Vols. 3, 4. N.p.: Bo Quoc Gia Giao Duc, Ban Su Dia, Vu Van Hoc Nghe Thuat (National Ministry of Education, History and Geography Division, Literature and Art Department), 1951.

———. *Dang Thanh Nien (1926–1927): Tap tai lieu va hoi ky* (The Youth Party: Documents and memoirs). Ha Noi: NXB Su Hoc, 1961.

———. *Lich su tam muoi nam chong Phap* (History of eighty years against the French). Ha Noi: XB Ban Nghien Cuu Van Su Dia, vol. 1 (1858–

1929), 1957 (2d ed.), vol. 2A (1930–1939), 1958, NXB Su Hoc, vol. 2B (1939–1945), 1961.

———. *Nguyen Trai.* Ha Noi: NXB Khoa Hoc Xa Hoi, 1969 (2d ed.).

Tran Huy Lieu, Nguyen Luong Bich, et al. *Tai lieu tham khao lich su Cach mang can dai Viet-Nam* (Historical reference material on the modern Vietnamese Revolution). Vol. 6. Ha Noi: Ban Nghien Cuu Van Su Dia XB, 1956.

Tran Huy Lieu, Van Tao, et al. *Tai lieu tham khao lich su Cach mang can dai Viet-Nam. Vol. IV: Phong trao dau tranh doi tu do dan chu va cac ching dang thanh lap sau Dai Chien lan thu nhat* (Historical reference material on the modern Vietnamese Revolution, vol. 4: The fighting movement for liberty and democracy and the political parties founded after World War I). Ha Noi: NXB Van Su Dia, 1958 (2d ed.).

Tran Thanh Phuong, ed. *Bac Ton cua chung ta* (Our Uncle Ton). Long Xuyen: NXB Tong Hop An Giang, 1988.

Tran Tu Binh, narr., Ha An, rec. *The Red Earth: A Vietnamese Memoir of Life on a Colonial Rubber Plantation,* trans. John Spragens, ed. David Marr. Athens, Ohio: Ohio University Press, 1985.

Tran Van Giau. *Giai cap cong nhan Viet Nam: Su hinh thanh va su phat trien cua no tu giai cap "tu minh" den giai cap "cho minh"* (The Vietnamese working class: Its formation and development from a class "of itself" to a class "for itself"). Ha Noi: NXB Su That, 1957, 1958 (2d ed.), 1961 (3d ed.).

Tran Van Giau, Dinh Xuan Lam, et al. *Lich su can dai Viet Nam* (Modern Vietnamese history). Vol. 4 (1919–1930). Ha Noi: NXB Giao Duc, 1963.

Tran Van Giau Tran Bach Dang, et al., eds. *Dia chi van hoa thanh pho Ho Chi Minh* (Geographical description and culture of Ho Chi Minh City). Vol. 1, *Lich su* (History). Ho Chi Minh City: NXB Thanh Pho Ho Chi Minh, 1987.

Treat, John Whittier. "The *Enola Gay* on Display: Hiroshima and American Memory." *positions* 5, no. 3 (winter 1997): 863–78.

Trinh-Quang-Quy. *Phong trao Lao-dong Viet-Nam: Le Mouvement du travail au Vietnam.* (The labor movement in Viet Nam). Sai Gon: [Self-published (?)], 1970.

Trung Tam Nghien Cuu Xa Hoi Va Phat Trien (Center for the Study of Society and Development, Dinh Xuan Lam, Duong Lan Hai et al.) *Nghien cuu Viet Nam: Mot so van de Lich su - Kinh te - Xa hoi - Van hoa* (Viet Nam studies: A few questions regarding history, economy, society, and culture). Ha Noi: NXB The Gioi, 1998.

Truong Nhu Tang. *A Viet Cong Memoir: An Inside Account of the Vietnam War and Its Aftermath.* New York: Vintage Books, 1986.

Tso, Shih Kan Sheldon. *The Labor Movement in China.* Shanghai, 1928. Reprint Westport, Conn.: Hyperion, 1981.

Tumarkin, Nina. *Lenin Lives! The Lenin Cult in Soviet Russia.* Cambridge, Mass.: Harvard University Press, 1983.

Turner, Karen Gottschang, and Phan Thanh Hao. *Even the Women Must*

Fight: Memories of War from North Vietnam. New York: John Wiley & Sons, 1998.

Ung Thu Ha. "Tim hieu cong nhan Bason trong su nghiep giai phong dan toc" (Tracing the Ba Son workers in the national liberation endeavor). Historical thesis, Tong Hop (now National) University, Ho Chi Minh City, 1989.

Ungar, Esta S. "Vietnamese Leadership and Order: Dai Viet under the Le Dynasty (1428–1459)." Ph.D. diss., Cornell University, Ithaca, N.Y., 1983.

Uy Ban Khoa Hoc Xa Hoi Viet Nam (Viet Nam Social Science Committee, Nguyen Khanh Toan et al.). *Lich su Viet Nam* (History of Viet Nam). Vol. 2. Ha Noi: NXB Khoa Hoc Xa Hoi, 1985.

Vella, Walter F., ed. *Aspects of Vietnamese History*. Honolulu: University of Hawai'i Press, 1973.

Vien Khoa Hoc Xa Hoi Viet Nam, Vien Su Hoc (Vietnamese Social Science Institute, Institute of History), Pham Nhu Thom, ed. *Hoi ky Tran Huy Lieu* (Memoirs of Tran Huy Lieu). Ha Noi: NXB Khoa Hoc Xa Hoi, 1991.

Vien Mac-Le-Nin (Marx-Lenin Institute). *Ky niem lan thu 65 Dai hoi Tua: Tinh doan ket chien dau vo san Viet Phap* (The 65th anniversary of the congress in Tours: The Vietnamese-French proletarian fighting solidarity). Ha Noi: NXB Thong Tin Ly Luan, 1986.

Viet Nam American Friendship Association, ed. *Transcript of the Proceedings at the Meeting in Celebration of the Second Anniversary of the Independence of the Republic of Viet Nam, 1947*. New York: VAFA, 1947.

Vo Nguyen Giap. *Unforgettable Days*. Ha Noi: Foreign Languages Publishing House, 1975.

Wakeman, Frederic Jr. "Mao's Remains." In *Death Ritual in Late Imperial and Modern China*, ed. James L. Watson and Evelyn S. Rawski, 254–88. Berkeley: University of California Press, 1988.

Walsh, Kevin. *The Representation of the Past: Museums and Heritage in the Post-Modern World*. London: Routledge, 1992.

Wang Gungwu, ed. *Self and Biography: Essays on the Individual and Society in Asia*. Sydney: Sydney University Press, 1975.

Watson, James, ed. *Golden Arches East: McDonald's in East Asia*. Stanford, Calif.: Stanford University Press, 1997.

Watson, Rubie S., ed. *Memory, History, and Opposition under State Socialism*. Santa Fe, N.M.: School of American Research Press, 1994.

Werner, Jayne S., and Luu Doan Huynh, eds. *The Vietnam War: Vietnamese and American Perspectives*. Armonk, N.Y.: M. E. Sharpe, 1993.

Whitfield, Danny J. *Historical and Cultural Dictionary of Vietnam*. Metuchen, N.J.: Scarecrow Press, 1976.

Whitmore, John K. "From Classical Scholarship to Confucian Belief in Vietnam." *The Vietnam Forum* 9 (winter/spring 1987): 49–65.

Wolters, Oliver W. *History, Culture, and Region in Southeast Asian Perspectives*. Rev. ed. Ithaca, N.Y.: Cornell University SouthEast Asia Program

Publications, 1999.

———. "On Telling a Story of Vietnam in the Thirteenth and Fourteenth Centuries." *Journal of Southeast Asian Studies* 26, no. 1 (March 1995): 63–74.

———. "Possibilities for a Reading of the 1293–1357 Period in the Vietnamese Annals." *The Vietnam Forum* 11 (winter/spring 1988): 92–147.

———. *Two Essays on Dai-Viet in the Fourteenth Century.* New Haven: Council on Southeast Asia Studies, Yale University, 1988.

Wood, Nancy. "Memory's Remains: Les lieux de mémoire." *History & Memory* 6, no. 1 (spring/summer 1994): 123–49.

Woodside, Alexander B. *Community and Revolution in Modern Vietnam.* Boston: Houghton Mifflin, 1976.

———. "Conceptions of Change and of Human Responsibility for Change in Late Traditional Vietnam." *The Vietnam Forum* 6 (summer/fall 1985): 73–111.

———. "An Enlightenment for Outcasts: Some Vietnamese Stories." In *Human Rights and Revolutions,* ed. Jeffrey N. Wasserstrom, Lynn Hunt, and Marilyn B. Young, 113–25. Lanham, Md.: Rowman & Littlefield, 2000.

Woolman, David S. *Rebels in the Rif: Abd el Krim and the Rif Rebellion.* Stanford, Calif.: Stanford University Press, 1968.

Wright, Gwendolyn. *The Politics of Design in French Colonial Urbanism.* Chicago: University of Chicago Press, 1991.

Wu Xiuquan. *Eight Years in the Ministry of Foreign Affairs (January 1950–October 1958): Memoirs of a Diplomat.* Beijing: New World, N.d.

Wyatt, David K. *Thailand: A Short History.* New Haven: Yale University Press, 1984.

Yamamoto Tatsuro. "Myths Explaining the Vicissitudes of Political Power in Ancient Vietnam." *Acta Asiatica: Bulletin of the Institute of Eastern Culture* (Tokyo: The Toho Gakkai) 18 (1970): 70–94.

Yoneyama, Lisa. "Critical Warps: Facticity, Transformative Knowledge, and Postnationalist Criticism in the Smithsonian Controversy." *positions* 5, no. 3 (winter 1997): 779–809.

Zagoria, Donald S. *Vietnam Triangle: Moscow, Peking, Hanoi.* New York: Pegasus, 1967.

Zinoman, Peter. *The Colonial Bastille: A History of Imprisonment in Vietnam, 1862–1940.* Berkeley: University of California Press, 2001.

———."Declassifying Nguyen Huy Thiep." *positions* 2, no. 2 (fall 1994): 294–317.

Index

Pages with maps and illustrations are indicated in boldface type.